Ethics and Society

P.K. Mohapatra retired as Professor of Philosophy from Utkar University where he taught for 35 years. Soon after his retirement, he was a Senior Fellow of the Indian Council of Philosophical Research from October 2002 to September 2004. A specialist in Philosophy of Mind and Philosophy of Values, he has also authored two other books entitled *Personal Identity* and *Concepts and Problems* and edited six books, prominent among them being, *Social Justice, Purusarthas* and *Perspectives in Analytic Philosophy.* A good number of his articles have been published in reputed journals of philosophy in India and abroad.

Dr. Mohapatra was the Vice Chairman of the Indian Philosophical Congress during 1994-97 and the General President of the All Orissa Philosophy Association in 1998. He is the Executive President of this Association since 1998. Also, he was the General Editor of *Utkal Studies in Philosophy* from 1994-2002.

Ethics and Society

AN ESSAY IN APPLIED ETHICS

P.K. MOHAPATRA

CONCEPT PUBLISHING COMPANY, NEW DELHI-110 059

Cataloging in Publication Data—DK
Courtesy: D.K. Agencies (P) Ltd. <docinfo@dkagencies.com>

Mohapatra, P. K. (Prafulla Kumar), 1942-
Ethics and society : an essay in applied ethics/ P.K. Mohapatra.
p. cm.
Includes bibliographical references (p.)
Includes index.
ISBN 13: 9788180695230
ISBN 10: 8180695239

1. Applied ethics. 2. Social ethics. I. Title

DDC 170 22

ISBN-13: 978-81-8069-523-0 (HB)
ISBN-10: 81-8069-523-9 (HB)

First Published 2008

Published and Printed by
Ashok Kumar Mittal
Concept Publishing Company
A/15-16, Commercial Block, Mohan Garden
New Delhi-110059 (INDIA)

Phones : 25351460, 25351794
Fax : 091-11-25357103
Email : publishing@conceptpub.com

Preface and Acknowledgements

The present book is an essay on the nature of the relation between ethics and society or the world at large. A crucial claim of the book is the claim that ethics is a condition of the world, like logic. What this means is that although, unlike logic, ethics does not determine what the world can contain and what it cannot, it certainly determines what the world *should* contain and what it should not. What the world should contain is what I call the ethically desirable (things, events, actions, conducts and so on). Things which constitute the fabric of the world may be of four types; namely things which the world ought to have, things which it ought not to have, things which it may or may not have and things whose presence in this world adds to its ethical value and status (though their absence does not make the world ethically poorer). Rajendra Prasad calls these four types of things obligatory, forbidden, permissible and recommended. Of these I call the first and the fourth the "ethically desirable". Although it is true that the world, as a matter of fact, does not contain all (and only those things) that are ethically desirable in my sense (for there are and can be many things in the world which are ethically forbidden and so undesirable), the major focus of this book is that philosophers and moralists could and should improve the moral status of the world by trying to minimize, if not totally eliminate, the number (quantum) of the forbiddens and increasing that of the obligatory and the recommended. Such a world would be a morally desirable world. And so it becomes (almost) a logical truth that a desirable world contains all that is ethically *desirable* and must not contain anything that is ethically forbidden. This is not a tautology since, besides containing ethically desirable things, the world may also contain many things that are desirable in other respects, e.g. things that are socially, politically or economically desirable, which may not be ethically desirable; but a thing's being ethically desirable would make it desirable in these other respects as well. This primacy of the ethical is what I strongly plead for in this project. And viewed from this perspective, ethics becomes a necessary condition of the world and the society.

The chapters that follow aim at bringing this into focus and suggesting how the world and society can be made a desirable one to live in. This, I contend, can be done by applying ethics (the ethical theories) in practical life and living up to it. While the above contention is mainly argued in the first chapter, the second chapter purports to show that application of ethics to society is not only imperative in the described way, it is also a matter of natural necessitation. For I argue to the effect that to be moral is as much *natural* for man as it is for him to be rational. I argue that *man is a naturally moral being* in the sense that every human person has the natural propensity to act morally unless otherwise constrained. In fact, man's moral nature follows *jointly* from his being rational as well as spiritual, both of which are shown to be constitutive of moral personhood. For while man's rationality makes us distinguish between what is moral from what is immoral, his spiritual faculty makes him *identify* with the moral and *alienate* from the immoral.

However, moral personhood and the essential morality of men has to be understood in tune with applied ethics, which is the central theme of this work that runs through all the chapters. For, human nature being as it is, the ethical theories not only need to be, but they *must* be, applied to solve intriguing problems of practical life. Indeed, I argue that every ethical theory—rather every theory worth the name—has a built-in applicability. A theory is meant to be applicable, and the one that cannot be applied is not, and cannot be, a proper ethical theory. Most of the value crises that contemporary society is facing, and ancient societies often faced, are because of non-application, or apparent inapplicability, of ethical theories to practical life: indeed it has often appeared that some celebrated ethical theories are inapplicable or, if applied, lead to consequences that are morally undesirable, even disastrous. It is argued that such predicaments are due to our taking the theories in their absolute, literal sense which, in turn, is because of our failure to balance between the spirit of the theory and the demands of the situation. Applied philosophy, taking this into proper account, would require 'justified violations' of the moral principles, on appropriate occasions, in order to get over the predicaments, for these predicaments arise because of the principles being followed literally and unexceptionably. The required violations only indicate the fact that moral principles are not absolute in the conventional sense, but defeasible under demanding circumstances.

Controversial cases, where celebrated moral principles seem to conflict, call for applied ethics which overcomes the conflict by *one* of the rival theories revealing that an arguably overriding capacity in these demanding situations. This feature of the moral principles, along with the idea of justified violations thereof, though mainly dealt with in the first chapter, also figures in chapter three and in the other chapters.

Does this idea of justified violation and the emphasis on the demands of the situation lead to relativism and denial of universality, absoluteness and objectivity of ethical theories and moral values? No, for it is argued that the absolute/relative distinction and the objective/subjective dichotomy, as have been customarily conceived, have been generally misconstrued. The third chapter exposes the futility of taking these distinctions in the absolute, literal sense and pleads for a liberal interpretation of them, which would show the ethical theories to be objective and yet fruitfully applicable to practical life. A theory being not objective in the absolute sense does not make it subjective. Taken in the absolute, literal sense, the described distinctions are only a philosopher's myth. Moral principles, in particular, admit of objectivity and universality of a secondary sort, in the spirit of what Nagel calls "objective tolerance" in his *The View from Nowhere*. And this is where lies the subtle distinction between metaphysical realism and moral realism.

With this sort of theoretical account of objectivity and application of moral principles, the next three chapters make use of applied ethics in the context of (human) rights and justice, rights of animals and nature or environment, as well as in the context of business and professional practices. For (I think that) applied ethics in all these areas has a specially justified necessity since controversies involving moral conflicts are characteristically present in all these spheres, which often lead to socio-moral crises.

Conflicts occur between rival rights of men—the fetus's right to life and the woman's right to privacy, a patient's right to know the state of his health and doctor's right (duty!) to secrecy in the interest of the patient's welfare. Conflicts occur between rival duties as well—between *sāmānya dharma* and *svadharma*, between universal duties and the particular duties of specific groups of men, between *sāmānya dharma* and *varṇa dharma*, that is; and this often leads to a corresponding conflict between general ethics and professional ethics. Conflicts also occur between the anthropocentric and the bio-centric approaches to nature, between instrumental value and intrinsic value of nature and environment. Conflicts are also encountered between ethics on the one hand, and business and professional practices, on the other—largely because of the latter's commitment to specific purpose and objective.

All these issues are laid bare and analysed for what they are. Liberal interpretation of values and rights and emphasis on their *necessity but defeasibility* put the theories in proper perspective and make their understanding and application possible and effective.

The contents and the contention of this work developed and consolidated mainly during my research as a Senior Fellow of the Indian Council of Philosophical Research during October 2002 to September, 2004. Lectures and discussions at Utkal, Poona and Ravindra Bharati universities during this period have considerably helped sharpen my ideas and arguments as have the writings of several eminent authors, which have been appropriately cited and acknowledged in this work. To these authors and the colleagues in the mentioned institutions I am grateful. And I am specially grateful to the I.C.P.R., New Delhi for awarding me a Senior Fellowship for working on this project.

P.K.Mohapatra

Rounak, HIG-194,
KalingaVihar, Bhubaneswar-751019
Ratha Yatra, July 16, 2007

Contents

1

Ethics and the World

There can be no absolute standards of value. If there is supposed to be any, it would be of no value, since such a standard would not be in keeping with the spirit of ethics, which is to promote the good life and provide effective guidance for such life. In the chapters that follow, I shall be arguing to this effect and present a model of ethical principles accordingly in their application to the different spheres of life and the world we live in. Ethical principles, I shall argue, are universal but *defeasible,* which means that no such principle is absolute and unexceptionable and each is subject to violation on morally justified grounds. I shall further argue that any actual body of ethical beliefs or any set of moral principles is not merely an exposition and/or analysis of some theoretical doctrines, but is intended to be a practical guide to living. Morality is thus a social affair and is essentially a matter of community concern. And this being so, application of moral principles to social situations of practical life is vitally important. In view of this, the focus of the present chapter is a close logical enquiry into the relation of ethics to the world of practical living which, I hope, will reveal the social significance and practical implications of ethical theories and moral principles.

Ethics as a Condition of the World

"Ethics does not treat of the world", said Wittgenstein in his *Notebooks,* 1914-16 (p.77e), "ethics must be a condition of the world, like logic." What did he mean? To be sure, logic is a condition of the world in the sense that it determines what the world can contain and what it cannot. The world can contain only that which is logically possible—though, as a matter of fact, not *all* that is logically possible—and cannot contain anything that is logically impossible. That is, anything the world may contain must be logically possible. Let us see how ethics can be said to be a condition of the world. It cannot be said that the world must contain only that which is ethically possible and cannot contain anything that is ethically impossible, for no sense can be given to the corresponding ideas of "ethically possible" and "ethically impossible". We can only speak of what is ethically desirable and what is ethically undesirable. Actions, conducts, motives, attitudes and intentions, plans, projects and policies of individuals or groups can be said to be, or judged to be, ethically desirable or undesirable. But then it cannot be said that the world must contain *all* that is ethically desirable and must not contain anything which is not. Ethics cannot be said to be a condition of the world in this sense, since as a matter of fact the world *does* contain a few things that are ethically *undesirable.* However, we can say and, in all fairness to him can take Wittgenstein to have said that the world *should* contain only ethically desirable things and *should not* contain anything that is not. Indeed, as a matter of fact, the world does not contain only the ethically desirables. Things that it does, or may, contain can be of four types: things that the world ought to have, things that it ought not to have, things that it may or may not have and things whose presence in the world adds to its ethical value, though their absence in the world does not make it ethically poorer. These four types of things (actions, conducts, occurrences) may be called obligatory, forbidden, permissible and recommended. I shall include the first and the fourth under what I call the "ethically desirable". In an ideal ethical world the number of the forbidden should be nil. But philosophers and moralists could strive to improve the moral status of this (actual) world by minimizing the number of the forbiddens and increasing the number of the obligatory and the recommended. Such a world would be a truly desirable world. Therefore, it is (almost) a logical truth that a desirable world contains only that which is ethically desirable and cannot contain anything that is ethically undesirable. Conversely, a world that does not contain any ethically desirable things, or contains less number of ethically desirable things than ethically undesirable things, would not be a desirable world.[1]

We thus make ethics a necessary condition of the desirable world. By this I mean that even if the world were desirable in some other respects, e.g. economic, political or even religious but not in respect of the ethical, it would not be a desirable world, whereas it being desirable in respect of the ethical would make it largely so in the other respects too. "Ethical goodness", says Rajendra Prasad, "is foundational to all other kinds of goodness in that its presence in any one of them heightens the latter's natural or distinctive value and its absence in the latter does the contrary".[2] A non-ethical goodness cannot sustain itself without being accompanied by some sort of ethical goodness. I shall call this the primacy of the ethical, which holds the key to applied ethics.

Applicability to the World

Now, if the purpose of ethics is to provide guidance for a morally desirable life, a moral principle must be such that it should not only be logically possible, but also empirically possible, to live

1. See Rajendra Prasad, *Varnadharma, Niskama Karma* and *Practical Morality* (D.K. Printworld, New Delhi in association with Department of Philosophy, Utkal University, 1999). p. 263. I owe considerably to this book for building up the arguments in this chapter.
2. *Ibid*, p. 263.

and act in accordance with it. In other words, it must be possible to apply moral theories to the world we live in. Indian philosophers have always believed that our ethical ideals are realisable[3]. The reason, I suppose, is that they are ideals we are expected to follow, we ought to follow, and anything, any standard, that is impossible to realise, cannot be expected to be followed by anyone. "Ought" must imply "can". One ought to do something only if it is possible to do it. This points to the significant fact that, contrary to the opinion of some modern writers[4], ethics works within the bounds of logic. For if 'ought' means 'can', then conversely 'cannot' means 'ought not', that is, if anything is impossible (cannot be realised or applied in life) then one ought not to try to achieve it. Ethics does not ask for the impossible. If we are enjoined to follow the ethical rules, it surely means that it is possible to follow these rules. It cannot be our duty to do what we are unable to do. Therefore an ethical value has reality only in its realisation or in its fulfilment. Value in Indian philosophy is generally construed as *iṣta* or 'that which is desired', the reality of which lies in the satisfaction of the desire. It is an end to be achieved, an ideal to be actualized. Values and ideals, which cannot be fulfilled or cannot be achieved, will remain abstract and utopian. Some Indian philosophers therefore have gone on to the extent of claiming that a value needs to be actualized before it can become truly a value.[5] And this is more particularly true of ethical values and ethical principles. Possible application of ethical principles to the world we live in not only defines the spirit of ethics but also makes ethics practical and world oriented. This is a prerequisite of applied ethics, which envisions a special connection between

3. See, for example, M. Hiriyanna, *Indian Conception of Values* (Kavyalaya Publications, Mysore, 1957), p. 245 and elsewhere.
4. Mckenzie, for example, repeatedly says in his *Hindu Ethics* (Ch. IV, esp. p. 242 and elsewhere) that ethical values are not to be judged on their consistency.
5. See Samkara, *Vedanta Sutra*, III.ii.38: *Prākbhoktṛ-sambandhātphalatvānu-papatteh.*

ethics and the world in the sense that an ethical theory has some sort of a built-in applicability to the world. For any such theory to be applicable to the world, the world must be such that (a) it must not make its application impossible and (b) the people in it must acknowledge it as a valid moral principle and be inclined to act in accordance with it. With these conditions satisfied, any theory that is still not applicable in practical life is not a good moral theory and will have nothing to contribute to the making of a desirable world. I shall argue that such theories will have to be toned down, even violated, in view of the world being as it is and human nature remaining as it is. This an exercise in applied ethics would do for a morally good reason. This will be "justified violation" of a moral principle. However, all cases of not acting in accordance with a moral principle are not cases of the principle being bad and inapplicable. Despite knowing a moral principle well enough, some people may fail to apply it, or act contrary to it, because of weakness of will or being overpowered by some sort of non-moral considerations; in these types of cases, the problem lies not so much in the theories and their applicability—this part is quite clear to the agent—as with the agent's mind set. A moral philosopher can emphasise the primacy of the ethical and persuasionally apply it to the weak willed person to make him do what he knows he ought to do. Although I shall obliquely deal with such cases later on, this needs more of a psychological exercise with which I shall not be much concerned. My concern here will be the first type of cases of inapplicable ethical theories, which I shall examine and analyse by considering some major Indian ethical theories and cases of moral conflicts their application may give rise to.

But before I proceed, a word about the way or ways ethical theories may be applied, and that will provide the key to the different ways in which ethical theories can be said to be applicable to the world. An ethical theory has a built-in applicability in the sense that it must be able to help us in judging, deciding and persuading others regarding what we ought to do and what we ought not to do. That it should have this sort of applicability is a *logical* requirement in the sense that it *makes* this an ethical theory. Accordingly, an ethical theory can be applied in three different, though interrelated, ways: *judgmental, decisional* and *persuasional* ways.[6] In tricky situations, where the choice of actions seems not so obvious or more than one action claim execution, one would need to apply an appropriate ethical theory (e.g. consequentialism) to judge which action of an individual or group (political, religious, or institutional) is right or wrong. Or, one can, on the basis of a theory, decide what he should or should not do under a particular situation. These two methods are interdependent in the sense that one would not decide to do *A* if he does not judge *A* to be right; and conversely, if one judges the action *A* to be right under a particular situation one will normally* have the proneness to decide to do *A* under that situation. To be able to do *that* one would have to consider which ethical theory would be relevantly applied in that situation and, if need be, one has to decide with *how much of rigor* or *stringency* this theory can be applied so that a proper balance could be maintained between the spirit of the theory and the demands of the situation; the former cannot be totally sacrificed, nor can the latter be totally ignored. Perhaps, being pitted between these, we may have to be satisfied with doing what is good enough or right enough in that situation—though it may not be absolutely the best or *the* right thing to do. We shall see that this we do for a morally justified reason. Thirdly, a theory can be used in the persuasional way when someone, himself convinced of the desirability of a theory, uses it to convince someone else to act in accordance with it. A more sophisticated version of this sort of application can be found to be implicit in Hare's *prescriptivist* theory of ethics; we will have occasion to discuss it in some detail in Chapter 3 below.

6. See Prasad, *ibid*, pp. 267-69.

* About the abnormal cases, shortly afterwards; we shall see that in such cases applied ethics assumes a more conspicuous importance.

As we shall see soon later in this chapter, Lord Krishna used the consequentialist theory in this persuasional way to make Yudhisthira tell the only lie of his life regarding the death of Aswasthama, son of Drona, in order that the latter would be forced to lay down his arms and get away from the war in desperation; this was thought necessary in the interest of winning the righteous war by the virtuous Pandavas, which could not have been possible with Drona in the opposite side. This way of applying ethical theories is also not unrelated to the first two; for one can persuade someone else to do ***A*** only if one is himself convinced of ***A***'s rightness, i.e. judges it to be right and can decide to do ***A***.

Justified Violations, Defeasibility and Applied Ethics

We must now proceed to examine some cases of ethical theories that are not applicable or difficult to be applied in actual situations and how applied ethics can be of help, if at all. To consider this, let us take the moral principle of truth-telling. In ancient Indian tradition (perhaps that is also true of ancient traditions everywhere), truth telling, and conversely not telling lies, was considered to be the highest kind of virtue—a *sādhāraṇa dharma* that no other *dharma* can override or defeat. This is what Krishna says in the *Mahabharat* and so says Bhisma several times in the *Shantiparva* of the epic. To be sure, truth telling is a great virtue; but taken in the absolute, literal sense, the theory becomes inapplicable or even morally disastrous, if applied. It is said of an ancient scholar that he would never open his lips in intellectual discussions on contentious issues and, if asked the reason for his silence, he would reply, "*anṛtāt bhayam*" (for fear of telling a lie i.e., saying something that might turn out to be false or inaccurate!). The other extreme is the case of the ancient *riṣi,* Kaushika, who had vowed to tell only the truth. It so happened that one day a group of innocent men were hiding behind a thicket near where the *riṣi* lived because they were being chased by some bandits. When the bandits came and asked the *riṣi* where were those men, he spoke the truth and the bandits looted and killed those innocent people. The scripture has it that the truthful Kaushika had to taste the horror of hell for having spoken that particular piece of truth. It is clear to the minimum moral common sense that such a theory is a bad ethical theory and needs to be toned down, even violated, in a demanding situation like the one described. That is why the very same Krishna had persuaded Yudhisthira to tell the lie about the death of Drona's son, Ashwasthama, in order that Drona, the invincible, may drop his arms and the deserving Pandavas could win the battle of *Mahabharat*. In fact, the *Mahabharat* prescribes such justified violations of the principle of truth-telling in five specific demanding situations.[7] Now, what is the ethical theory which, being applied here, makes the violation of this celebrated moral principle morally justified? Surely this is consequentialism, judging morality of actions on the basis of prizable consequences. The same goes for the other celebrated principles of non-stealing (*asteya*) and non-killing (*ahimsā*). The great *riṣi* Viswamitra made a justified violation of the former when he stole some meat to save the lives of his starving family members, while Bhisma gave a similar treatment to the latter when he commended that scriptural owl for breaking hundreds of eggs laid by a poisonous snake, thereby preventing calamitous loss of human lives because of numerous deadly poisonous snakes that would have hatched out of the eggs. Since a great moral good resulted from this, the so-called *adharma* committed by the owl was as good as, or rather better than, the normally considered *dharma* of non-killing. Classical Indian theory of *dharma* considers such violations of celebrated moral principles not only permissible but also commendable. Violations in Viswamitra-like situations are justified as *āpad dharma* or duty

7. *The Mahabharat*, Vol. 4, '*Karnaparva*", p. 398: 31-32. The conduct of a marriage ceremony, the process of sex between couples, the attempt to save someone's life, the attempt to prevent somebody's everything being snatched away and prevention of danger to a *bramhin's* welfare are the five specific situations where telling lies would cause no sin.

in emergent, calamitous situations. It is a matter of moral significance that it is not always irrational not to do what conventional morality wants us to do, nor is it always rational (approved by moral rationality) to act as per the moral commandments in the received sense. Take, for example, the maxim that to forgive is divine. The *Mahabharat,* which is naturally expected to assent to this*, has implicit instruction to the contrary. Prahallada says this to Bali regarding the moral virtues of forgiving:

> But forgiving in all conditions is not allowed, even for the wise people: *tasmāt nityam kshyamā tāta panditeirapi varjitā.*
> (*The Mahabharat*, Vol.II.p.1022: 8)

A blanket commandment to forgive, and a literal adherence to this commandment, cannot be morally justified. For forgiveness granted to every offender, irrespective of whether or not he sincerely realises his guilt and repents and hence deserves forgiveness, may be morally counter-productive on occasions and even undesirable, for:

> He who always forgives all offenders indiscriminately acquires many defects; his servants, enemies as well as people unrelated to him do not take him seriously and rather disrespect him, and no one behaves with him in a humble manner:
>
> *Yo nityam kshyamaté tāta, bahun doṣān saḥ bindati/.*
> *Bhrutyāḥ paribhavantyenamudāsinastātharayaḥ//.*
> (See *ibid.*p.1022: 7)

Forgiveness is morally justified only if it is extended on morally justified grounds, i.e. when extended to the offender

* For it holds *kshyamā* to be of the highest authority: *kshyamā dharma, kshyamā yajña, kshyamā veda, kshyamā śrutam*; Forgiveness is morality, forgiveness is sacrifice, forgiveness is the vedas, forgiveness is revealed truth. (*The Mahabharat,* Vol.II, pp. 1027:35).

who is really deserving of it. Forgiveness, like most moral values, is a conditional virtue which admits of justified violation in demanding situations.

Moral values instantiate that important kind of things, i.e. principles and relations, which hold necessarily, though, on occasions, they may be defeasible in overriding circumstances when another competing value demands precedence. The necessity of values is a weaker sort of necessity that is different from the strictly logical form of necessity, which is absolute and unexceptionable. For ethics, unlike logic, is a product of the society, which aims at promoting values common and conducive to effective and desirable social living. In this sense it operates in the empirical level of social process and so moral principles grow out of taking due note of the peculiarities and relevance of particular cases of moralising. The appropriateness of a value to be pursued, thus, cannot be thought apart from social situations. The normal situational fact is that people live as members of the society, which runs through various circles of interaction which, in turn, demand "various kinds and degrees of cooperation, competition and conflicts".[8] Moral values, like truth-telling, therefore, need to be pursued accordingly. It would not be reasonable to tell the truth to an enemy or even to a business competitor. A business boss is not being dishonest if he does not speak the 'whole truth' in a press conference. Nor is an ailing patient untruthful when she responds with "Fine, thank you!" to a visitor's courtesy "How are you?" as she would *be* in responding in a similar manner to her physician's query. Withholding the truth in such situations would not be a blanket violation of the virtue of truth-telling, for defeasibility of a virtue under demanding circumstances does not and cannot turn this virtue into a vice at all. In demanding situations, like the one in which Kaushika spoke the truth, a considerate, confident, lie would have been a better—a *morally* better—alternative to an

8. J.L. Mackie, *Ethics: Inventing Right and Wrong*, (Penguin Books, London, 1977), p. 182.

undesirable revelation of truth. And this would have been a proper example of 'justified violation' of a (conventional) moral principle—sanctioned, as we have noted, by scriptures and masters of reputed traditions. This is not, however, to lapse into unfettered relativism; for the violations are *justified* by a balance between the spirit of the principle and the demand of the situation, without which ethics cannot be a social affair which it is primarily supposed to be. Perhaps because of considerations like these, Mackie has warned by saying: "A prudent man will not squander his limited stock of convincing lies, but use it sparingly to the best effect".[9]

One may see a tension here between prudence or self-interest and moral reason which I have taken to be the justification for violating a principle on appropriate occasions. Sidgwick, for example, saw this tension to be irresolvable. But the tension is only apparent; it will lose its apparent strength when it is seen that egoism or the self-interest theory is a moral theory that occupies an important place in any viable moral system. For everyone, *in his own interest*, should desire that there be a moral system. A parallel can be drawn from the area of business ethics (of which we have more to say in a later chapter): If the aim of business is the maximization of owner value, an ethical conduct of business (i.e., taking care of customer satisfaction, maintenance of quality, maintaining reasonable profit margin and employees' welfare etc.) will achieve this purpose in the long run, though this may result in short term losses. So it is in its own interest that business should be ethical. *Good ethics results in good business*, as advocated by Milton Friedman and others. Thus, what is important is a viable moral system based on cooperation and reciprocity even amidst conflicts and competitions. And even if an existing moral system is found not to be suitable to one's self-interest one should try to modify it and not destroy it or run away from it. This brings us back

9. *Ibid.*, p. 183.

again to the significance of justified violations of moral principles which points, in turn, to the fact that moral values are necessary but defeasible.

The conventional theory that moral values are absolute and not violable under any circumstances is formally known as rigorism or the theory of duty for duty's sake. But despite its profundity and respectability in both western and eastern ethical history, rigorous pursuit of this theory is questionable in principle. To say the very least, the theory is not universal. It is true that people are normally lauded with moral credit for doing things from a sense of duty, but this is not the case on all occasions. We may sometimes justifiably praise somebody (morally, i.e.) for not doing what normally was his duty and we may, also justifiably, even blame him (morally) had he done what was his duty just for the sake of doing his duty without caring for consequences and despite knowing well enough that it would lead to disastrous consequences. In addition to our example of Kaushika and his truth telling, we may take another example from the area of professional ethics. A doctor, as a normal human being, is normally obliged to convey the correct information about the state of his patient's health to the patient as well as to his family members. But if the patient is suffering from a terminal disease, like blood cancer or brain cancer and if, in addition, the patient's father has serious cardiac history, then withholding the correct information about his patient's health, or even passing on an incorrect information, would be morally praiseworthy. But passing on the correct information, though it is the duty of the doctor as a normal human being, would not merit moral credit, but rather in view of the catastrophe on the family, if it happens to occur, would make him worthy of moral condemnation. Insisting steadfastly on doing his duty and passing on the correct information would make him not only a duty-fanatic but a bad professional too; for professional ethics demands a certain sort of secrecy in the interest of an avoidable moral catastrophe. The compulsions of his professional ethics, which requires him to maintain the described secrecy, would defeat and override the competing ethics of truth-telling, though a universal duty it otherwise is. Sometimes, in situations like this, not to do one's duty may become one's duty; by not passing on the correct information he would be doing what it is his duty *not to do*. This was so aptly expressed by Rajendra Prasad in his *Karma, Causation and Retributive Morality*.[10] The concept of duty may thus merit modification and a conventional duty, thereby, may warrant violation as justified by the demands of the situation without making any considerable departure from the spirit of the theory. Defeasibility and justified violability, in our view, must define the nature and spirit of moral principles.

On the point of what I call justified violation and defeasibility of moral principles, a possible but recurring doubt will have to be got out of the way. We have seen that violation of a celebrated moral principle may be called for *as morally justified* under demanding situations, but we have also been insisting that the demands of the situation must be properly balanced with the spirit of the principle at issue, which must not be sacrificed and made totally subservient to the former. It must be remembered that the aim of ethics, and hence of every moral principle, is to promote values common and conducive to practical life and to provide effective guidance for moral living. And application of ethical theories must be made accordingly. But applying a principle in its absolute literal sense, we have seen, would in effect be contrary to the spirit of the principle and would lead to morally undesirable consequences (like the loss of innocent lives as a result of truth telling by Kaushika). That is why, toning down or even violating these principles, say of truth telling, will be morally justified in the sense that its result would be morally desirable and hence in keeping with the spirit of the principle. Withholding the truth or even telling a lie on the part of Kaushika in the described circumstances would not strictly be considered violation of the spirit of the principle of truth

10. Published by the ICPR, New Delhi in 1989, p. 268.

telling which (the spirit) is, after all, meant to promote moral good; and saving the lives of innocent passers by, even at the cost of telling a (morally desirable) lie, can never be anything other than moral good. In making such (justified) violations, we would not be making an exception to the *morality* of the principle, but only to the scope of its application[11]. There are, here, two principles in conflict, namely truth-telling and saving the lives of innocent people. The former is *defeated* under the circumstances and is overridden by the later, which is a more comprehensive value with higher authority. In the face of this, revelation of truth is morally undesirable and hence is not morally justified. This does not mean that truth-telling under normal circumstances would cease to be a virtue; this only means that truth-telling, like most moral principles, is a defeasible moral principle, violable under appropriately demanding situations. Later on, I shall argue that the same applies in the case of the conflict between *svadharma* and *sādhāraṇa dharma* in the tricky situation that Arjuna faced in the battle of *Mahabharat,* and that in the interest of fighting a righteous war Arjuna's *svadharma* had an arguably overriding capacity. Because of this, I would also like to argue, Yudhisthira's telling the lie about Aswasthama's death had the overriding claim in the interest of winning a righteous war which is morally justified, and which could not have been possible without his telling this lie. Tricky situations of conflicts of principles, though few, are not rare and ignorable in the complexities of practical life, and these situations call for sophistication, in the form of exercising critical power, in moralising. Violation of the absolute form of moral principles in the greater interest of preserving the spirit of the principles is an important element of this sophistication and is thus a significant aspect of applied ethics.

Absolute Standards Account for Inapplicability

It may be asked now: if the absolutistic version (should we say,

11. See Rajendra Prasad. *ibid.* p. 272.

literal version) of these celebrated theories are thus bad ethical theories—because inapplicable or disastrous, if applied—how and why our great seers had tended to stick to them? It is mainly because they had failed to know the subtle nature of *dharma* (or duty). To know this, I would say, is to know when to follow a *sādhāraṇa dharma* (duty of all men) and when to make a justified exception to it, to know to what extent and with what stringency one has to follow a moral rule and when to make an exception to it without sacrificing the spirit of the principle and without ignoring the demands of the situation. Kaushika failed in this and Viswamitra too would have failed had he allowed himself and the members of his family to die of starvation rather than living on stolen meat.

Besides this, there is another important factor, which makes an ethical principle inapplicable or unattractive. Generally ethical theories are formulated by men of extraordinary nobility and exemplary strength of character, who set the moral standards too high for the common man with normal moral faculties to reach these standards. Thus, if a normative ethical theory keeps its moral norms so high that "they become unreachable for the common man, prescribe principles he cannot emulate or recommend actions he cannot perform, it is bound to be dissuasive".[12] Indeed, in a very reasonable sense, such theories cannot be called *normative* ethical theories in as much as their "norms" fly far away from the normal. As Rajendra Prasad makes the point, a normative ethical theory must pertain to what ought to be and what ought to be done *as well as* what normally is and what normally is done, because the concepts of *normative* and *normal* share the common parentage in the concept of *norm*. As a result of long communicative use to do different kinds of jobs they may develop different logical (i.e. functional) characters and obscure their family resemblance, but their parentage can never be obliterated. It is not suggested that the

12 Prasad, *ibid*, p. 270. I have adopted this argument from Professor Prasad, whose influence on this chapter is considerable and compelling.

norms of the ethical theories should be easy and soft so that no effort would be necessary to live up to them. All I wish to say, which I have put forth as a condition of applied ethics, is that living up to ethical norms must be possible not only logically but also empirically in the world we live, move and have our being. A Platonic picture of the moral order as a single system of actually existing perfect prototypes (as found, for example, in the Divine Command theory and in the Natural Law theory) is useless and unhelpful. For, "it succeeds in creating an indubitable and infallible authority of the prototype only by (stipulatively) defining it so and by making it altogether distinct and separate from our ordinary fallible thinking and acting, but thereby making it useless for improving our actual [moral, PKM] practice".[13] Guidance for a good moral living, which a normative ethical theory aims at giving, is needed more by the ordinary man than by a savant or a saint. Indeed, as some Indian moral philosophers have made it clear, ethics and ethical standards are not applicable in the case of these liberated souls. "It is obvious", says Mckenzie, "that in a certain sense ethical categories are inapplicable. He who has attained *moksa* is beyond good and evil"[14].The *Chhandogya Upanishad* points out that no evil can cling to a knower just as no water can cling to a lotus leaf (iv.14.3); the saints with the purity of their liberated souls can do nothing moral or immoral. The ethical teachings of the Upanishads are relevant and rather necessary for an individual's preparation for this liberation. It pertains to this lower stage of life of the ordinary man. The saint who is untouched by evil or good can afford the luxury of the most arduous moral standards, which *he* can follow but no ordinary man can. In the austerity of moral absolutism, where only angels revel, mortals are likely to falter. And in the fact of occasional failures lies the key to all that goes to make the significance of

13. Kurt Baier, *The Rational and The Moral Order*. (Open Court, Chicago and La sale, Illinois), p. 199.
14. John McKenzie, *Hindu Ethics*, Reprint Corporation. Delhi p. 77.

human freedom and moral accountability. For only in the possibility of doing something wrong that someone's conduct can be morally judged; and one who just cannot do anything wrong is outside the scope of the moral scanner. It is because of this that the Buddha pleaded for an ethical code known as *madhyamārga* or the middle path. He has very rightly said that it is pointless to lay out a road on which only the extremely sturdy can walk. An exalted but inapplicable ethical theory is like a marvelous mansion with cracks on its roof; it will be held in high adoration as long as one is not going to live in it. What is required, therefore, is that the described gulf between the infallible moral standards and the actual moral practice is bridged, so that the Platonic prototypes would be brought down to earth and applicable to society and the world at large. That is why, Baier pleads for construing the moral order as a social order and morality as essentially applicable to society. A social order, Baier goes on to say, is a certain character or quality possessed by societies, which may possibly be very different from each other, but qualify as a moral order by virtue of sharing the same social order (*ibid*).

Logical Consistency and Applicability

A moral theory, like any genuine philosophical theory, must be logically consistent. Just as it is impossible to think illogically, so also a logically indefensible normative theory cannot provide any guidance for a moral life and hence for what I have been referring to as a desirable world. Only by making our moral theories logically consistent (free from "cracks in the roof") can we apply them to human life for the promotion of the good life. The function of moral philosophy, as that of philosophy, says Rajendra Prasad, must not be reportive but analytic and reconstructive, by which our ethical theories can be made logically consistent, wherever necessary, and applied effectively to the world. Hence the justification of 'justified violations' of exalted theories of morals. Although, we have seen, there have been some cases in classical Indian ethics where this sort of exercise has been taken resort to, yet this has not been so in many of our celebrated theories of morals, especially as envisaged in our epics and the *Bhagavad-Gita*. By way of illustration, I pick out two cases of what I call bad ethical theories, one of which, because of flawed logic, could not be effectively applicable and inevitably led to several moral crises, and the other, because of its exalted absolute standards, led to morally disastrous consequences, when applied. The former is the theory of *dharmas* (duties) in the *Bhagavad-Gita* and the latter is the principle of promise keeping of Bhisma in the *Mahabharat*.

Let me briefly deal with the latter first. *Bhisma pratijñā*—the promise keeping of Bhisma—is a proverbial moral ideal in India's scriptural tradition. Bhisma was promise bound to protect the throne of Hastinapura and be loyal to the king, and he kept this promise till his last breath. But in the process of his promise keeping he was forced to do what Dhrutarastra desired him to do and even had to fight against his dearest Pandavas, despite knowing fully well that King Dhrutarastra and the heir apparent to the throne, Duryodhana, were on serious immoral path. What is worse, even after the deceitful game of dice, when the virtuous Droupadi was shabbily treated and was going to be disrobed in public by the wicked brother of Duryodhana, Bhisma, the paragon of virtues and *dharma,* remained a helpless spectator. Even when asked by wailing Droupadi whether it was right and in accordance with *dharma* on the part of Yudhisthira to put her on stake, after having lost his freedom and hence his agency, in the game of dice, Bhisma pleaded inability to answer her question on the plea that the meaning of "*dharma*" was too deep and subtle[15] to admit of a clear answer. This may be so with the meaning of *dharma*; but our moral common sense cannot accept disrobing of a virtuous lady of a great family—for that matter any woman—in public as a *dharmic* action in

15. *The Mahabharat*, Vol. II, *Dyutaparva*, p. 898.

any sense of the term, much less can it accept the fact that Bhisma, whom Lord Krishna used to describe as the repository of *dharma*[16] ("*dharma mayonidhiḥ*"), did not have enough knowledge to answer Droupadi's question and prevent the ghastly immoral attempt to disrobe her. It was a different matter that Krishna prevented the disrobing of Droupadi, but morality was disrobed that day and nobody tried to prevent that. At any rate, it was Bhisma's literal adherence to the abstract theory of promise keeping which not only kept him from preventing this particular act of immorality, it also kept him from preventing a great moral disaster—the destruction of a great royal dynasty! His violating this principle under these demanding circumstances would have told us a different story, most certainly about a morally desirable world.

Dharmas, Conflicts and Defeasibility

I now turn to *Gita* theory of *dharma* that recognizes two types of *dharma—svadharma* and *sādhāraṇa dharma*—both of which constitute a very fundamental normative structure of classical Indian ethics. First, let us consider *svadharma* or what is also known as *varṇadharma* (one's duty as a member of a particular *varṇa*). It has been maintained in the *Bhagvad-Gita* that, for a balanced and effective functioning of the social system, God created four *varṇas* of men and assigned to them four different types of duties or *dharmas*. The duties of a person belonging to a particular *varṇa* is called *varṇadharma* or his *svadharma*: for the *Brahmins* it is worship, teaching and preaching, for the *Kshyatriyas*, to rule over and protect the country, for the *Vaiśyas*, diligence, tread and commerce and for the *Śudras* it is to work for the other three castes, presumably to enable them to perform their duties effectively, thereby facilitating effective division of labour. Krishna says in the *Gita* that he made this assignment of the different *varṇadharmas* on the basis of *gūṇas* (nature,

16. *Ibid.*

qualities) and *karmas* (natural dispositions to act in certain ways): "*gūṇa karma vibhāgasaḥ chaturvarṇam mayā sruṣṭam*".[17] Besides the four types of *svadharma,* there are a set of general duties called *sādhāraṇa dharma,* i.e. duties which are obligatory for all men irrespective of their *varṇa.* These are the ones like truth-telling, non-killing and non-stealing etc. Both these types of duties—*svadharma* and *sādhāraṇa dharma*—are supposed to be obligatory, a kind of categorical imperative, which are best performed in a *niṣkāma* way or desireless manner—with no desire or concern for consequences. Whether any action can at all be performed in this manner is a debatable question, but that will constitute the subject-matter of a separate chapter or paper. My present concern is to examine the necessity of these imperatives and their applicability.

It has been shown already that the duties like truth-telling, non-killing and non-stealing, which come under *sādhāraṇa dharma*, are not applicable if taken as obligatory (for their application in some situations lead to morally disastrous consequences), and should therefore be applied with exceptions under suitably demanding situations. We have now to see the logicality of the *varṇadharmas* or *svadharmas* being obligatory and categorical as claimed by the authors of this theory. But here we are stopped by a puzzling problem—a moral crisis—that results from the inevitable conflict between the two moral principles, *svadharma* and *sādhāraṇa dharma,* both of which are claimed to be obligatory. This is very significant, for it is *because* Arjuna faced this crisis and declined to fight in the battle of *Mahabharat* that Lord Krishna had to elaborate the *varṇadharma* theory and tried to apply it persuasionally to convince Arjuna that it was his *svadharma* as a *kshyatriya* (prince) to fight and defend his country from the wicked influence of his adversaries. Yes, it was his *svadharma* as a prince to fight, argued Arjuna, but it was also his *sādhāraṇa dharma,* duty as a man, not to kill! How can he fight a war

17. *Bhagavad-Gita* IV. 13.

which inevitably involves killing people, that too his own relatives and venerable elders? What exactly was his duty here—*svadharma* or *sādhāraṇa dharma*? The *Gita* seems to have no satisfactory answer to this, no *logical* solution to offer. (Indeed, the *Gita* has left many questions unanswered, but I have no scope here to address to this issue). The only answer we are offered to this crucial moral crisis arising out of the conflict between the two forms of *dharmas* or duties is that Arjuna should follow his *svadharma* as a Kshatriya and fight in the war, even if he would have to kill people, including many of his own kinsmen. The conflict here was a conflict between (Arjuna's) *svadharma* and (his) *sāmānya dharma* and Krishna's exhortation virtually meant that the former should override the latter. But one suspects that Krishna did not offer any reason for justifying why should this *sāmānya dharma* or *sādhāraṇa dharma*, which is normally thought more important as a *mānava dharma*, or a universal duty of men, be allowed to be superseded by what may be dubbed as a sectarian duty. Instead, he simply went on extolling the *varṇa dharma* as absolute and inviolable. Arjuna must perform his *svadharma* of fighting the war and must not worry about killing his adversaries or causing their death; it was even pleaded that killing he would not be doing, because they (their souls) are immortal or (alternatively) all his sins including the sin of killing would be waived or redeemed if he took shelter in the Lord (Krishna). (*Sarvadharmān parityajya māmekam śaraṇam braja//Aham tvām sarva pāpebhyaḥ mokṣayisyāmi mā sucha//*). Put in other words, Krishna argued to the effect that either Arjuna would not kill them (who are *amrutasya putrāḥ)* or even if he would, the sin of his (act of) killing, in fact all his sins, would be redeemed in his surrender to the divine. The irony of the *Gita* theory of *dharma* is that the whole theory is devoted almost exclusively to emphasise the importance of *svadharma* and very little attention is given to *sādhāraṇa dharma* or *sāmānya dharma*. Arjuna's question as to why should he perform this specific duty in preference to his universal duty of non-killing and non-killing of his kinsmen (*kūla dharma*) remained unanswered or inadequately answered, anyway. Instead of offering any logical counters to Arjuna's arguments, and when his arguments apparently failed to convince[18] the latter, Krishna cast a sort of spell (!) on him and revealed to him the cosmic form (*viśwarūpa*) and an overwhelmed Arjuna was made to fight. Instead of persuasionally applying an ethical principle to convince Arjuna to do what Krishna thought he (Arjuna) ought to do, the latter only used a non-moral method of emotional persuasion. Perhaps Krishna would have done better had he argued for the violation of the *sādhāraṇa dharma* of non-killing here in the interest of fighting a righteous war (Arjuna's *svadharma*), which would have been a morally justified violation, and Arjuna's *kshyātra-dharma* would have had an arguable overriding capacity.

It might be objected that as a matter of principle, a *varṇa dharma* can't (be said to) override a *sādhāraṇa dharma* on the ground that the former is a sectarian duty or a professional duty while the latter is a universal duty[19]. It will be said, that is, while a professional duty or a sectarian duty is limited to a specific group of people, a universal duty is binding on all men. It may be said further that one can opt out of a profession* and so be not obliged to perform the specific duty prescribed for the

---

18. "*Hato vā prāpsyasi swargam, jitvā vā bkokshyasé mahim//Tasmāt uttiṣtha Kountéya yudhāya kritanischayaḥ"//.* (If you die in the battle, you will go to heaven, and if you win, you'll enjoy mastery over the kingdom; therefore arise, Oh son of Kunti, and be determined to fight) mocks at the theory of *Niṣkāma Karma* and "*Sarva dharmān parityajya māmékam saraṇam braja//Aham tvām sarva pāpebhyaḥ mokshyayisyāmi mā sucha*" (Give up all *dharmas* and stake shelter in me, I shall free you from all sins) smacks of persuasion and indoctrination rather than argumentation.
19. See for example Rajendra Prasad, *Karma, Causation and Retributive Morality*, p. 257 and elsewhere.

* If *varṇnadharma* is determined by *gūṇa* and *karma*, a person can very well change his *varna* to which he might have happened to belong and become worthy of another *varṇa* by virtue of his *gūṇa* and *karma*. A critique of *svadharma* as *swabhāvaja* and hence unchangeable is detailed in what follows.

professionals in question, but no one can opt out of one's universal duty that is imperative for every man, since no one can opt *not to be* a man if he happens to be one.

Prasad's argument to this effect is fairly cogent but, I suspect, enigmatically simplistic. And this is so for two reasons. My first reason for finding it enigmatic is that Professor Prasad himself has lately been a recognized champion of the theory of 'justified violation' of moral principles, and this apparently absolutistic characterization of *sāmānya dharma* as not defeasible by *svadharma* and the similar absolute distinction between *sāmānya dharma* and *svadharma* does not go well with his (justified) violability theory. And my second reason is Prasad's implicit admission of possible defeasibility of each of the two forms of *dharma* by the other. For he resents the failure of the *Gita* theory of *dharma* by alleging that it "does not provide any clear cut principle to determine when a *sāmānya dharma* can supersede a *varṇa dharma* or *vice versa,* though it does admit that on occasions one can supersede, or be superseded by, the other." (*Ibid*, p. 292) Quite true, the one form of *dharma* can override and be overridden by the other form of *dharma*, and this is admitted not only by the *Bhagavad-Gita* but generally by the bulk of our scriptural traditions and especially, as we have seen, by the *Mahabharat.* For this reason, I maintain in this work that moral principles and ethical theories are universal but defeasible, that they are violable in demanding situations, and this applies to all forms of ethical theories. The compulsions of a paradigmatic righteous war meant for establishing *dharma (dharma samsthāpanārthāya)* evidently warranted a Kshatriya's *svadharma* the overriding capacity over his *sāmānya dharma* of non-killing and also of protecting his kinsmen.

Critique of Svadharma as Swabhavaja

Now for the logicality of *Gita*'s theory of *svadharma* or *varṇa dharma.* As said above, *svadharmas* are supposed to be obligatory by natural necessitation, for the *Gita* defines a *svadharma* as born out of the nature of the members of the particular *varṇa*. This much at least is the implication of a *varṇa dharma* being defined as *swabhāvaja*.[20] The assumption is that the four classes of people belong to four different "natural kinds", as it were, and the *guṇas* (qualities) and *karmas* (actions), which form the basis of this division of each class are strictly limited to or typical of it and different from those of other *varṇas*. It is advised that one ought to do what is required of him as per his own *svadharma* and not try to do what is that of some body else belonging to a different *varṇa*, which is *paradharma* (somebody else's duty). The *Gita* even has the injunction that it is better to die while performing one's own duty (*svadharma*) than trying to do what is the duty of another person of a different *varṇa* (*paradharma*), because the latter is fraught with fear.[21] And he who performs his *svadharma* incurs no sin[22], even if the consequence of that action turns out to be harmful in any way, whereas he who takes resort to *paradharma* is considered to be doing something sinful; such a person should be dissuaded or disallowed from performing *paradharma* and even be punished, if he does perform this. Eklavya, the tribal youth, a *śudra*, was not permitted to learn the art of archery from Drona because that was not his *svadharma* and Sambuka, the tribal chief, was killed by Rama for performing *tapaḥ* (meditation) which was not his *svadharma*!

Now let us see how this important ethical theory, being based on flawed logic, became inapplicable or, rather, could not be effectively applicable and led to undesirable consequences, when applied without qualification. The theory, as I see it, is based on two basic assumptions: (1) The four *varṇas* (classes or castes) are exclusive natural kinds and (2) one's *varṇa dharma* is determined by one's own nature or *swabhāva*. From these

---

20. *The Bhagavad-Gita*, Ch. XVIII, 42-44 and elsewhere.
21. *Ibid*, Ch. XVIII, 47.
22. See Sri Aurobindo, *Essays on the Gita*, p. 497 and also Samkara, *Gita Bhasyam*, p. 433.

premises it naturally follows that (3) what is natural to one is obligatory to him and *vice versa.* We can easily see that this theoretical framework leaves us with two options, each of which is unacceptable: Either (a) what one is naturally disposed to do is always morally right (so is one's bounden duty) or (b) it could be sometimes right and sometimes wrong, the theory has no criterion for the distinction between what is right and what is wrong (there is nothing to tell what one ought to do from what one ought not to do). But while (a) is an obvious untruth (b) is self-defeating for the theory. Thus, by *reductio ad absurdum*, we have good reason to conclude that (1) and (2) are weak assumptions of the theory. We have reason to ask why the natural must be the determinant of what is one's duty or what is right for one to do? And the *varṇa dharma* tradition—*Gita, Mahabharat,* and *Manu Smruti*—has no answer to this, nor do we find any reason (logical) offered. On the contrary, classical Indian tradition puts a fair amount of emphasis on self-control and self-purification, which suggests that it does not consider human nature to be morally sacrosanct and unerring. Therefore it remains an open question as to why should naturalness determine one's duty?*

Besides, it is a matter of common experience that despite our clear knowledge of right and wrong, *dharma* and *adharma*, quite often, by natural impulse, we refrain from doing the right thing and take resort to wrong doing. Duryodhana's oft-quoted confession that, although he knows very well what is *dharma* and what is *adharma*, he has neither the inclination to stick to the former nor the disinclination from doing the latter,[23] is a clear indication of this fact of nature (human nature), which definitively falsifies the theory of natural necessitation (*swabhāvajatā*); one is not only not always necessitated but not

* The basic spirit of the argument has been adopted from Professor Rajendra Prasad, *ibid,* pp. 16-17.

23. "*Jānāmi dharma na cha mé pravṛtti//Jānāmyadharma na cha mé nivṛtti*"// Vidyaranya Swami, *Panchadasi,* p. 192.

even inclined to do what he knows he ought to do. It is odd and perhaps disappointing that the *Gita* did not have anything to explain, much less remove, this possibility of akratic abstention from one's duties and akratic indulgence in non-duties or wrong doings. This, however, can be explained and applied ethics, in its persuasional form, can try to remove or at least lessen, the occurrence of immoral actions under akratic conditions. Akartic abstention from duties and indulgence in non-duties is certainly an act of immorality; but this is no cause for despair. A moral philosopher, perhaps with a bit of psychological deconditioning, could use the agent's awareness, if not explicit guilt, that he has done something contrary to what he knows is moral, to strengthen his moral will. This may not guarantee cent percent success; but it would surely have the effect of minimizing immoralities issuing from weakness of will. Besides, I think the problem here is a problem regarding the connection between what one believes to be moral and what he is motivated to do. Normally, to accept or believe that ***X*** is morally desirable is to be motivated to do ***X*** or act in accordance with ***X***, if ***X*** is a moral principle. Taken in a strict sense and omitting the qualification "normally", it would go in the way of ethical internalism, which sees a *necessary connection* between beliefs and motives. But the inadequacy of internalism is right on the surface, demonstrated by the not so unusual akratic actions coupled with awareness of their immorality. Beliefs and motives are thus not necessarily related. But this is unworrying. For it is possible to salvage a logical or conceptual relation between them by unravelling a weaker sort of logical relation that is weaker than logical necessity but stronger than mere contingent connection. A kind of phenomenon, say pain, need not occur always in the presence of another, namely, pain behaviour, but it still is logically, i.e., conceptually dependent on pain behaviour since, as Wittgenstein has so aptly pointed out, if nobody ever behaved as if he/she was in pain or said that he/she was in pain in a sincere tone of voice, then the word 'pain' would never have found a place in our language. It is thus logically impossible (in the weaker sense of "logically") for pain to occur *always* in the absence of pain behaviour. Evan Simpson makes the point thus:

> It is possible to rescue a conceptual connection between beliefs and motives by specifying logical relations weaker than logical necessitation. We can say, for example, that one kind of thing *logically depends* upon another if it is logically impossible for things of the first kind always to occur in the absence of the second, but logically possible that the first should sometimes occur alone. This is a logical relationship, but unlike necessitation it does not make it logically impossible for the first thing to occur without the second also occurring.[24]

These are instances of that important kind of relations, which are *necessary but defeasible*. And this more appropriately holds in the case of moral matters. (I have said above that in a similar way moral values are universal, though on occasions they may be defeated and overridden by other competing values). I shall therefore go to some extent* with ethical externalism and keep the qualification "normally" to say that moral beliefs and motives for appropriate actions are *normally* related by way of this described weaker logical relation. And that is quite enough to say that, few exceptions notwithstanding, *to accept X as morally desirable is to be motivated to act accordingly*. Because of this, we will be surprised if somebody acts contrary to what he believes to be moral. If this is so, an ethical theory can be *judgmentally* applied in practical situations, for to judge ***X*** to be right is to decide or be motivated to do ***X*** or act in accordance with ***X***. The cases of akratic weakness are understandable exceptions but could, in principle, be improved upon as we have shown. It would thus depend on the moral reformer how effectively he can persuasionally apply a moral principle to

24. "Between Internalism and Externalism in Ethics", *Philosophical Quarterly*, Vol. 49, No. 195, April, 1999, p. 203.

* For I have reasons to believe that both externalism and internalism are inadequate for giving a proper account of the relation between beliefs and motives. See Chapter 2 for more on this.

remove the weakness of the agent's will and with how much of success.

Anyway, because of factors like exclusive natural division of the *varṇas* and *a priori* assumptions of natural necessitation of them, the *svadharma* theory could not be effectively applied in a consistent manner. On the contrary, a strictly formal and literal adherence to it led, in some cases, to glaring injustice and immoralities. It was grossly unjust for Drona not to accept Eklavya as his disciple just because he was not a *kshatriya,* though he would have made a very worthy disciple and proved to be an equally great archer, if not greater, as Arjuna. It was also equally wrong and unjust not to allow Karna—otherwise a man of a great personae and valour—the status of a *kshatriya* prince simply because it was not publicly known that he was a *kshatriya* by birth as much as any of the Pandavas. The watertight division of the *varṇas* and the consequent exclusive *svadharma/ paradharma* distinction was not only logically unsound but also socially and culturally unwarranted. Rajendra Prasad very naturally wonders what a great tragedy it would have been for India as well as for the entire world if prince Goutama were to be prevented by a Lord Krishna from becoming a recluse because that was not his *svadharma*!

A good normative ethical theory is viable if it is consistently applicable in all *relevant* cases—*not in all* cases indiscriminately. The *varṇa-dharma* theory was certainly based on sound theoretical considerations of *gūṇa* and *karma*, but ran into serious practical problems by assuming these to be fixed and *a priori*. As a matter of fact, human nature being what it is, it cannot be assumed to be fixed and static. What is natural for a man is an empirical matter and can be determined only in a probabilistic manner on the basis of what he does and how he behaves. The proponents of the *varṇa-dharma* theory, Lord Krishna in particular, would have done much better by taking these facts into consideration and allowing justified violations of the theory in reasonably demanding situations. This would surely have led to a better world, a morally desirable world.

2

Moral Personhood

Natural Propensity of Man to Act Morally

If it is a logical truth that a desirable world must contain all that is ethically desirable and must not contain anything that is ethically forbidden, application of ethics (ethical principles, that is) to society is an essential imperative. For given the fact that the world contains a few things that are ethically forbidden and undesirable, only by applying ethics (in the way suggested above) philosophers and moralists could try to make the world morally desirable by minimizing the quantum of the forbidden and increasing that of the morally obligatory and the morally recommended. It is my firm contention that application of ethics to society is not only imperative, it is also a matter of natural necessity. While I have adduced fair enough reasons for the former contention in the first chapter, it will be my effort to argue for the latter in this chapter. To this purpose, I shall try to show that to be moral and to tend to act morally is as much natural for man[1] as it is for him to be rational. I shall argue, therefore, that man is a *naturally moral* being in the sense that every man has the natural propensity to act morally, unless

1. I shall use "man" in the sense of "person", presumably in the sense in which Aristotle defined man as a rational animal, and ignore the rather dubious distinction, made by Locke, between 'man' and 'person'—the former requiring a human body for its application and the latter defined in terms of consciousness "that *makes* a person".

otherwise constrained. It will be shown further that human nature being as it is—characterized by a natural propensity to act morally—and ethical theories being as they are—having a built-in applicability—these theories not only need to be, but they must be, applied to solve intriguing practical problems in society. It thus needs to be examined why and how a person is a moral being and is naturally so.

Persons as Naturally Moral

The theory of moral personhood that I want to present is based on the fact that morality supervenes on personhood in as much as the reality of value supervenes on the reality of consciousness. For consciousness, which essentially characterizes personhood, has two prominent aspects which, in a way, define personhood; those are *rationality* and *spirituality*. In respect of the first, man is capable of reason and reflection. And because of this feature, human consciousness necessarily contains what is called 'personal stance' which is adopted by one person towards another who, in turn, is capable of reciprocating this stance. As Strawson implied[2], to be a person is to treat others, who are like oneself, *as* persons. Rationality makes us recognize not only the distinction between oneself and others but also their essential interrelation; it accounts for (explains?) that reciprocal personal stance, which necessarily characterizes us, persons. By virtue of spirituality, the second important aspect of human consciousness, human beings are capable of reflective self-transcendence, which is the capacity to go beyond the confines of one's own interests and recognize values in others. Moral personhood is a necessary outcome of these two aspects, rationality and spirituality, of human consciousness. Thus if man is rational and spiritual by nature, then it follows that man is naturally moral. It is because of this that acting morally is

2. P.F. Strawson. *Individuals* (Methuen, London 1962) p. 99. "It is a necessary condition of one's ascribing states of consciousness, experiences, to oneself... that one should also ascribe them, or be prepared to ascribe them, to others who are not oneself."

congenial to human nature and on the few occasions when one refrains from morality or acts in ways contrary to moral expectations, one does find it *alien to one's nature and inclinations*, to say the least. This should be evident from the rather familiar fact that normal human mind is prone to conducts and actions that are considered good and virtuous, and to get along well with things and systems of thought that are true rather than false or erroneous. As an old Buddhist verse puts it, human mind has a "natural partiality for truth, which we all believe will ultimately triumph over error and ignorance". Man is not only a rational being with the power to know and appreciate moral values, but given his freedom unhindered by constraints of any sort, he would identify with what is morally valuable, and act and strive towards realization of it. In what follows I shall spell out in some detail this fact of morality as the natural offshoot of rationality and spirituality.

Rationality and Moral Personhood

Let us consider the fact of rationality in man. What is involved in man's being rational and how it bears upon moral personhood? When man is said to be rational it is meant to be so much an essential characterization of man—indeed a defining feature thereof—that any body trying to question this by asking "Why should I be rational?" would be asking an utterly improper question, because in trying to answer this question he would be giving *reasons* for his being rational! We would be presupposing rationality, that is, in our attempt to justify our being rational. The resulting justification of rationality, whatever we may come up with, would thus be inevitably circular. Thus it is, in a way, futile to ask for justification for man's being rational. But this shows "not that rationality lacks a necessary justification but that it needs no justification because it can't intelligibly be questioned unless it is already presuppsosed."[3] All this accounts for the definition of man as a rational being. The fact that many

3. P. Singer, *Practical Ethics*, 2nd edn. (Cambridge Univ. Press, 1993), p. 316.

people in fact are irrational or, at any rate, some times behave irrationally, is irrelevant to this definition. For what is meant here is that men are *capable* of rationality, that is, *capable* of being fully rational, though—because of factors alien to human nature—at times they may not be acting rationally. In this respect, to be rational, like to know, is a capacity concept *a la* Ryle—and hence the rational being need not always exercise the faculty of reason but *can* do so on appropriate occasions. The fact that some of us are very irrational some of the times, or even most of the times, in actual life should be absolutely unworrying. To such deviant pointers, eminently raised by Bertrand Russell, Antony Flew appropriately replied that "... to be rational, *in this sense of [being] capable of rationality*, is not merely not inconsistent with, but is a precondition of being irrational...", very much in the same way as "only a moral being, a *being capable of morality and immorality*, can be truly said to be actually immoral."[4] We would not say of a chimpanzee—even a systematically trained one—or of a sophisticated machine, or of a robot endowed with what now is fashionably described as artificial intelligence, that it is behaving irrationally, for it is incapable of behaving rationally and irrationality in the strict sense of these terms. Just as only people with a sense of logic can be said to be illogical and be properly reprimanded or criticized for being so, i.e. for being not logical of which they are capable, only rational beings, with a sense of discrimination between what is rational and what is not, can be said to behave irrationally and be held accountable for doing so. Because of this, actions of beasts, babblers and insane adults which, though may *happen* to be good or bad, useful or harmful, can never be termed as rational or irrational, much less moral or immoral; since responsibility cannot be ascribed to them and commendations or condemnations will not apply. Freedom and morality are semantically inalienable and in the obvious lack of

4. *A Rational Animal* (Oxford, the Clarendon Press, 1978), p. 90; emphasis added.

freedom in the described case, attribution of moral responsibility would be gratuitous.

Rationality thus being the presupposition of personal consciousness, reasoning is a distinctively human activity. Reason governs actions as well as theorizing. That is, we all are capable, by virtue of rationality, not only of theoretic discriminations of sorts, but also of judging what we should do and what we should not, what is good and right and what is not. Further, our actions that are governed by reason are responses made to our desires and, as Aristotle insisted, one can respond too much or too little to one's desires. The correct response lies somewhere between the two extremes. This is the doctrine of the golden mean. It is a meta-ethical statement about the form of certain moral concepts that to every virtue there are two distinct vices, the two extreme responses to one's desires. Reason steers clear between the two and locates the virtue. The distinction between the two extreme responses on the one hand and the correct response on the other is the distinction between what can be called the *desired* and the *desirable.* The desirable is what one values, or what any one would value, under all normal conditions. Being driven by passion, I may act upon a desire, e.g. to supersede a more deserving colleague which, deep within my inner self, I find alien and hostile because it is not in keeping with reason. My being motivated by such a desire, which I really disvalue, would create for me a moral predicament, not uncommon in human history and the rational struggle to get over it by attaining an "ideal consistency" between what I value and what I desire is a distinctive mark of personhood [5]. By acting upon the described desire I might appear to have been free to do what I desired to do, but this would be not only an irrational but a puerile view of freedom since, far from being free, I would be

5. For an elaborate analysis of the distinction between desiring and valuing, see B.H. Baruah, "Person and Value: A Sketch for a Theory of Moral Personhood" in *Persons, Mind and Value* ed. S.K. Mohanty (Decent Books, New Delhi-DSA Philosophy, Utkal Univ. 2000).

really impeded from being the person I want to be, if I acted on a desire which is hostile to what I value as a rational being. A genuine moral reason, as we shall elaborate in the next chapter, derives from what we value, from what we desire, from the nature of the case rather than from *our* nature. Thus rationality of persons is inseparably connected with morality or moral personhood. For as we see, morality is a distinctively rational affair in the sense that moral concern is grounded on reason. This makes persons, who are constitutively rational, naturally moral and endowed with intrinsic moral worth.

The other connected feature that follows from the person being rational is evaluative consciousness, which is characteristic of personal consciousness. That means that persons are conscious of others, the world and themselves in terms of moral and religious values. "Those things mean to them in certain ways, as having some significance."[6] Moral reflection, by which we engage in moral evaluation of ourselves, our actions and those of others, is thus constitutive of personhood; for moral reflection is the activity of rational agents and only persons are rational agents.

Moral reflection is an intellectual operation aimed at judging the moral worth of human actions and intentions. The objects of one's moral reflection may be one's own intention, actions as well as those of others. The results of such reflections are usually expressed in the form of moral judgements. Being endowed with the capacity of reason and reflection, a person often reflects on the rightness or wrongness, goodness or badness, morality or immorality of his actions before performing these actions, in which case the actions become proper objects of moral accountability. It is not that every person, every rational being, does engage in this act of reflection *always* before doing anything he does. Quite to contrary, moral reflection is not the same as moral action nor is moral action necessarily preceded by moral reflection. It is quite possible, indeed often the case,

6. *Ibid.* p. 9.

that men do things, which may turn out to be morally right and commendable without at all reflecting on the morality or otherwise of such actions before performing them. People often do such things because of their familial and societal habits and conditioning. Such unpremeditated actions, more prevalent in unsophisticated and intellectually naïve societies, are nonetheless subject to moral commendation or condemnation. A properly reflected action, however, gets a clear edge and is often more deserving, at least on the well-known principle that a Socrates dissatisfied is better than a pig satisfied. For if one simply happens to stumble on to what is the moral thing to do, one does it by fluke without knowing that one is doing so. And when one acts in this way, one gets no or not much credit for this. But when one does it with proper reflection, with full knowledge of what one is doing, one gets full credit for it and one's action is more properly moral, if I am allowed this adjective. The 'deserving trait' of moral reflection is further explained (evidenced) by the fact that, other conditions being fulfilled, moral reflections would lead to moral actions. However, in some cases, despite reflecting on the morality of an action ***X*** and judging that ***X*** ought to be done, a person may not do ***X***, because the actual doing of ***X*** requires fulfilment of certain other conditions, besides judging that it ought to be done—conditions like absence of hindrances, external and internal, incapacity of the agent, physical and physiological, and so on. But if these other conditions are fulfilled, "then one's judging that one ought to do ***X*** suggests that one would do it." This is how Rajendra Prasad explains the very intimate relation between moral reflection and moral action.[7] However, I would like to think that the "suggests" in the above quotation has all the strength of "implies". It is rather odd that Prasad seems to underplay this point, for Prasad himself goes on to say thereafter that other conditions being fulfilled, "We would then be

7. *Karma, Causation and Retributive Morality*, (ICPR, New Delhi, 1989), p. 2.

surprised or disappointed if we find that one does not do what one says [read 'judges', PKM] one ought to do. And *our surprise and disappointment will be more logical than psychological*".[8] This "logical surprise" at one's failure to perform the moral action ***X*** despite one's reflection that it is a moral action which one ought to perform clearly indicates the logical link between moral reflection and moral action by virtue of which people will resort to moral actions because of their moral reflection, unless obstructed by non-occurrence of the other required conditions. What kind of "logical" link are we talking about, it may be asked, if moral reflections do not always lead to moral actions, if moral beliefs and motives for actions are not necessarily related? To be sure, I have been talking somèwhat within the confines of externalism in ethics by espousing the thesis that one can accept (have the belief) that ***X*** is morally desirable and yet that this *alone* can't provide the motive for doing ***X***. The link, I suppose, can be construed as a conceptual connection, weaker than logical necessity but much stronger than mere contingent relation, very much in the way Evan Simpson suggested in his article "Between Internalism and Externalism in Ethics".[9] We can say for example, Simpson points out, that "one kind of thing [moral action in this case, PKM] logically depends upon another [moral reflection here, PKM] if it is logically impossible for things of the first kind always to occur in the absence of the second *but logically possible that the first should sometimes occur alone*."[10] This sort of logical relationship has been recognized in other areas of philosophy as well. Wittgenstein's notion of criterion, on which mental states are by nature expressible in physical behaviour, even if they are not always so expressed, may be a fitting case. Pain is typically, though not invariably, connected with pain behaviour. I have agued elsewhere[11] that it is not at all a case of contingent

8. *Ibid*. Emphasis added.
9. *Philosophical Quarterly*, Vol. 49, no. 195, April 1999.
10. *Op cit*, p. 202. (emphasis added).
11. See my *Concepts and Problems* (Cuttack, 1998), Ch. 12. p. 107ff.

relation, because though it is possible for pain to occur unaccompanied by pain behaviour, it is impossible for pain *never* to be expressed in behaviour. The impossibility of massive error makes Davidson argue that "belief in its nature is veridical", for most, if not all, of a person's beliefs must be true, although it is not a matter of necessity that any particular belief be true. I have adduced a similar view[12] that it is *necessary* that persons should have mental states though it is not necessary that a person should have *this* or *that* particular mental state. These are instances of that important kind of relationships, which are necessary but defeasible but which do not, for that reason, cease to be necessary and degenerate into contingency. In view of this, and given the weaker sense of logical dependence outlined above, we can say that it is necessary that anyone having a moral belief will *sometimes*, or quite often, be motivated to act accordingly—not necessarily that he will always be thus motivated. Thus, internalism fails and externalism fails too. The lack of logically necessary relation between beliefs and motives, between moral reflection and moral action, should be absolutely unworrying, for *pace* externalism, the fact is that moral motivation is included in the moral beliefs of people, that moral action flows from moral reflections, if of course there are no defeating situations obstructing the actual performance of the action. Simpson again: "It is part of making moral judgements that one is *sometimes* moved in virtue of the contents of those beliefs."[13] All this point to the fact that men with moral reflection are naturally inclined to act morally, and since moral reflection is the act of rational agents, persons are prone to act morally by virtue of their rationality, which is constitutive of their nature.

Our natural propensity to act morally is so strong and so compelling that it is often considered an improper question to ask "why act morally?" or "why be moral?" Besides the dubious reason (for rejecting the question as improper) that our ethical

12. See my *Personal Identity* 2nd edn. (Decent Books, New Delhi, 2000).
13. "Between Internalism and Externalism in Ethics" *op cit*, p. 203.

principles are by definition overridingly important,[14] the more important reason, important for the present purpose, is that this question be rejected on the same ground that we must reject the other question, "why should I be rational?"[15] The question "why should I be rational?", one can easily see, is a logically improper question, a question that should not, rather cannot, be asked for the simple reason that in asking this question one would be questioning something (i.e., rationality) that is normally, nay logically, presupposed. Therefore the question is really a logically improper question, since in trying to answer it one would be giving *reasons* for being rational. As we have argued above, we would have to presuppose rationality in trying to question rationality. Now, is the question "why should I be moral?" as much improper as the question "why should I be rational?" To be sure, to be rational is a part of the definition of being a man/person. Can we say that to be moral is also a defining feature of man? Would the question then be taken as presupposing the very same thing (morality) it purports to question? Yes, if the "should" in question is taken as a moral "should". For in that case one would be asking for *moral* reasons for one's being moral, and this would be absurd. However, as Singer rightly points out, it is not necessary to interpret the question as a request for an ethical justification of ethics. The "should" here need not mean a moral should. "Why should I act morally?" can simply be asking for reasons for one's actions without any specification about the *kind* of reasons asked for. There may be several non-ethical points of view from which we may demand reasons for actions, e.g. self-interest, public etiquette or aesthetics (aesthetic considerations). And whether to act morally from considerations of ethics, self-interest, etiquette or aesthetics would be a very open question, not

14. Singer, *Practical Ethics* 2nd edn. p. 315. Singer considered this as a dubious reason, since it conflicts with universalisability, which, by general admission, is a more natural feature of ethical principles.
15. *Ibid*, p. 316.

committed to the ethical point of view. Non-question beggingly, it is (may be interpreted as) "a question about the ethical point of view asked from a position outside it."[16] Given the conception of ethics as in some sense involving a universal point of view, the question "why should I act morally?" would be asking for reasons for transcending self-interest and acting on universalized judgments—from the point of view of the impartial spectator or ideal observer. We thus come back here to what we described as "reciprocal personal stance", which we claim to be constitutive of personhood as a result of the person being a rational agent. Kant is eminently noted for trying to demonstrate that to act rationally is to act ethically. Moral personhood is thus the direct offshoot of the person's rationality.

Spirituality and Moral Personhood

Let us now consider the impact of spirituality on the making of moral personhood. If it is because of rationality that we adopt the reciprocal personal stance and treat others as persons as we are, it is the faculty of spirituality that endows man with the distinctive capacity of reflective self-transcendence, the capacity to rise above the ethos of self-interest and egocentricity. Unfailing moral personhood, which requires freedom from egocentricity, depends upon spiritual sustenance. Admittedly the basic function of reason is to discern between oneself and others and to judge egoism as ethically inferior to altruism. But as we have seen above, merely judging that the latter is good and valuable is not necessarily or even invariably connected with one's actually being motivated to realize this good. Merely having the valuational system, which no doubt is the first important aspect of moral personhood, is not enough to have one's motivational system oriented accordingly. One has to *identify* with the value judgement in order to be so motivated; the identification has to be typically relevant to moral motivation.

16. *Ibid*, p. 317.

And such morally relevant sort of identification is possible only when it is characterised by spirituality. For in identifying with a value judgement "the agent is not just emotionally attached to the judgement of value but is in spiritual accord with the judgement of value".[17] Moral motivation is possible through spiritual endeavours.

What I want to drive home is the point that reason, unaided by spiritual endeavour, does not *eo ipso* facilitate morality or lead to moral action. In order to realize unfailing moral personhood, an agent must buttress his evaluation system with a distinctively spiritual urge for self-excelling. His motivational system must add to itself this unique spiritual urge for self-excelling which is not intrinsic to his evaluation system. More importantly, this spiritual urge is not only extrinsic to the agent's evaluation system, it is extrinsic to rationality itself.[18] For the attainment of unfailing moral personhood, rationality must be complemented by spirituality, both of which are distinct, though essential, aspects of personal consciousness. If we may put it this way, rationality, in so far as it promotes (is responsible for) the evaluation system in us, is the necessary condition of moral personhood whereas spirituality, in so far as it makes us identify with the value judgement or the moral point of view and orients our motivational system after that (the judgement of value, i.e.,) is the sufficient condition thereof; for the latter, in the company of the rational faculty in us, goes on to complete the making of unfailing moral personhood.

The more important fact, which must be noted with emphasis, is that spirituality, though extrinsic to rationality, is not extrinsic to personhood, like rationality. It is an innate potentiality which, when actualized or realized, leads the person to rise above his self-interest and egocentric ethos. To the extent to which this realization of spirituality is effected, moral personhood gets developed in the direction of perfection. The

17. B.H. Barua, *Persons, Mind and Value*, p. 36.
18. *Ibid*, p. 32.

control of our motivation system by our evaluation system can be a matter of degrees depending on the extent of this realization. The evaluation system can evolve and change drastically and moral paradigms can and do change because of this. The prevailing wisdom of a culture is a good source of value paradigms, which shapes our motivation after them. But to draw from this the general theoretic conclusion that moral personhood, even personhood, is a matter of degree and subject to gradation, as some have done,[19] is not only far fetched but odd and counter-intuitive. Moral personhood, like personhood, is an all-or-nothing concept, and the unfolding of it through evolving value systems cannot interfere with its intrinsic pristinity. Spiritual self-excelling, which makes this unfolding possible, is an innate capacity, which gets realized through intellectual maturity and in response to changing cultural ramifications. It is by virtue of this faculty of spirituality that the person is a reflective self-evaluator. If Heideggar said that persons are beings whose being is in question in their being, the spiritual urge for self-transcendence underlies their life of self-appraisal that leads to self-transcendence or self-excelling. As discussed earlier, while rationality makes us distinguish between wanting as desiring and wanting as valuing, between the *preya* and the *shreya,* as so aptly envisioned in the Indian value systems, spirituality makes us *alienate* from the former and *identity* with the latter. Reflective self-appraisal involves alienating or disvaluing something of our common nature, which Nerlich describes as "person-contingent" features,[20] such as some specific needs and desires, moods and manners, which form the first order features of ordinary life. The first order desires that persons have largely part of their human nature, which constitute the basic nature of a person. But humans would not be persons if they were to be

19. E.g., Baruah and Mohanty respectively in *Persons, Mind and Value*, especially, p. 30.
20. G.C. Nerlich, *Values: Speculations on the Ethical Life of Persons*, (Oxford, the Clarendon Press, 1989).

constituted of, and confined to, only the basic features with which the moral being in them refuses to identify. For persons are distinguished from other beings by virtue of the fact that they are capable of having higher order intuitions and attitudes towards their first order desires from a valuational point of view. This distinctive feature, which tells a person from a mere human being, is what Frankfurt calls "second order desires".[21] Second order desires mark the distinctive character of persons as reflective self-evaluators and it is in their ability for reflective self-evaluation that the real freedom of the person lies. For freedom consists, not in acting upon our basic desires but in being able to translate our higher order desires into actual motivations for actions. "The free agent has the capacity to translate his values into action; his actions flow from his evaluative system".[22] Compulsive behaviour, like that of a kleptomaniac or of one under coercion or hypnosis, are un-free, being responses to desires that claim fulfilment independently of the agent's evaluation system. By taking resort to reflective self-appraisal, the person—the moral person—exercises his freedom and breaks away from his basic desires and inclinations, which he finds alien to his nature, and identities with the others, which he values and glorifies. He wants to be different from what he happens to be. Thus Frankfurt:

> "Besides wanting and choosing and being moved to do this or that, men may also want to have (or not to have) certain desires and motives. They are capable of wanting to be different, in their preferences and purposes, from what they are…No animal other than man, however, appears to have the capacity for reflective self-evaluation that is manifested in the formation of second-order desires."[23]

---

21. H. Frankfurt, "Identification and Wholeheartedness", in F. Schoeman (ed), *Responsibility, Character and the Emotions* (Cambridge, CUP, 1987).
22. Gary Watson, *Free Will* (Oxford Univ. Press, 1982).
23. *Ibid*, p. 7.

Freedom of the individual, which is the driving force of self-excellence, is the prerogative of persons. It lies at the root of the urge to moral perfectibility and goes to the making of what I have been referring to as unfailing moral personhood. It is in quest of freedom that the person is engaged in reflective self-evaluation and as such is an embodiment of value. For because of his ability to be free, the ability to identify with the value judgement and motivate himself to live in conformity with it, that the person is able to transcend the level of mere human existence. The self-transcendence or personal self-excelling requires that the person's motivational system be controlled by his valuational system or evaluation system with which he identifies—his reason has to control his passion. The evaluation system that we persons have, it must be reiterated, is not or need not be static and fixed. It is a faculty we all are endowed with, and each of us is capable of developing and making progress with it by exercising the freedom to expose ourselves to new and changing values and circumstances. On its part, therefore, the evaluation system can evolve and go through drastic change—all through the exercise of our critical power of self-appraisal. This is how moral *progress* is possible. Moral progress is possible by moral striving, and moral striving that aims at moral perfection (attainment of perfect moral personhood) is, we have seen, not just rational but spiritual. And the capacity to exercise spiritual self-transcendence, as well as the freedom that leads to it, is explained by the fact that persons are capable of having second order desires.

The capacity to have and satisfy second order desires makes the person a normative being. For second order desires are higher order normative self-attitudes and as such are judgements upon our basic desires on the basis of valued norms. These judgements, which involve retrospective assessment of our already formed basic nature—our actions, inclinations and emotions—are caused by an attitude of self-appraisal and the urge for self-excelling, the spiritual urge we all are potentially capable of. "Because of higher order self-attitudes of normatively well developed kinds, a human subject considers herself, or what she does, an object of value for herself, an *itre pour soi*, or what is properly a person."[24]

The conclusion to which we are drawn from the foregoing considerations is that moral personhood is a joint offshoot of man's rationality and spirituality. As rational beings we discriminate between what *is* and what *ought to be* (if the former happens to be what ought not to be), we distinguish between what is desired and what is desirable, we know that altruism is preferable and worthwhile. As spiritual beings we identify with the latter and alienate from the former. And because of the spiritual urge we rise above self-interest and ego-centricity* and are motivated to act morally from the universal point of view. Both these faculties combined, make us not only aware of the moral, but also motivated to *be* moral, to act morally. Rational discernment of the moral from the immoral and spiritual urge for self-excelling put us naturally on the path of moral progress and moral perfection. Thus moral inclination is innate to persons, who are naturally or constitutively endowed with the capacity of rationality and spirituality. By virtue of this, we inherit our moral standards and go on improving these standards, replacing one (or one set of) standard(s) by another which may be found to be better under changing social and cultural scenario. Our intrinsic moral sense enables us to gather the acquired ability for improving and developing the moral standards, by living upto which we march towards moral perfection. Indeed this is

24. B.H. Baruah, *ibid*, p. 19.

* In so far as self-interest leads to, or becomes indistinguishable from selfishness and egoism. Self-interest, however, need not have only this connotation. It is certainly different from selfishness and can be rationally justified. Indeed self-interest can be morally sanctioned whereas selfishness can never be. And as long as self-interest does not affect the interest of others, it can have moral as well as rational justification. For example, it is quite rational and not at all immoral to carry an umbrella when it is raining, but obviously immoral if you snatch away somebody else's umbrella to protect yourself from rain and allow the other fellow to get drenched.

what moral philosophy is all about. "Much of moral philosophy should be seen as just a continuation—more self-conscious and more sustained—of this project of improvement that all of us are engaged in well before we have even heard of philosophy,"[25] much in the same way as we all think and speak in accordance with the principles of logic even without our being aware of it. That means, for a person there can't be any question about his having or not having any moral standards, it is only a matter of his having *this* or *that* moral standard. We are now in a position to see that the question 'Should I be moral?' or 'Why should be I moral?'—like the other question 'Should I be rational?' or 'Why should I be rational?'—is a logically improper question, which cannot be asked without involving self-inconsistency.

There is thus no alternative to our being moral, which is also evident from some compelling facts about human nature, like (1) that *we all have benevolent and sympathetic inclinations* that make us concerned about the welfare of others and (2) that we all have *a natural conscience* which gives rise to the feeling of guilt when we do something we know is wrong.[26] Awareness and acceptance of ethical standards is bound to make us live upto them. And on Hare's persuasive account of ethics, one's acceptance of ethical standards is likely to lead one to arouse similar moral feelings in others. Ethics has the primary function of promoting values common and conducive to the members of the society, and ethical judgements do this by commending and encouraging actions performed in accordance with these values. Further, ethical judgements must be concerned with the *motives* of (right) actions, not just the rightness of the actions, *pace* Kantianism and virtue ethics, because this is a good indication of the tendency of an action to promote good or evil, and also because it is here that praise and blame may be effective in altering the tendency of a person's actions. It is here also that applied ethics can begin to get a firm foothold. For praise and

25. James Griffin, *Value Judgment* (Oxford, the Clarendon Press, 1996), p. 1.
26. See Peter Singer, *Practical Ethics*, p. 327.

blame can change a man's moral evaluation system, which is a very good means of changing his moral behaviour. In this sense morality can be taught and our natural propensity to act morally can be properly propelled to bring about a desirable moral order. Like learning counting or knowing how to go on, morality can be taught in order that our intrinsic moral sense could be sharpened to effect unbridled, spontaneous moral actions and build up unfailing moral personhood.

While we say that morality can be taught and needs to be taught in order to change man's moral behaviour, moral evaluation or moral reflection, which is a natural human disposition, cannot be taught. It happens with sufficient intellectual maturity in the person, and intellectual maturity is a potential faculty of man as a rational animal—an essential prerogative of man. Moral personhood is thus a matter of natural necessity. For morality, as we have seen, is a rational affair and since rationality is constitutive of personhood, morality becomes intrinsic to personhood. That means, if one accepts that it is morally obligatory to do an action *X* one is committed to doing *X*, whenever it is necessary, and one will be self-inconsistent if he does not do *X*.[27] However, commitment and requirement of self-consistency do not often act as enough motivation to act morally as required of moral personhood. I shall cite the opinions of two prominent contemporary philosophers in this context before I come to a modest clash with them and fortify the conclusion of this chapter, adduced in the foregoing paragraph. The first view, which is stated as under, is that of Thomas Nagel:

> To say that altruism and morality are possible in virtue of something basic to human nature is not to say that men are basically good. Men are basically complicated; how good they are depends on whether certain conceptions and ways of thinking have achieved dominance, *a dominance which is precious in any case.* (emphasis mine).

27. As Rajendra Prasad points out in his *Karma, Causation and Retributive Morality*, p. 329.

And he goes on to add with apparent indignation:

> The manner in which human beings have conducted themselves so far does not encourage optimism about the moral future of the species.[28]

With a similar note of indignation, though with less explicit desperation and sense of pessimism, Rajendra Prasad writes:

> It can be said of most modern Indians that they censure injustice only fearing that they may be victims of it and not because they shrink from committing it.[29]

This, incidentally, is a well-known remark made by Thrasymachus, about the nature of the average man in Plato's *Republic* (p. 609; see also p. 608).

I find the indignation expressed in the above passages absolutely unworrying, *al beit* apparently unsettling to the general trend of this chapter. For what it purports to highlight in effect is only the distinction, I have drawn attention to, between one's knowing to discern the moral from the immoral and one's identifying with the moral. As I have shown, the former is because of our rational faculty while the latter is because of the spiritual urge endemic in human nature. The few occasions, in which some people are likely to act to the contrary, displays the exceptions rather than the features of normalcy. Such deviant actions and behaviour, we have seen, are hostile to our nature and from which we understandably tend to *alienate* deep within our inner self; these exceptional (im) moral conducts are because of obvious extraneous factors, prominent among which are kleptomania and akratia or weakness of will, which make the subject act against his best judgement. The oft-quoted confession of Duryodhana "*jānāmi dharma na ca me pravṛtti, jānāmyadharma na ca mé nivṛtti*" is a glaring case in point, too

28. *Possibility of Altruism* (Oxford, 1970), p. 144.
29. *Karma, Causation and Retributive Morality*, p. 345.

familiar and self-explanatory to create a flutter. It has also been argued that both these faculties of rationality and spirituality are present in us in the dispositional sense and need to be made occurrent by sufficient intellectual maturity and meaningful social living, which plays an important catalytic role in the process of moral progress and perfection. Interestingly, Rajendra Prasad alludes to this in the very first essay of the cited book (p. 2). Although moral reflection may not, in some cases, lead to moral actions, as Prasad and Nagel rightly point out, it cannot be denied that the former is intimately related to the latter. For other conditions being fulfilled, one's judging or reflecting that one ought to do the action ***X*** would lead to one's doing ***X***. We would be certainly surprised, even disappointed—as Prasad and Nagel seem to be—if one does not do ***X*** *despite* one's judging that one ought to do it. But, as should be quite clear from the forgoing by now, this has nothing to impair my contention (indeed the fact, which I have laid bare) that man is naturally moral and is inclined to act morally by his very nature and dispositions.

3

Morality, Objectivity and Applicability

If persons are naturally moral and if reciprocal personal stance is an essential constituent of personal consciousness, as we have seen, then the moral values that we hold and live up to must be objective and generally applicable. That means, moral principles must be objectively valid, which are not affected by personal peculiarities or individual perspectives. Bulk of the history of ethics has proceeded on this supposition, which has been largely strengthened by the requirement of universalisability of moral principles and theories—a requirement sought to be met by intuitionism and utilitarianism alike, by altruism as well as the self-interest theory. Because of this, moral realism, absolutism, intuitionism and deontology have occupied major concerns in ethics rather than relativism, non-cognitivism and even consequentialism. But the supposed objectivity, on its part, has generated more problems for itself and for morality despite its attractiveness and wider appeal. For objectivity in the received sense claims to apply ethical theories unexceptionably without regard for the specificities and peculiarities of individuals and situations. Genuine moral reasons, accordingly, are thought to be the ones derived from the nature of the case rather than from our own nature. An objective value is thought to be there (in the objective world) independently of our valuing it or judging it as a value. It appears that we cannot avoid the desire for objective values: that desire is a feature of our humanity; we crave for objectification as a result.

Objectivity and Moral Scepticism

However, such requirement of objectivity in the case of moral values has often been self-defeating (and this, we shall see later on, points to a major distinction between moral realism and metaphysical realism). For in moral reasoning, i.e, judging things (actions, conducts and even agents) as value (or valuable) individual perspectives can never be gotten rid of, though could only be maximally minimized. The role of the will in moral valuing can hardly be wished away, however hard we try to "step back" from the act of valuing. In the realist's search for moral *knowledge* our desire to have an objective view, no part of which is the product of some peculiarity of ourselves or of our perspective, may thus be a craving for the utopia that can never be realized. The craving for an objective view, backed by principles valid from a point of view with no peculiarities whatsoever, is virtually a view from nowhere, a view with no principles to judge with; and with no principle to judge with, the objective mind could not judge at all.[1] The hope for genuine objectivity is at once held out and snatched away! The dilemma glares at us: if a view is objective, it cannot judge something to be value or disvalue, and if it judges, it cannot be an objective view. We have met this spot elsewhere, in fact at several points in the history of thought. One such spot was Bradley's view on thought and reality: If the reality is to be known, it will have to be known through ordinary discursive thinking, the inevitable function of which is to proceed through the way of judgment, which "moves by the machinery of terms and relations" and so cuts across reality into the 'that' and the 'what', thereby destroying its original unity; the judgment that then purports to reunite the separated inseparables is condemned as "a deceit, a

1. See Thomas Nagel, *The View From Nowhere* (Oxford Univ. Press, N.Y., 1986), p. 118.

device, a mere practical compromise".[2] The conclusion to which Bradley was drawn from this was that what thought can give us is only an appearance, but not the truth. Likewise, the search for objectivity for moral values would lead, as it often has, to moral skepticism: it can not only result in scepticism about objective moral values[3], but scepticism about morality itself, if morality and objectivity are thought of as essential invariants. Nagel puts it very succinctly as follows:

> However often we may try to step outside of ourselves, something will have to stay behind the lens, something in us will determine the resulting picture, and this will give grounds for doubt that we are really getting closer to reality.[4]

This is as true in the case of the realists' search for knowledge as it is—or rather more so—in the case of our search for objective moral values. What we see here is a predicament of principle—a predicament we get entangled with in our attempt to face a problem that both demands and resists a solution. Our search for objectivity is a case where we crave objectivity and know that we cannot attain it. For the problem here is the problem of how to combine—since we cannot preclude it—the perspective of a particular person in the world with an objective view of that same world, the person and his point of view included.[5] It is a problem that everyone with the impulse to transcend his particular points of view will have to face. Besides being a compelling reason for moral scepticism*, this craving for objectivity also presents the other problem of applicability of moral principles. We have seen in the first chapter that ethical theories, taken in their absolute literal sense, are found to be

---

2. F.H. Bradley, *Appearance and Reality* (Oxford Univ. Press, 1963, first published in 1895), p. 28.
3. J.L. Mackie, *Ethics: Inventing Right and Wrong* (Penguin, London, 1977).
4. *The View From Nowhere*, p. 68.
5. *Ibid*, p. 3.

* Other alternatives are also there, as I shall spell out later in this chapter.

either inapplicable in practical life or, if applied, lead to consequences that are morally undesirable or even disastrous on occasions. And taking these theories in this sense is an implicit symptom of the craving for objectivity that has not unjustly, though somewhat mistakenly, occupied major concerns of ethicists and moral philosophers. However, I think that the threat of moral scepticism and inapplicability of moral theories are only illuminating pointers. For morality is something we cannot care less and the purpose of ethics is to provide guidance for actions in practical life. Hence the craving for objectivity that seems to pose an apparent threat to morality and its applicability stands in need of analysis and understanding. What has gone wrong with it and where and why? In what follows I shall attempt an answer to this and, to this purpose, set myself to the task of ethical analysis of the concept of objectivity, especially as it applies to moral values.

Universalisability vis-à-vis Objectivity

Before I attempt an analysis of the concept of objectivity for understanding the claim of objectivity of moral values, I propose to examine the contentious notion of universalisability and its implications. This I want to do for two reasons: Firstly because, on the most common understanding of morality, a moral judgment needs to be universalisable in order to qualify as a moral judgment; and in this sense universalisability is a test criterion. The second reason, which is more to the point here, is that the requirement of universalisability has been a major factor responsible for the craving for objectivity of moral values and for the related claim that moral judgments must be objectively true. Universalisability as a test criterion of moral judgments is supposed to provide a rationale for *universal applicability* of value predicates, because of which Kurt Baier, for example, was led to observe that moral principles admit of no exceptions, that the moral point of view based on universalisability provides an objectivity and disinterested perspective for resolution of conflicts of interests. "Universalisability", says Baier, "involves conforming to rules even when doing so is unpleasant, painful, costly or ruinous to oneself".[6] Now, while the first of the above claims about universalisability is perfectly innocuous and beyond dispute, the second claim calls for careful examination. Does universalisability imply objectivity of the moral values? If so, in what sense? My first approach to this would be that, although it is quite tempting to assume that objectivity is semantically inalienable from the concept of universalisability, this has not passed as an undisputable fact. Mackie, for one, has drawn attention to several subjective elements in universalisability.[7] I leave the defense of Mackie to himself, who is quite capable of justifying his stand on this. My plea for adding to the controversy is my apprehension that, *as stated*, the doctrine of universalisability cannot be always true and that, if it cannot be true always, it loses the force it claims to have for promoting the case for objectivity of moral judgments and moral values. To be able to see the point I want to make, let us examine the doctrine as stated by its proponents. R.M.Hare, who is eminently known as the author of the notion of universalisability, held that moral judgments are universalisable in the sense that a person making a moral judgment is committed to making the same judgment in any relevant and similar situation. Expressed in another way, moral judgments are universalisable in the sense that anyone who judges that an action is right or wrong, good or bad, ought or ought not to be done, is committed to taking the same view about any other relevant and similar action. The crucial concept, then, is "relevantly similar". A situation is relevantly similar to another if there are a set of properties, **x**, which it shares with that first situation and **x** was the person's reason for making the moral judgment in that other situation originally. And if any situation resembles the first one in respect

6. Kurt Baier, *The Moral Point of View* (Cornell University Press, Ithaca, N.Y, 1958), p. 307.
7. J.L. Mackie, *Ethics: Inventing Right and Wrong*, pp. 97-102.

of this limited set of properties, **x**, *that* makes us compelled to make the same judgment here or, otherwise, to withdraw the judgment made in the first case. Universalisation, thus, implies that each moral judgment we make creates a moral principle: If our reasons for approving a certain action was a set of features, **x**, *that* creates for us the principle that all actions having **x** are right. However, although this makes reasonably good sense, the principle can be shown to be false if, in a new situation, some feature, **n**, within the set of features, **x**, could prominently stand out as a reason *against* and defeat the principle of universalisation. This defeating feature, which was nonetheless present in the first case, was not enough to defeat our reasons in favour, but in the new case appears in a greater degree to act as a strong enough reason to defeat our earlier reason in favour. To borrow an example from Jonathan Dancy,[8] the action in the first case, let us suppose, was kind and generous but "a bit thoughtless". Apparently this last feature was ignored and the action was approved for its kindness and generousity (*not for its thoughtlessness*). The action in the second case is just as kind and generous but "grossly thoughtless", which is enough reason to disapprove the action. The doctrine of universalisability is thus found to be false, despite the presence of all the three said features. Perhaps, the defenders of universalisability would like to change the account of "relevant similarity" and broaden the universalisability base by including the reasons against, in addition to the reasons in favour, as the point of resemblance. This, Dancy points out, may dispose of the original problem but would be vulnerable to new sorts of counter-examples. For instance[9], suppose a man knocks down a woman with his car and then takes her to the hospital, pays for the exuberant hospital expenses, looks after her and so on. Because of this we approve of his subsequent/post accident actions as marks of regret and

8. *Moral Reasons* (Blackwell, Oxford, UK and Cambridge, USA, 1993), p. 80.
9. Dancy, *ibid*, pp. 80-81.

admission of guilt and accountability. But we would not be committed to approve of another man behaving in exactly similar manner under similar circumstances with the ulterior motive to seduce the woman away from her husband. Are we going to say here that the fact that the first person had no ulterior purpose of seducing the woman *was* among our reasons for approving his actions? This would only be a naked attempt to shield the first judgment from the threat of counter-examples and, by implication, protect the universalisability principle from being falsified at *any* cost. One is here reminded of Flew's snubbing accusation[10] of "death by a thousand qualifications" directed against the theologian's fright for falsification. Are we not trivializing an otherwise fine principle, the principle of universalisability, by going on including additional reasons, even negative reasons (like absence of the ulterior motive for seduction, in the above example), only for the purpose of protecting it from falling short of objectivity? I shall shortly argue that by not being objective and universal in application the principle of universalisablity would not cease to be a sound basis of moral judgments, nor does it become subjective or relative for that matter. On the contrary, frequently changing the notion of "relevantly similar" and shifting the universalisability base would tend to be relative and trivially inclusive. And why must we do this? Is it just to protect the principle behind a moral judgment as universal and unexceptionable? Hare and Baier seem to hold on to this, for which they could be charged with conservatism. Hare hopes to derive ethical principles entirely from the semantics of key moral terms like 'good' and 'ought'; indeed as cited above, the example of universalisability has been generally thought to be semantically inalienable from the concepts of objectivity and universality. And because of this, such a view is open to the

10. A.G.N. Flew, "Theology and Falsification" in *Body, Mind and Death*, eds. Flew and McIntyre (Macmillan, London.)

charge of linguistic conservatism, and Hare seems to be well aware of this.[11] But this tendency for generalism and literal adherence to objectivity is no better than a parody of philosophical circumspection. Generalism has in fact been the cause of many bad moral decisions, some of which I have cited in the first chapter. Such bad decisions are usually the result of ill judged attempts to fit what we are to say in one particular occasion to what we had said on another occasion; it could be the unjust decision of a person who insists on this on this occasion because of having made a similar decision on another (putatively similar) occasion.[12] The resemblant features, which characterize relevantly similar actions or situations, are not something fixed and limited, nor are all of them equally important in every case. As we have seen, one of the features in the set of resembling features (e.g., the feature of thoughtlessness of an action) may stand out as a reason against calling the action right in a particular case. So reasons may function in new ways in new situations, and if this is not taken due note of, bad decisions will inevitably result. An example can explain: pleasure can be taken as a reason for doing an action because it gives pleasure—normally, that is,—and this can be justified as a universalised moral principle as it is in psychological hedonism. But sometimes, though not generally, it can be a reason *against* doing it. Hunting of animals, even if pleasant to the hunter, can never be considered an approved action. Ray Hattersley has a better example which is more explanatory in the case against generalism:

> I have long supported whoever it was who said that the real objection to fox hunting is the pleasure that the hunters get out of it.... If killing foxes is necessary for the safety and

11. See his *Moral Thinking,* (Oxford, the Clarendon Press, 1981), Ch. 1, sec. 5.
12. This is a main point made by John McDowell in his "Non-cognitivism and Rule Following" in Holtzman and Leich (eds), *Wittgenstein: To Follow a Rule* (Routledge and Kegan Paul, London, 1981), pp. 41-62.

> survival of other species, I—and several million others—will vote for it to continue. But the slaughter ought not to be fun.[13]

What this points to is the fact that pleasure, though a universalisable reason for action, can't be reason in all cases; what it further points to is that slaughter of a dreaded species (threatening the existence of some other species), though universalisable, can be a case of immoral action *if it is done for fun.* The point is that slaughter ought not to be done for fun. A morally sanctioned act of slaughter can *cease to be* moral if it is done for fun. Thus, what is not so important in making moral judgments is the question "which other case does this case best resemble?" as the question "what is *the nature of the case* before us?" Dancy again:

> Of course a comparison with other cases may help us to decide how things are here, just as a long experience of car engines may help us to diagnose the fault this time. *But this decision or diagnosis is still essentially particular*. It would be surprising if a long and varied moral experience did not serve to sharpen one's sensitivity for the future. *But in neither case is* one's first question what one can say here is consistent with what one *has said elsewhere. The crucial question is how things are in the case before us.* [14]

A moral judgment, we have said, generates a moral principle. Moral principles can, therefore, be learnt in particular cases. And we may add, generalism, in encouraging the tendencies not to look hard enough at the details of the case, can lead to over-simplistic and dubious decisions. Thus the semantic consideration, that has guided many a moralists to club together the concept of universalisability and objectivity, has been very misleading in locating the logic of universalisability. The fact

13. *The Guardian*, 21 April 1990. Quoted by Dancy in *Moral Reasons*, p. 61.
14. *Ibid*, p. 63 (emphasis mine).

rather is that universalisability, far from being meant as an abstract principle and a wholistic ground for moral judgments and values, is wedded to taking account of the peculiarities of the particular situations in deciding the morality or otherwise of an action and in discerning values from disvalues. This should be quite evident from the crucial concept of *relevantly similar* situations and actions involved here. And that enables us to apply a moral principle in *all relevant cases—not in all cases* indiscriminately. Whether a particular situation is relevantly similar to any other situation for making the relevant moral judgment depends crucially on the *nature of the case* rather than the apparently oversimplified features overviewed as common to both the situations. You can generalize a principle taking the specific factors into consideration, and not making abstractions from them. M.G. Singer aptly opines:

> The generalization principle must be understood in the sense that what is right for one person must be right for every relevant and similar person in relevantly similar circumstances.[15]

The minimum that is required is that moral judgments are universalisable subject to the proviso that the conditions are similar or remain the same. If so, their interests, purposes and ideals are taken into account—*pace* Hare and even Kant—because these factors also constitute the relevant conditions making the situations relevantly similar. What should guide the generalization—and this is the force of objectivity and impartiality involved—is what is the nature of the case rather than what is our nature. What determines a value for me is not what I am inclined to do or believe by my nature, but what merit lies in the nature of the object valued. And what is the merit of the case is what conforms to our moral sense,—intuitionism in ethics is entitled at least this much to tell us. The dictates of our moral intuition normally lead us to notice

15. *Generalization in Ethics* (Alfred A. Knop, N. Y. 1961).

the merit in the case as distinct from what one is inclined to think of the case. We adopt a maxim for its own sake, not for our purposes. In other words, we act not so much as to serve our inclinations as out of respect for some features of the maxim. Hare is perfectly right in saying that whenever we commend we have in mind *something about the object commended,* which is the reason of our commendation.[16] With these provisos, Hare and even Kant are entitled to their forms of universalisability. Moral judgments are universalisable if it is determined that others who are relevantly similar to me not only could act in the way I am acting but also that they *should* do so (Hare), or if it is determined that my maxim could stand as a law for all rational beings, that all rational beings *could* act on the maxim (Kant). What must not be lost sight of is that ethics is empirical, a product of social life, and so moral principles grow out of taking account of the peculiarities of particular cases of moralising. Abstract generalism and literal objectivism are often impediments in their understanding and applicability. Universalisability, it must be borne in mind, is *not universalism;* to say that a moral principle or a moral judgment is universalised is not, therefore, to say that it is universal.

Claims of Objectivity: An Elucidatory Note

Having thus delinked the notion of universalisability of moral judgments from generalism and, I hope, from objectivity in the conventional sense, let us look a bit more closely at the logic of "objectivity", which will eventually throw light on the nature of objectivity required, if at all, of moral values and moral judgments. In what follows, I am going to argue that objectivity admits of several senses in several contexts, and much of the ongoing debates about objectivity of moral values, I am inclined to think, have been largely due to confusion between, or non-recognition of, these different senses. To forestall my contention, I think it appropriate to put forth the statements of two recent

16. *Language of Morals* (Oxford, 1952), p. 130. Emphasis added.

writers on this contentious issue: Jonathan Dancy, before discussing objectivity, begins "with a discussion of *the sort of objectivity properly attributable to moral values and reasons*"; (*Moral Reasons*, p. 144.) and David Brink, while outlining what some call "global subjectivism" and some others "sophisticated realism", expressed the view that "once we understand the *objectivity obtainable in the sciences*, we can see that ethics is or can be every bit as objective as the sciences". (*Moral Realism and the Foundations of Ethics*, Cambridge Univ. Press, 1989, p. 6) [Emphasis added in both the quotations]. With these statements regarding the "sorts of objectivity" properly obtainable in different disciplines, which are self-explanatory, let us begin our enquiry into the question of objectivity and that of objectivity of moral values.

Moral Realism and Objectivity

The theory that moral values are objective is what normally goes by the name of "moral realism", and moral realism is viewed as a special case of metaphysical realism. And since realism in any discipline typically believes that there are facts and truths of a certain kind which are independent of human thoughts and theorizing about them, moral realism is committed to the belief that there are moral facts and truths that are objective and independent of our judging them as values or disvalues. Realism about the external world (metaphysical realism) takes the claims of common sense physical theories and those of the natural sciences literally and holds that the scientific terms refer to *real* features of the world and that (advancement in) the sciences provide us with more and more accurate *knowledge* of the world. Similarly, moral realism takes the moral claims literally, i.e. *as* claims that *describe* moral properties of people, of actions and of institutions and takes these properties to be *real and objective* properties which obtain independently of our moralizing or moral theorizing. According to it, not only there are moral facts and true moral claims that purport to state moral facts but also often *do* state such facts and refer to real properties, as the result of which we can and do sometimes have moral beliefs and moral *knowledge.* Although this has been the more generally accepted theory of moral values—represented by Price, Prichard, Sidgwick, Moore, Broad and Ross—this has been considerably eclipsed by twentieth century emotivism and non-cognitivism spearheaded by A.J. Ayer, R.L. Stevenson and R.M. Hare. But J.L. Mackie[17] has lodged by far the most conspicuous recent attack on moral realism and the objectivity theory and somewhat less expressedly and more circuitously, this has been done also by Thomas Nagel[18]. Because I consider Nagel's scepticism to be less expressed and rather subdued by his tacit recognition that *a complete picture of the world requires modification of the form of objectivity*[19], I will address to Mackie's scepticism more elaborately, though allusions to Nagel's view on objectivity will inevitably occur at a later stage of this chapter, especially in course of presenting my account of a proper analysis of objectivity as applied to moral values.

Understanding Mackie

When Mackie began his book with the bold declaration that "there are no objective values" and went on to argue that the theory that values are objective is based on an error, this—very much like the subtitle of his book—struck many as a startlingly unconventional approach to moral values. This is not surprising, because this was an expressed challenge to moral realism with which most of us are familiar and comfortable and there is thought to be, perhaps because of semantic considerations,

17. *Ethics: Inventing Right and Wrong.*
18. *The View from Nowhere.*
19. *Ibid*, p. 6 and also in Ch.VIII. Note especially his statement that "objectivity need not be all-or-nothing" (p. 148), which is meant to tone down his scepticism expressed earlier (p. 68): "However often we may try to step outside ourselves, something will have to stay behind the lens, something in us will determine the resulting picture, and this will give grounds for doubting that we are really closer to reality".

among other things, an undeniable close connection between realism and objectivity—though, as we shall see, realism about value is not exactly the same as realism about what there is and about empirical facts. Mackie backed up his contention by arguing that if values *were* objective, they would surely be parts of the fabric of the world and that, since we don't find them as such, values would have to be things (entities or qualities or relations) of a queer sort.[20] And presumably since admission of these would be commitment to intuitionism, which "has long been out of favour" and is otherwise "implausible", the objectivity theory must be false and unacceptable. Mackie's moral scepticism is thus a scepticism about the *objectivity* of moral values, which should be carefully distinguished from, and must not be confused with, or taken as, scepticism about *morality* and moral values as such. For such confusion would not only lead a critique of Mackie seriously astray but would also expose a poor understanding of moral values, as is apparent in some writings on Mackie's position. Bernard Williams,[21] for example, seems to argue that scepticism about objectivity of moral values and scepticism about moral values as such (our everyday moral convictions) "hang together" and, because of this, attributes to Mackie the view that "moral considerations have no place in practical reasoning", if his error theory is right. Williams says so presumably on the ground that since for Mackie morals are no candidates for knowledge, his moral scepticism must upset our everyday moral convictions. But I think this sort of criticism is both a misrepresentation of Mackie's contention as well as an improper understanding of moral values. To take the latter point first, William's argument will stand here only if moral values are to be taken as objective by definition; but this is certainly a case of improper identification, for "Are values objective?" is neither an improper question nor is Mackie's

---

20. *Ethics: Inventing Right and Wrong,* Ch. 1 sec. 9.
21. "Ethics and the Fabric of the World" in Ted Honderich (ed) *Morality and Objectivity* (Routledge and Kegan Paul, London,1985). pp. 204-5.

opening statement "There are no objective values" a contradiction in terms. Besides—and that brings us to my first point against Williams's—Mackie expressed scepticism about the *objectivity* of moral values, and *not* about moral values as such*, as should be clear by now from the foregoing.

In fact, Mackie in the said book is quite serious about our everyday moral convictions, which he considers as having important bearings on practical reason. A similar confusion is also seen to be endemic in some other responses to Mackie's error theory. Simon Blackburn, while claiming that Mackie should have avoided *moral* (because erroneous) views altogether and taken resort to what he calls "shmoralising" instead of moralizing, seems to have equated "moral" with "erroneous" and to have attributed this view to Mackie[22]. But this, I repeat, is to miss the point, for Mackie did not say that all moral reasoning was based on error, but only the objectivity theory *was*, the theory that moral values are objective *was*. Hence the comment that "there is something fishy about holding an error theory, yet continuing to moralise"[23] is unfair to Mackie and uncalled for, to say the least. The least that Mackie would be committed to have said is that to moralise is to objectivise (in the stronger sense of the term, to be spelt out soon in this chapter). The confusion and the resulting misrepresentation of Mackie's position is yet again apparent in Hare's otherwise excellent account of Mackie's position, with which I find myself in considerable agreement, when he is seen to conclude that Mackie's endeavour is "self-defeating" on the contentious ground that "He [Mackie] first said that moral judgments are all false, and then told us how to decide which moral judgments should we accept"[24]. But, once again, all that Mackie can be

* It is odd that Williams fails to see this, for he goes on to say that Mackie's error theory meant "very roughly to be that of taking moral values to be objective", *op cit*, p. 204.

22. Simon Blackburn, "Errors and the Phenomenology of Value" in Honderich (ed), *ibid*, p. 2.
23. *Ibid*, p. 4.
24. R.M. Hare, *"Ontology in Ethics"* in Honderich, *ibid*, p. 53.

(dis!) credited with is the view that moral judgments, *if they claimed to be objective*, are false—***not*** that all moral judgments are false.

However, my salvation exercise is not to be taken as a clean chit to Mackie in whatever he has said about the objectivity of moral values and his error theory thereabout. For I suspect that despite Mackie's splendid display of the absurdity of realism and useful analysis of the concept of objectivity as applied to moral values, certain defects of detail cannot be ignored in his way of presenting the issue at stake. To revert to his queerness argument alluded to above, Mackie is seen to have attributed to the objectivist a sort of ontology that, in order to be objective, moral values *will have to be* real relations, properties, facts and even entities of some kind, existing out there as parts of the fabric of the world; that if such things are not found existing in the world then these values must exist somewhere somehow to be grasped by the intellectual faculty of intuition, if not knowable through common observation. Such sorts of claims of realism are queer and implausible, and Mackie rightly rejects them. But in rejecting them he has inadvertently given a fair amount of concession to an opposite ontological position of antirealism, which is grounded on the equally implausible supposition of *non-existence* of moral facts (properties and relations etc.) out there in the world, *as if* the discovery of some such things in the world would have obliged him to grant objectivity to some moral values at least. This sort of ontological mode of presenting the issue is familiar and primitive. And in this way of philosophizing, which has become quite fashionable of late, we talk of realism and antirealism with perfect ease; but it is often not clear what exactly is meant by them.

For one thing, antirealism can be ambiguous between rejection of realism and idealism (or subjectivism), both of which are distinctively different positions. Holding on to the former, one is content to deny the existence of certain facts, properties and relations out there, *not* to relegate their existence to somewhere in the mind of the observer, which is the latter position and which is not content simply with denying their existence in the external world. Correspondingly, ethical antirealism can mean rejection of the realist theories that values are ontologically objective, and it can also mean—suggested ironically by the subtitle of Mackie's *Ethics*—the theory that moral values are subjective inventions. In this second sense it may be a commitment to ethical subjectivism or a sophisticated form of ethical realism, treating values somewhat like Platonic forms. While declaring that there are no objective values, Mackie's intention may be taken to be putting forth the former position but never to be espousing the latter. In fact, far from straying into subjectivism or Platonic 'idea-ism' with respect to values, he takes considerable conceptual strain to defend our everyday moral convictions and took deliberate care to protect them from the shadow of subjectivism and moral scepticism. But while this part of his thesis comes out clearly enough in his *Ethics,* his arguments, especially the argument from queerness, dressed in ontological make up, failed to offer a rational defense of moral convictions, to which quite evidently he was deeply committed.[25] Rather his ontological mode of arguing and thinking duped him to concede, *al beit* indirectly, that values *could* exist somehow somewhere; his argument that they would in that case be entities or relations of a queer sort accessible to intuitionism, which is "out of favour" and implausible, serves only as a subterfuge. Besides the argument from queerness, the other support for Mackie's moral scepticism is what he calls the argument from relativity—the argument that social groups or different groups in the same community differ about values and moral codes, that values and moral codes change from time

25. I am almost in entire agreement with Hare's argument to this effect (*ibid*, p. 53). though I sharply differ from his attribution, *because of this*, to Mackie the view that moral judgments are all false (see note 24 again); for besides being a gross misrepresentation of Mackie's skepticism, such attribution clearly does not follow from his posing the issue in the ontological mode.

to time—which tells against objectivity of values. But the argument that disagreement and/or relativity undermines objectivity is neither unquestionable nor independent of the sense in which objectivity is understood.[26] Mackie himself points out that disagreement among historians has nothing to affect objectivity of historical facts.[27] We can also add similar counters against relativity: the fact that boiling point is relative to altitudes and atmospheric pressure has nothing to show that boiling point is not an objective fact. Even the fact that we feel hot if we dig into freshly cooked puree and cold when we touch ice does not affect the fact that this is a universal feature with sentient beings. Obviously, disagreements of particular types are anathema to moral objectivity and Mackie rightly points out some such relevant disagreements. But the question more to the point here is: what kind of objectivity it is that is relevant and applicable to morality and whether disagreement about and relativity of morality (moral codes and commitments) will affect this objectivity. An elaborate enquiry into the concept of objectivity is therefore in order.

Objectivity and Independence

Objectivity, as I have already indicated, has the broad sense of being understood in terms of independence. Metaphysically speaking, things and beings of the external world are said to be objective in the sense that they are independent of the mind's (our) thinking about them or theorising about them; they would be there anyway, irrespective of our thinking or knowing about them. This is a philosophical position, which can be described as metaphysical realism. Speaking from the ethical point of view, values are objective or actions and conducts (of individuals and institutions) are objectively right or wrong if they are so, independently of our judging them to be so. They would be so

26. S.L. Hurley elaborately argues to this effect in his "Objectivity and Disagreement" in Honderich (*ed) Morality and Objectivity*, pp. 54-97.
27. *Ethics: Inventing Right and Wrong*, p. 36.

anyway, whether or not particular moral judgments are made or *despite*—and this is a speciality of moral realism*—some of us making judgments to the contrary, perhaps by acting on impulse or inclinations. But while this understanding of objectivity in terms of independence is innocuous and rather trivial, the concept, in its application, has displayed two sorts of implications. For a convenient starting point, let me call these implications *literalism* and *liberalism*. In the literal sense, our intellectual history has equated 'objective' with 'real', 'universal', 'absolute' and 'unexceptionable' in its application. Objective reality of **x** (a thing, a fact, a property or relation) requires **x** to be absolutely independent or "purged" of all peculiarities of the perspectives of the observer or the agent. Moral values in this sense are supposed to be entirely agent-neutral, which is taken as true value or truly objective value. But this is a kind of objectivity, which, even though appealing and often craved for by philosophers (including moral philosophers), is elusive and utopian. Philosophers have craved for it knowing well enough that they cannot get it. We have seen the likes of this in the Cartesian quest for certainty, in Plato's quest for the ideal state and in Hegel's model of the Absolute. In moral philosophy the model of literal objectivity has been reflected in the quest for absolute standards of values (or absolute values) and moral behaviour. The search in each case has ended in scepticism for the obvious reason that the objectivity sought was not gettable. We have argued in the first chapter that such searching for, and sticking to, literal objectivity in the realm of values has created serious problems in the application of many of our celebrated moral principles. Yet the quest has rather obstinately continued over the ages. In recent times, Nagel displays a somewhat similar search for objectivity and inevitably

* We could say on impulse or inclination that **x** is wrong which it is not or which most of us would say it is not, but we do not say on impulse or inclination that something is unreal which it is not or which most of us would say it is not.

espoused scepticism[28], as that sort of objectivity is nowhere to be found. Nagel's problem was "how to combine the perspective of a particular person inside the world with an objective view of that same world, the person and his view included".[29] As Dancy precisely pointed out, this was seen to be a problem because Nagel saw the subjective/objective viewpoints as in essential tension, which both demands and resists a solution.[30] Partly reminiscent of the Kantian discomfort with the thing-in-itself that nevertheless exists and is yet supposed to be unknowable and inaccessible to the understanding, Nagel's problem was how to achieve absolute detachment from the specifics and peculiarities of the knower's perspectives, nothing—literally nothing—of which should remain to infect and corrupt the objective view of the world. But search for this sort of objectivity very soon lands him up in scepticism evident in his remark that—

> However often [read *hard*] we may try to step outside ourselves, something will have to stay behind the lens, something in us will determine the resulting picture, and this will give grounds for doubt that we are really getting closer to reality.[31]

The idea of "stepping outside" from one's perspectives of knowing in order to have an objective knowledge of the world lays bare an inevitable antilogy which cannot be gotten rid of, and yet we want to get rid of it. Nagel wants to adopt both the subjective and objective viewpoints and strives to surmount the tension between them that is nonetheless insurmountable. A typical spot and puzzle situation that Wisdom finds philosophers often entrapped in.[32] The tension, I suspect, is largely because

28. T. Nagel, *The View from Nowhere*.
29. *Ibid*, p. 3.
30. *Moral Reasons*, p. 144.
31. *Ibid*, p. 68
32. John Wisdom, "Philosophy and Psychoanalysis", in his *Philosophy and Psychoanalysis* (Basil Blackwell, London, 1953).

of the picture of an extreme opposition between subjective and objective and taking the latter in an absolute, literal sense. Surface semantics of course suggests this uneasy picture, but actual usage and particularistic analysis would undermine the opposition and ease the tension. Liberated from literalism, objectivity of the view of the world would be seen to be compatible with the subjective perspective of a particular person knowing the world. Taking a liberal view of objectivity, our knowledge of the external world, though inevitably interfered with by our subjective experience and personal perspectives, would nevertheless be objective in the sense that it would be open to inter-subjective verification and agreement, and that is where universalisability gets a firm foothold. Our knowledge of the secondary qualities, such as colour and sound, is a very good case in point. Colours (perception of them, i.e.) are conditioned by sentience, to be sure, but that does not make the colour ascriptions subjective, nor would it justify denying the description of objective knowledge to them. The whistling noise of a passing train, though likewise influenced by our auditory conditions, is nevertheless an objectively occurring noise, intrasubjectively recognized as the sound of a passing train. Neither the colour (red, for example) nor the sound (of the passing train, for example) can be said to be cent per cent genuine to the fullest satisfaction of the sceptic's demand for absolute objectivity; but that does not make our use of colour-and sound-words meaningless and our colour-and sound-statements false, nor does it make the fact of things being (called) red and particular sounds being (called) what they are a mere matter of subjective appearances. It is for this reason that moral values have often been considered analogous to secondary qualities.[33] The reason for this secondary quality model of value awareness is that ordinary evaluative thought presents itself as a matter of sensitivity to aspects of the world.

33. For example, Mackie, in *Ethics* and McDowell, "Values and Secondary Qualities" in *Morality and Objectivity*, ed. Honderich.

Objective Tolerance: The Secondary Quality Model of Value Awareness

I am rather inclined to think that moral values have a strong reason to be treated as objective in the described sense. For values are essentially connected with the agent's will and yet equally essentially are universalisable in the sense in which we have seen them to be, far from being objective in the absolute, literal sense. Thus, like the secondary properties, moral properties such as wrongness or rightness of actions are objective in the liberal sense or in a secondary sense, if we may so call it.[34] Objectivity of wrongness is because of its independence: the action would be wrong independent of our judging it to be so and *despite anybody's judging it not to be so,* since its being wrong is a matter of inter-subjective agreement. It can further be said that 'wrong', like 'red', has an objective property or disposition to arouse a response in us; 'red' creates a typical colour experience while 'wrong' causes in us a certain response, an attitude of disapproval or condemnation. To put it in a more objective phraseology, a thing being red has the property of looking red while an action being wrong has the property of not-to-be-doneness built into its nature. This property in both cases is not only out there but also is intrinsic in the colour (redness) and the value (wrongness). In this sense values are shown to be both *objective and intrinsically related to the will.*[35] Because of the latter, we have to admit, as McDowell does (*op cit*), that values cannot have primary objectivity or what I have been calling absolute or literal objectivity. Primary objectivity, as it has been pictured, has to be defined in terms of absolute independence, a view that is completely free from the peculiarities of the (individual's) perspectives of knowing, judging and theorizing, as Nagel demands of it. But as Nagel

34. Jonathan Dancy (*ibid)* makes the distinction between primary and secondary objectivity that is virtually the same as what I mean by literal and liberal sense of objectivity.

35. See Dancy, *ibid*, esp. pp. 156-57.

himself is forced to see, this would have to be literally a view from nowhere and hence would not be a plausible view at all,[36] since "something must stay behind the lens", "something in us will determine the resulting picture". In the face of this difficulty, which is a difficulty of principle, Nagel settles for a less ambitious strategy that he calls "objective tolerance"[37], which is that we should be content with the views/principles "which would not be rejected by the objective mind" (the mind with no peculiarities of perspectives). Absolute or primary objectivity, on the contrary, will demand full endorsement (not mere non-rejection) by the objective mind. Moral values cannot have this sort of objectivity simply by virtue of the fact that they are intrinsically related to the will, just as an absolute objective view of the world cannot be possible since any view of the world would have to presuppose its existence and hence knowability.* Values, therefore, must admit of a weaker sort of objectivity that can be called secondary objectivity in order for them to admit of a plausible understanding or significance and possible application to the world. (More of this soon later on). Thus McDowell: "Evaluative 'attitudes' and states of will are like, say, colour experience in being unintelligible except as modification of a sensibility like ours". In this way McDowell showed values to be both objective and intrinsically related to the will. We must, therefore, part company with literalism in the matter of objectivity of moral values, which by no means is parting company with *objectivity* but is only a justified switch-over to the secondary sort of objectivity or what I have been calling a liberal view of it. Primary objectivity, which diehard realists crave for, even if there can be no view of it, is

36. *The View From Nowhere*, p. 68.
37. *Ibid*, p. 130 ff.

* If Kant and Strawson are of any guidance, "understanding maketh nature" *al beit* out of given materials, but the given materials cannot be incorruptibly *given;* and the view of the world, paradoxically, cannot be a view *of the world* but a *view* of the world—as knowable, i.e., identifiable and reidentifiable.

unattainable and as such inapplicable to values and indeed to anything in the world; and so the search for it is irrational, to say the very least. Thomas Nagel *did* see this, which is evident from his recognition of and settling for "objéctive tolerance", but his apparently obstinate preference for absolute objectivity not only lands him up in scepticism ("something will stay behind the lens") endemic in conventional philosophizing, but also forces him to discriminate between agent-relative values (which can have only secondary objectivity) and agent-neutral values which he claims to be true value of which the former is alleged to be a distortion.[38] This is certainly a mistaken idea, since both sorts of values are recognized kinds of objective values and, though the agent-neutral values are usually more objective than the agent-relative ones, the latter, on occasions, can compete with the former and sometimes defeat the former. But with absolute objectivity as his dominant model, Nagel finds it hard to show this, which nonetheless was one of his main objectives in this book.[39]

Craving for Absolute Objectivity: Sources and Solution

Why, then, is this obstinate obsession with absolute objectivity, particularly when values can never have this sort of objectivity (because of their being essentially related to the will)? Why, indeed, is this recurring category preference when distinct categories or forms of objectivity are a fairly recognized fact? I suspect that this is because of certain confusion or confusions involved in our understanding of the concept of values and the claims of objectivity thereof. Let me refer to this preference for absolute or literal objectivity as "the preference". The first confusion that, I think, is responsible for the preference relates to our understanding of the concept of value. It is the confusion

38. See Dancy's exposure of Nagel's weakness *ibid*, pp. 153-54.
39. See Dancy, *ibid*, ch. 9 sec. 3. Dancy points out that because of this, "Nagel's form of moral realism is construed in such a way as to diminish its own chance of success." (*Ibid*, p. 154).

between two senses in which we quite familiarly understand the concept. The concept of value has two dimensions and accordingly it can be understood in two different ways: "value" can mean, 'values people hold' or it can mean 'values things have'.[40] The distinction is also due to the fact that value is a function involving both a subject who values and an object (action or agent) that is valued. In the former sense, value is an activity of the rational mind and as such is subjective, and in the latter sense it is an object out there, having reference to something beyond the valuing subject. Although we are quite aware of this ambiguity involved in the meaning of value, the mind's proneness to opt for what is objective in preference to anything subjective leads us to confuse the two senses of value or rather assimilate the subjective sense to the objective one and thus to take value as objective, independent of the mind's function of valuing or making value judgments.

The second confusion leading to the preference for absolute objectivity is what I think to be the confusion between two senses of 'independence', which quite obviously, define objectivity. To return to the secondary quality model of value awareness, secondary properties like colour and sound are essentially phenomenal and so they could not be instantiated without there being minds for them to appear to. In this sense they are dependent on the mind perceiving them. Likewise, Mackie and McDowell point out, values are related to the will without which they could not be experienced or be made aware of. But, we have seen, this does not prevent them from being objective in the secondary sense. This objectivity they (redness and wrongness alike) earn because of their *independence,* independence from the mind or will knowing or making colour statements or value judgments. An object can be objectively red even if nobody is actually looking at it. It is there anyway, independent of any particular experience. Similarly an action can be objectively wrong even though nobody is actually making

40. See S.K.Mohanty, *Persons, Mind and Value*, ed. himself, p. 88.

any judgment about it; it is there anyway, independent of any particular value judgment. This, as we have seen, is secondary objectivity which the secondary properties and moral values can at best be credited with. But the mind's proneness to prefer anything independent and objective to anything that is relative and dependent (hence subjective) leads us on to regard values as objective in the absolute, literal sense. The proponents of absolute objectivity appear to overplay the ideas of independence which these properties (secondary and moral) do in fact enjoy. But here, I suspect, an essential confusion is involved between two senses of independence. The first is the sense—call it the 'weak sense of independence' ***(wsi)***—in which redness or wrongness would be there anyway, independent of any *particular* experience. The second is the sense—call it the 'strong sense of independence' (***ssi***)—in which redness or wrongness would be there anyway, independent of any *possible* experience. Values and secondary properties are independent and hence objective as per the ***wsi*** and can never be so as per the ***ssi***. For the fact that a thing can be red even though nobody is actually looking at it has nothing to show that there could be colours of which there could be no possible experience by anybody, and the fact that an action could be right or wrong even though nobody is actually judging it to be so has nothing to show that actions could be right or wrong even though no possible judgement could be made about them. Absolute objectivity could be attributed to values only at the risk of confusing between the two senses of independence thus discerned and assimilating the ***wsi*** to the ***ssi,*** which are evidently discernible, as shown above.

Perhaps because of confusions of the described types—which may be one reason, there are other reasons also,—the preference for absolute objectivity has gained ground. But a rational account of moral values and moral reasons for valuing facts, properties and actions would reveal that moral values have a secondary sort of objectivity. By accepting secondary objectivity for values, it is shown that values are both objective and intrinsically related to the will, which means that values being objective is not entirely incompatible with their being related to, and dependent on, the valuing subject in anyway. This is how I take McDowell to have wanted to highlight and emphasize the crucially important fact that our moral values are normative as well as causal[41] (causally related to the will, i.e.). But it is because of the fact that values do not "pull their own weight in the causal story" that people are often persuaded to abandon objectivity as redundant to the world,[42] which is seen to be the case with Mackie for an example, (*Ethics*, ch.1). Abandoning objectivity of values, as Mackie expressedly does, or claiming that objectivity in this case does not matter, as Hare seems to do, purportedly point to the unreality (ontological) of the values and this we have seen to be the denial of objectivity to them in the literal sense. For, Mackie makes it abundantly clear when he says, "...my thesis that there are no objective values is specifically the denial that any such *categorically imperative element* is objectively valid. The objective values which I am denying would be action-directing *absolutely,* not contingently ... upon the agent's desires and inclinations.",[43] and "The difficulty of *seeing* [as Hare complained, PKM] how

41. This is where lies an essential difference between values and secondary properties, like colour, despite both being dispositions to cause typical responses in the observer. For, as McDowell points out, value as a disposition elicits merited responses in us. This is also explained by the fact that wrongness or rightness of actions cause an attitude of disapproval or approval and the corresponding response of condemnation or commendation, which is not the case with observation of secondary qualities. So even if the analogy between moral qualities and secondary qualities is quite "tempting", R.M. Hare cautions against pressing the analogy too far, for it would obliterate this important difference between the two. "The reaction which, according to this sort of phenomenalist view of morality, 'produce' the moral quality", says Hare, "are attitudes such as approval and disapproval. *But these, unlike the perception of something red, are subject to our reasoned choices*". (*op cit,* p. 47) Emphasis added.
42. Courtesy Dancy *(ibid*, p. 157).
43. *Ethics: Inventing Right and Wrong*, p. 29. (Emphasis added).

values could be objective is a fairly strong reason for thinking that they are not so."(*ibid*, p. 24). This he says with apparent sympathy for Hare. This difficulty of not 'seeing' how values are objective, because they do not exist as part of the fabric of the world, issuing in fact from metaphysical realism confused with moral realism, is justifiably countered by accepting secondary objectivity for moral values. For one thing, values are thus shown to be part of the objective world, to which our valuings are responses; and for another, in being intrinsically related to the will and the valuing mind, they are not required to be absolutely objective and entirely independent of our valuing responses. Viewed from this perspective, far from being unreal or unattainable, objectivity of moral values can be 'seen' to be there in our rational account of how or when an action is wrong,—how we rationally determine or satisfy ourselves, as we do more often than not, whether an action is wrong. It is quite possible to arrive at a moral conclusion, even though that conclusion is not a statement of fact about what exists in *rerum natura.* Ethical rationalism does not essentially require ethical realism, as Hare has clearly shown.[44] Hare argues:

> People become realists and insist that the quality of wrongness has to be part of the fabric of the world, because they think that unless this is so, there will be no way of rationally deciding such questions. But are they right to think this? They think it only because they are victims of a prejudice that is almost universal among moral philosophers.[45]

The prejudice, Hare points out, is a prejudice about rationality, which is that those procedures are rational—and only those are—which lead to making of statements. Hume, of whom Mackie seems to have been an ardent follower, was clearly a victim of this prejudice; for he insisted that nothing can be an object of reason if it is not statable in terms of truth and falsehood,

44. "*Ontology in Ethics*", in Honderick (ed.) *Morality and Objectivity*, p. 48.
45. *Ibid,* p. 48.

agreements and disagreements to *real* relations of ideas or *real* existence and matters of fact.[46] Hare, for whom the function of moral judgments (our valuings, i.e.) are essentially *prescriptive,* thinks that we can rationally decide what to do and what to ask or advise others to do without having to depend solely on the factual elements, which may be nonetheless there in the process of reasoning. However, when Hare said that ethical rationalism does not need ethical realism, it has to be understood with some caution. For I think what he had in mind in saying that ethical realism is not required, or does not matter, in a rational account of morality is moral realism *as a specific case* of metaphysical realism, which demands absolute objectivity and independence for moral values. This is evident from his eagerness to "get away from the supposedly ontological question which allegedly divided the realist and anti-realist"[47] and from his argument, directed against Mackie, that "we need not worry about whether moral facts and moral qualities exist".[48] This is surely the purported existence of moral qualities absolutely independent—ontologically independent—of the valuing mind or will, and Hare was right in denying this sort of realistic claim. (And Mackie too was right in doing so). But this is not to deny the claims of moral realism altogether and surely this is not what Hare wanted to do. For he is seen defending a form of realism regarding moral facts and moral qualities, which is evident from his claim that—

> Doubtless they are not part of the fabric of the world. But the realists would not disagree. They would rather say, 'of course the moral properties are not physical properties and moral facts are not physical facts, *but all the same they are real properties and facts.*'[49]

46. See his *Treatise*, III, 1, i.
47. Hare, *ibid,* p. 47.
48. *Ibid*, p. 48. This would be also evident from the passage last quoted.
49. *Ibid*, p. 48 (Emphasis mine).

In what sense, then, are the moral facts and moral qualities "real"? Surely, in a liberal sense or what I have been discussing as the secondary sense, in which they can very well be conceived as objective and real. In this sense, moral realism can be thought delinked from metaphysical realism. David Brink has interesting arguments to show that one can be a metaphysical anti-realist but a moral realist and vice versa.[50] "Moral realism," for him, "is roughly the view that there are moral facts and true moral claims whose existence and nature are independent of our beliefs about what is right and wrong" (*ibid,* p. 7),—although these facts and qualities are not parts of the world; nor do they exist somewhere else somehow –, and he tries to show why moral realism is not amenable to standard metaphysical objections (in *ibid*, chs. 2-4). Moral facts and moral claims are real and true independent of our beliefs about what is right and what is wrong; to be real they do not have to be parts of the fabric of the world nor that of some supernatural world. Moral realism, thus construed, says Brink, is neutral between subjectivism and objectivism (see *ibid,* pp. 20-21). This is a significant pointer because, though it is in a way customary to associate moral realism with objectivism and anti-realism with subjectivism about values, an acceptable theory of values must be at equal distance from ethical subjectivism and ethical objectivism, both of which are extreme stereotypes. Brink's preference for moral realism that cuts across these extremes does not conclusively show that moral enquiry is possible only on realist assumptions. But, Brink points out; "realism provides a natural explanation, a justification of the way in which we do and can conduct ourselves in moral thought and inquiry." (*Ibid,* p. 24). At any rate, if the foregoing discussion of objectivity is to hold, one need not espouse anti-realism in moral matters simply on the ground that one abandons objectivity in the absolute, literal sense and realism in the metaphysical or ontological sense. Acceptance

50. *Moral Realism and the Foundations of Ethics* (Cambridge Univ. Press, N.Y. 1989), esp., chs 2-4.

of "objective tolerance," a secondary form of objectivity or what I call objectivity in the liberal sense can and does provide justification of moral realism and objectivity of values.

Applicability and Objectivity

It is in a way necessary to justify realism and objectivity of morality in this way since only in this way, i.e., only in taking objectivity of morality in this sense that moral theories can have application to the world. As shown in the first chapter, ethical theories have a built-in applicability to the world, firstly because, like every genuine theory, ethical theories being practically applicable is a *theoretical* requirement, and secondly because ethics is meant to provide guidance for practical living. It has been argued that the requisite conditions[51] being satisfied with regard to the nature of the world and of the people in it, if some ethical theories are not, or seem not to be, applicable to the world, the theories must suffer from some theoretical defect. And this defect we have shown to be an unqualified adherence to *absolute* objective standards of morality: taken in this absolute, literal sense, many of our celebrated moral principles or ethical theories were seen to be either inapplicable or, if applied, leading to consequences which were morally undesirable or even disastrous. Driven by an insatiable craving for absolute objectivity, our *riṣis* and saints have set their moral standards much too high to be possibly met by the common man, who naturally fails to live up to them though, ironically, ethics is meant for and needed more by the common man. If morality is to be taught, it is not the liberated savants or saints but the common man who is to be taught what is right and what is wrong, what is good and what is bad. And the teaching of ethics carries with it the applicability of the moral principles that we are expected to live up to. If we are taught the virtues of a principle or a set of principles, whose application to the world is impossible or questionable, the principle(s) in question would

51. See page 19 and elsewhere in Chapter 1.

hold no attraction for us, however lofty and profound they are made out to be; we would hold them in high esteem, but shrink within if required *ourselves* to live in accordance with them. This only points to the unreality, and hence unattractiveness, of absolute objectivity, which stands in the way of applicability of ethical theories. As we have seen, the desire to work towards absolute objectivity is the desire to work entirely "from outside" (Nagel), independent of any peculiar perspective of one's own, a desire to have a view from nowhere. To be sure, such desire is incoherent, but it is not necessary for, and not any part of, a rational account of morality. Dancy has argued that such a desire is no part of what he calls "Hegelian objectification"[52], which pleads for adequacy of what Nagel has described as "objective tolerance" and what I have been referring to as objectivity in the liberal sense for the purpose of having a rational understanding of moral principles and conducting ourselves in accordance with them. In fact any fruitful exercise in moral theory is an exercise in this Hegelian objectification and that is why Dancy declares that if our moral reasons can survive the process of this weaker sense of (Hegelian) objectification they will have all the objectivity they are expected to have. (See *ibid*, p. 135). Thus, to repeat, applicability of moral principles, which is an essential part of the spirit of these principles, requires not literal objectivity but liberal objectivity in respect of these principles. Our moral principles need not be applied unexceptionably; they must be applied by taking both the demands of the situation and the spirit of these principles into proper consideration. For in this lies a rational account of moral principles. Of course, rationality requires consistency in judgment and practical application of a principle in all cases. But while this is innocuous, it is in the danger of leading us to, as it has in most cases of conventional theorizing, imposing an abstract requirement of consistency on our moral principles and, for that matter, on rationality which, in turn, would lead to a

52. *Moral Reasons*, p. 152.

sort of generalism, the danger of which we have indicated above. Given this view of consistency, what would be required for our moral practice to be rational is some general principles under which particular moral judgments are subsumable. Such flair for a "subsumptive"concept[53] of rationality and consistency, which Hare, for example, displays in his otherwise ingenuous account of universalisability[54], and the consequent generalism it leads to, has the tendency to generalize on the basis of limited resemblances (between several cases) and ignore the peculiarities of particular problems and situations which call for variant choices and explanations. The rigidity of this view of rationalism and consistency makes it not only implausible, but it also makes several moral principles inapplicable because of their alleged "inconsistency". I have argued that consistency and rationality truly demand that we apply our principles to all *relevant* cases, *not to all* cases indiscriminately. For this purpose, a weaker sense of consistency and a weaker sense of objectivity is strong enough. Mackie's emphasis on the importance of our moral convictions, not to be affected by his denial of objective values, is a tacit acceptance of objectivity of moral values in this weaker sense in preference to the supposed absolute objectivity, which he has expressedly denied. Any possible criticism (we do indeed come across several of them) that Mackie allows a smooth entry to objectivity through the back door that he resisted at the front door is not only too simplistic but is symptomatic of a common confusion between the two senses of objectivity discerned above—a *common confusion* to which Nagel fell prey as well, as we have just seen; for how else does one account for his acceptance of "objective tolerance" as well as his scepticism expressed in his concern that something still will stay behind the lens, that something in us will determine the resulting picture? This is clearly because of his attempt to

53. Thanks to Dancy (*ibid*, p. 82 ff) for the phraseology and also the spirit of the argument.

54. *Freedom and Reason* (Oxford University Press, 1963).

run the two senses of objectivity simultaneously. Though he accepted the reality of the secondary form of objectivity and Hegelian objectification, his dominant model still remained to be that of primary objectivity and absolute objectification with which he seems to have confused the former, as Dancy has categorically alleged (see Dancy, *ibid*, pp. 151 and 153).

What follows from the foregoing as a matter of conclusion is this: if objectivity is semantically tied up with morality, it is a matter of practicality that moral values be objective in a secondary sense, in the described liberal sense and not in the absolute, literal sense. For sticking to the latter would make our moral principles either inapplicable or applicable only at the risk of leading to morally undesirable consequences. Inapplicable moral principles are not only uninteresting and not ethical theories worth the name, but are detrimental to the spirit of ethics, whose prime objective is to provide guidance and directions for moral living in practical life; and the last requires that ethical theories must be applicable, and applicable effectively, to deal with problems of practical life. This much is implied by our claim that ethical theories have a built-in applicability. We fall back, therefore, on a liberal and weaker sense of objectivity in respect of moral values and moral principles, which have the merit of explaining better our moral principles and their applicability to the world.

4

Ethics of Rights and Justice

We talk nowadays of rights with so much of emphasis and importance, of rights of so many varieties and variations and of rights of so many different species—humans, animals and inanimate things—of the present generation to which we belong as well as of future generations to which we don't, that the talk of rights has assumed the status of a *lingua franca* in the contemporary global society. We speak of rights with a lot of emotions and committed passion, and the few of us who do not do so—consciously or unconsciously—would perhaps have no right to be part of a smart society. Yet, it might appear surprising that there has been no mention of rights in some of the major scriptures and religious texts of antiquity. The universality and objectivity that the concept of rights is claimed to have is hardly borne out by history, nor has it passed for a claim that is beyond question in contemporary writings (as we shall soon be able to see). There was not even a word for 'right' in any classical European language until the fourteenth century. It was not until several centuries later that a word for "a right" was introduced into some Asian languages. Further earlier, Aristotle never talked of rights and there is no mention of rights in the modern sense of the term in ancient Greek society and Greek classical texts. Nor do we find any mention of rights in traditional Confucian Chinese society. However, this is neither surprising nor degrading the importance and moral significance of rights in the lives of men and nations. This is *not* surprising because the awareness of, and claim for, rights are social inventions which came much later as a social necessity and therefore the very notion of rights, being imbedded in the fabric of particular societies, is not strictly objective or absolute but dependent on social decisions and policies. MacIntyre, on these considerations, calls rights "moral fictions" which claim an objectivity which they do not in fact have.[1] We shall have more to say on this later on. But irrespective of whether rights are taken to be objective and absolute or relative and conditional, there is a wide-ranging agreement that rights play an important role in our social and moral life. Rights, they say, provide the minimum standards for interaction among people, "a moral 'floor' below which we would not want to sink in our interaction with one another". Study of rights, therefore, has a crucial significance in a proper understanding of the moral universe.

RIGHTS: JUSTIFICATION, STATUS AND RIGHT-MAKING PROPERTIES

Justification of Rights

Demanding social situations, especially certain undesirable happenings in recent history, not only gave rise to the awareness of rights of men but also called for justifications thereof. The question of *justifying* rights, so that they can be properly claimed by right holders, became largely important because of several perplexing events in recent history. Nazi Germany tried to subvert, enslave and even exterminate the Jews and the Gypsies by applying state laws. Blacks were systematically and even legally discriminated against in the pre-Civil Rights America. And apartheid was legally perpetuated in the *Raj* regulated South Africa. The fact that such deliberate mistreatment of human beings could be effected without needing to violate state laws

1. Alasdair MacIntyre, *After Virtue*, (Duckworth, London, 1981).

led to alarming concerns and generated serious brainstorming. It called for a *philosophical justification* of human rights; rights must have some deeper foundation, it was increasingly felt, which must be independent of particular governments or societies, which may recognize or fail or even refuse to recognize them. For this reason several theorists have tried to provide a firm foundation for human rights which could justify the claim that people *do* have certain fundamental rights which are primary and inalienable, even if the governments in authority fail or refuse to acknowledge that. They saw these rights as belonging to people simply by virtue of their very *nature*, by virtue of the fact of their being human beings. Hence the description of human rights as *natural rights.* Two of the most influential political documents of our age—*Declaration of Independence by America* and *Declarations of the Rights of Man and Citizen by France*—projected the notion of rights as the cornerstone of political organizations and social reconstruction, not only of their countries but of the world at large, not only for *their* men and citizens but for the entire humanity. Quite recently, during the second half of the last century, the world witnessed a major resurgence of interest in the notion of human rights. The Civil Rights movement in America during the nineteen sixties and onwards has had a great moral impact not only on that country's political and social life, but had profound reflections on the global situation. This is borne out by the fact that foreign policies of nations thereafter came to be largely shaped by expressed emphasis on human right violations by mutual adversaries. Like Marxist ideology being undermined by critiques as "false consciousness,"[2]—indeed, "ideology" in he Marxist context was not taken very kindly but often considered as a word for abuse—nations have tended to ennoble their own foreign policies by leveling charges of human rights violations against rival nations. America *versus* Russia in its USSR days and Pakistan *versus* India even to date can be taken as cases in point. Other examples

2. See Karl Manheim, *Ideology and Utopia* (Routledge and Kegan Paul).

(of mutual accusations of human rights violations) are not scanty in recent political history.

The foregoing has enough indication that our discussion of rights is centering round *human rights,* which are also called natural rights, and so it will be in what follows in this chapter. I have two reasons for this. The first, which concerns the meaning and implication of "rights", issues from the fact that rights exist because we are moral beings and so are naturally obliged to guard the moral value of our being by voluntary observance of the moral law. And since persons have free choice and have the ability to voluntary observance of the moral law, only persons can be properly said to be the right holders or the subject of rights. This must be the primary sense of rights by which I wish to mean that other forms of rights, like animal rights and rights of inanimate things such as nature and environment, are significant in a secondary extended sense.* Besides, the reason for the primacy of human rights concerns the reason or justification for such rights, which is that the subject being simply a human being ensures that he has these rights. These rights are seen as belonging to people simply by virtue of their very nature; in this sense these rights can be described as *swabhābaja* (born out of nature) very much as the *Bhagavad Gita* considers *svadharma* as *swabhabaja* (see Ch.1. p. 37 ff). Such characterization is more truly applicable in the case of human rights, which are taken for granted as *natural* rights of men. Indeed as we shall see, some of these rights—the more fundamental of them—are so very essentially human that no one has the right to renounce them voluntarily, since they are

* I will not, however, go to the extent of denying that animals have rights and that cruelty to animals, though wrong, are not violations of animals rights, as Austin Fagothey for example argues in his *Right and Reason* (C.V. Mosby Company, Saint Luis, 1972, p. 198). For this contention, which treats cruelty to animals as "offence against the creator, *who has provided man with these creatures to be used for any reasonable and good purpose they can serve"* (my emphasis) is an open commitment to anthropomorphism, which I take as neither tenable nor defensible.

more like one's moral duties. My second reason for choosing human rights for discussion under 'rights'—which is not unrelated to the first—is that only human rights can properly be considered as inalienable and even absolute, for such rights are entailed by some fundamental characteristic or group of characteristics of human nature. These characteristics, by virtue of which persons have the rights they are said or supposed to have, are what I propose to call the "right-making properties", which some have also called right-conferring properties[3], which are possessed only by men and not by animals and inanimate things.

Right-Making Properties

These properties are so called because their presence in us justifies our holding the rights in question; they confer on us the relevant rights. The fact that these right-making properties are distinctively human will be clear in the course of delimiting these properties. It is not that all or any of the properties of human nature are right-making, but only those without which human beings would not be human beings. Two criteria are usually used to determine such properties: First, "the more essential a property is to being a human, the stronger it will be a right-conferring property"[4] And second, "right-conferring properties are limited to those characteristics which are morally good or [at least, PKM] morally neutral".[5] The first criterion purports to exclude those properties which are inessential or accidental, without which one's being human will neither be affected totally nor even be diminished. For example, consider one's ability to snore or speak in loud voice. Because one is capable of doing these, one does not and cannot be said to have the corresponding right to snore or speak in loud voice;

3. See L.M. Hinman, *Ethics: A Pluralistic Approach to Moral Theory* (Fortworth: Harcourt Press, 1997), 2nd Edn.
4. *Op cit.*
5. *Op cit.*

restricting one's freedom for these activities will in no way affect one's being a human being. But restricting freedom of expression and even expression of religious beliefs will affect his being a human person. The second criterion, which is expressly normative in nature and which points to the moral dimension of the right-making properties, purports to exclude features of persons which are definitely immoral or morally undesirable. I may be capable of being jealous, violent and harmful to others, but they do not confer on me the right to be jealous, violent or to cause harm to others. Duryodhana's self-confessed *nature* of indulging in *adharma* and refraining from *dharma*—even if it can be shown to be true in the case of a sizable number of persons—cannot confer on him (or them) the right to do so. His (their) doing so, therefore, is subject to moral condemnation. Restricting my freedom to indulge in these not only would not diminish my humanity but also would rather groom me in accord with my inherent human nature, which we have shown to be naturally moral (Ch.2 above). Now, considering these criteria for selection of legitimately right-making properties, human properties like rationality or the ability to think and judge, autonomy or the ability for free choice and voluntary action, the ability to be a self or a person and the ability to value and to have projects and plans are the most prominent candidates which are distinctively human. No parallel properties can be attributed to animals and inanimate things to count as right-making or right-conferring. Perhaps a third reason can also be adduced by pointing to a very important fact that right implies duties which are *morally* obligatory on the part of others or the society, without which the right holder cannot possibly exercise the rights he is entitled to. These other members of the society are usually called right observers whose duty it is *not to interfere* with the exercise of the rights in question by the right holders and, if need be, to *cooperate* by providing or creating the conditions conducive to such exercise. For this reason I prefer to call these other members of the society "right promoters", who promote the right by performing both these negative and positive duties. In a very important sense, non-performance of such duties would make the holding of rights pointless, for it would then be like holding on to a theory which cannot be applied in practice. Obligations to promote the rights are essentially moral and belong to beings whose nature it is to be moral, among other things. It is this ethical fact that provides the firm substructure of the rather oft-stated *cliché* that rights and duties are correlatives and complementaries—a *cliché* it would be if divorced from its moral background. With these inevitable facts of correlativity and complementariness between them, rights and duties *primarily* relate to persons or human beings. Confucius, once asked to say what is the true moral law, replied in one word "Reciprocity"; and it is this reciprocity or what we have described as "reciprocal personal stance" (Ch.2 above), which binds the right holders and the right promoters rather logically or conceptually together: if I have a right to something, others have the corresponding duty to promote or facilitate the right and *vice versa.* The paradigm right holder is therefore the human person. Rights of animals and inanimate things do make significant sense, but, in the absence of the desired reciprocity, particularly in respect of the corresponding duties (which cannot properly be applied) on the part of (in the case of, i.e.) these supposed right holders, such rights I would designate as secondary ones. It can even be said that the language of rights put some logical constraints that make it difficult to coherently talk of rights of animals and inanimate things. Joel Finberg, for example, would say this of the things like nature or the environment that though on moral grounds we could act for the sake of, or on behalf of, animals, it is impossible to act on behalf of inanimate things like nature or the environment since there would, in this case, be no "behalf" or "sake" to act for.[6] There is also the further difficulty, which applies to animals as well, that we cannot properly speak of *duties* which we have seen to be an

6. See Hinman, *ibid*, Ch. 7.

essential correlative to rights and the latter's meaningful application. For duties are *moral* obligations to be fulfilled by moral beings or valuing beings, which animals are not. The proposal to talk of rights in these cases as well as in the case of human persons with the same strength and significance would be rather dubious and a bit over ambitious. I shall therefore stick to treating human rights as primary and human beings as paradigm right holders, and confine my discussion to these rights in this chapter and defer the analysis of animal rights and environmental rights to a subsequent chapter.

Some Theories of Rights Considered

Let us now consider and assess how different theories wanted to view the nature and foundations of rights (or natural rights) which people are eminently entitled to. Several theories have tried to provide a foundation for the rights of men, which could justify the claim that people *do* have certain fundamental rights even if (independent of the fact that) governments and societies may fail or refuse to acknowledge that. Four different theories have been offered: e.g, rights as self-evident, rights as divinely founded on God's will, rights as founded on natural laws and rights based on some characteristics of persons such as freedom, rationality and valuing power etc. In other words, four main approaches to justifying natural rights have been made by these theories: (1) appeal to self-evidence, (2) appeal to divine decree, (3) appeal to natural law and (4) appeal to human nature.

The first approach is obviously reflected in the *American Declaration of* the *Bill of Rights* (1777) and the *United Nations Universal Declaration of Human Rights* (1948). While the former declared that people's possessing certain inalienable rights like rights to life, liberty and pursuit of happiness was simply "self-evident", the latter offered no arguments whatsoever for its long list of human rights which it took simply for granted. The philosophical support for this theory in recent most writings comes eminently from Ronald Dworkin[7] and Robert Nozick[8], who consider the existence of rights to be self-evident and taken for granted. I am inclined to believe that (what we call natural) rights are obviously self-evident. Hinman's objection that (if rights were self-evident) how could the founders of the United States approve of slavery despite their emphasis on the right to liberty[9] can be explained away as a case of *akaratic action* (acting against one's best judgments) which, as such, cannot constitute a generic feature of human nature. Don't we sometimes (or even some of us most of the times) act against our best judgements? Once again, Duryodhana's confession (that could well be the confession of many of us) "*Jānāmi dharma na ca mé pravṛtti//Jānāmyadharma na ca me nivṛtti*" is a glaring illustration of the moral compunctions of an akratic mind for having to act contrary to what is naturally (self-evidently) just and moral. Natural rights are self-evident, for (a) they are in conformity with human nature and (b) human nature and (human) rights have both been shown to be morally substrated,— (a) argued elaborately in chapter 2 and (b) argued precisely just above.

The other theory, generally found in some earliest theories but eminently explicit in Locke's *Two Treatises of Government,* sees the rights as divinely ordained. Interestingly, the claim for divine foundation for the rights of citizens was adduced as a counter to a similar claim by the crown for *its* powers, since anything less would fail to override the so called rights of the monarch. What, then, would justify a choice between two counter claims of divine sanction for competing rights? Keeping in view the primacy of the ethical as detailed in chapter 1, I suggest that it is *morality* or the moral aspect of the foundation of rights that makes the difference. For the major attractiveness of the divine tradition would, rather *should,* lie in the fact that it

7. *Taking Rights Seriously.*
8. *State, Anarchy and Utopia* (Basic Books Inc. N.Y. 1974).
9. *Ibid.*

places the rights (of the citizens) firmly on the basic structure of the moral universe. If rights came from God, they belong to the deep structure of a religious world rather than to its superficial structure. As I have argued elsewhere,[10] in its deep structure, religion and divinity are really authentic and indistinguishable from morality. Thus rights being self-evident and divinely founded I see to be only two aspects of what I take to be the same theory, based on the moral nature of man. In view of this, the non-theists (atheists and agnostics alike) need not fight shy of taking rights seriously on the perfunctory plea of their being divinely ordained.

The third theory that (natural or human) rights are founded in natural law, I reckon, is also compatible with, or better explained in terms of, the moral account theory with which I have aligned the self-evidence theory and the divine foundation theory of rights. For in an important sense the rights based on the natural is necessarily good if the natural is what comes from what is wholly good, that is God (uncorrupted by evil). I am well aware that appeal to natural law in order to be morally dressed up does not have to have a theistic foundation; in fact I am largely in agreement with Rajendra Prasad's view that morality and belief in God are logically distinct.[11] But I am quite sure that a theistic account of rights in terms of a natural order fares better than its non-theistic counterpart. The non-theistic approach to natural order need *some* way of establishing that the natural order is fundamentally good in order that it can serve as a justification of rights, and this it cannot do without committing some sort of naturalistic fallacy.[12] The fourth theory, call it the Human Nature theory, proceeds from the existence of some right-making properties in persons to the existence of the corresponding rights to which persons are said to be entitled.

10. See my *Concepts and Problems*, (Cuttack, 1988), Ch. 10. See also my *Religion and Social Change* (Cuttack, 1992), Introduction.
11. "God and Morality" in *Indian Philosophy Today,* ed. N.K. Devaraja (Macmillan India).
12. See Hinman. *ibid.*

Notwithstanding the circularity this may seem to involve, this theory is of a kind with the other three in virtually holding that we have some rights simply because we are human beings and are in possession of human nature. This is what constitutes a strong common ground for rights provided by these theories. And this, as my arguments above would strongly imply, provides a prominent moral justification for the rights we hold. For man being a naturally moral and valuing being, anything issuing from human nature will have to have moral underpinnings.

Rights are Moral in Nature

T.M. Scanlon expressed the view[13] that morality is a mutually beneficial constraint among rational persons. There is a fair amount of truth in this contractualist interpretation of morality in which one sees significant reflections on rights and obligations. We have seen that obligations, negative and positive, are moral constraints on the right promoters in relation to the right holders' entitlement and that is what makes rights *moral* in nature and conception. Likewise, rights, which demand moral obligations on the part of others, are moral constraints on oneself in the sense that it is limited by duty. One can exercise one's right only up to the point where one's duty to others supersedes one's right; for a right would cease to be a right if it adversely affects the rights of others. Each of us is endowed with some rights to fulfil his purpose, but the society as a whole has an end to achieve in the general interest and none of us should pursue his objective in a way which would frustrate the social goal. Thus J.S. Mill:

> The moral rules, which forbid mankind to hurt one another (in which we must never forget to include wrongful interference with each other's freedom) are more vital to human well-being than any other maxim.
>
> (*Utilitarianism,* p. 316)

13. *Morality by Agreement* (Oxford, 1987), p. 3.

And Hare, who considers the wider domain of morality as essentially including the crucially important area of rights and obligations, suggests that:

> Within the general area of morality marked out by the use of "ought" and "must" there is a smaller field of obligations and rights, distinguished by being person-related and by being… *overridable.*
>
> *Moral Thinking* (Oxford, 1981) p. 153 [emphasis added]

This smaller domain is a distinct but central domain of morality dealing with principles of justice and of rights and obligations that present themselves as constraints on conduct and as such are overridable or defeasible, depending on the relative strength of each other. One's right, therefore, is a moral power to do or omit something depending on someone else's right and/or on one's own duty towards others.

On the Status of Rights

However, the question of whether rights are overridable or overriding is an important issue on which writers on rights are sharply divided. The protagonists of natural rights are the 'strong rights' theorists who consider rights (by which they want to mean natural rights or for whom natural rights form the paradigm case of rights, anyway) to be primary* and overriding all other considerations, including other types of moral considerations. By contrast, the defenders of the notion of rights as principally *moral* in nature consider rights to be secondary, which can be overridden or superseded by other moral considerations such as utility, duty or moral agreements like the social contract. Although my account of rights as a moral power and as basically

* By 'primary' these strong rights theorists mean rights to be absolute and infallible. This is in sharp contrast with my claim, made above, that natural rights are primary in that it not only recognizes the existence of other secondary rights but also envisions the possibility of these natural rights being overridden, as I shall show later on.

so in virtue of their being correlative to duties would draw me closer to the latter (let me call it the "moral nature" view of rights, by which I mean that rights are *moral* in nature), I differ from the proponents of this view in their characterization of rights as secondary and overridable. In fact I differ from the protagonists of both the views for holding on to exclusive views on rights, which, I believe, results in a distorted and incomplete understanding of our moral life. To be able to prove my point, let me briefly state and examine the position of the 'moral nature' theorists *vis-à-vis* the 'strong rights' theorists and see in what sense they consider rights as secondary and overridable.

The notion of natural human rights, the theory that rights are primary and absolute, has been subjected to criticism from three prominent points of view: the utilitarian, the Kantian tradition of deontology and the protagonists of contractualism. All three of these, though they take rights to be moral in nature, argue to the effect that rights, even the natural human rights, are only derivative ethical concepts, subservient to and dependent on some other moral considerations like utility, duty and agreement such as social contract.

Since the time of Bentham, utilitarians have been considering ethics as suspect if it took rights as primary. For them rights are justified only insofar as they are compatible with maximization of utility. But if we have a right to a property and, in addition, if a strong religious sentiment is attached to it, the 'strong rights' theorist would consider this right as inviolable and inalienable, even if its transfer to the government or the public sector means greater benefit to the society as a whole. 'Strong rights' theorists like Dworkin,[14] therefore, have maintained that considerations of utility can never override basic rights (right to property and right to religion in this case).

In Kant one finds two distinct approaches, one subjecting rights to subservience to duties, which he considers more moral,

14. Ronald Dworkin, *Taking Rights Seriously*.

and the other considering rights as dependent on or justified by respect and self-respect they help promoting. Duty comes first and rights follow from duties, the first Kantian approach holds. It is kind of odd that the deontologists prefer to ground rights on duties and not conversely, because there are some duties, which Kant himself regards as "imperfect duties", and which do not entitle any body to have any corresponding rights. Hinman cites the example that I may have a duty to donate to the poor, but that does not entitle any poor man to claim a right to a part of my money and property. Kant also claims that each of us has a duty to himself, but that does not make any sense of the claim that we have a right against ourselves. The second approach of Kant to rights, which is perhaps more familiarly Kantian, is the primacy of respect. "Respect humanity, whether in others or in oneself" is one important version of the categorical imperative, and it follows from this, though partly, that *failure to respect one's own rights* is a moral failing. Like the citizens of Feinberg's "Nowhereville",[15] people who never know how to claim anything as a matter of right would be missing that sense of self-respect, which is the moral minimum for a good life. Conversely, in the absence of a sense of respect (for oneself as well as for others), rights would be non-existent and without any sense. For "it is claiming that gives rights their special moral significance", says Feinberg. However, this project of Messrs Kant and Feinberg to place respect somewhat at the apex of a moral universe and to make rights subservient to respect does not seem to be acceptable beyond question. A sense of respect both for others and for oneself certainly adds to the dignity of the person, but the converse does not seem to be holding, not at any rate universally. For renouncing self-respect and giving up one's rights for the sake of one's duty towards others and for the society would not diminish the moral dignity for the person, but it is rather often considered an ennobling act and indicative of extraordinary strength of character. The greatness of

15. Joel Feinberg, "Nature and Value of Rights".

renunciation and self-sacrifice has often passed as a distinctive trait of oriental and medieval western morality. The Indian idea of *aparigraha* (non-acceptance or no claim to anything) has always remained an inspiring moral ideal. The well known prayer of Bhima Bhoi, an eminent saint poet of Orissa, to redeem the whole world, to alleviate the sorrows and sufferings of the people, even if that meant *his* rotting in the hell—"*mó jivana pachhé naraké padithāu, jagata uddhāra pāu*" (*Stutee Chintamani*, verse 27:7)—has made him a moral role model for many. Besides, in view of the criticism, often made, of the rights tradition for being individualistic and even anti-communitarian, non-claiming of rights in the interest of the welfare of others and of the society at large has an interesting significance.

Whereas Kant and his deontologist followers made right subservient to duty and respect, the contractualists in ethics see rights as existing in so far as they provide the minimum moral requirement for a moral community grounded in an implicit contract entered into by the members of the community freely and rationally. This approach has the merit of avoiding, or at least lessening, the criticism often made that the rights tradition is too individualistic and even anti-communitarian. The Indian tradition of *aparigraha* is an implicit detractor of the rights tradition for this reason. But the principle of making rights grounded on contract too cannot be universalized. For though many rights may originate in contracts, not all rights can be said to result from contracts and no right can be wholly grounded on contracts alone. Wherefrom the parties to a contract get the *right to enter into the contract*? It may be asked. Is it because of a prior contract? This can't go on *ad infinitum*! "Contracts receive their binding force from something existing prior to [and other than, PKM] all contracts, the moral law, which requires the observance of just pledges and agreements", says Austin Fagothey[16], who goes on to add the further argument that non-renunciable rights like the right to life cannot be the results of a

16. *Rights and Reason*, pp. 201-2.

contract, though the right to protect and preserve the right to life may be, I would like to add. For a contract can be broken, but the right to life cannot be "contracted away."[17]

In the light of the foregoing discussion on conflicting claims about the nature and status of rights, let us attempt an honest assessment of the rival theories. Both the 'strong rights' theory and the 'moral nature' theory give illuminating revelations regarding the importance and moral significance of rights. While the former rightly regards the natural human rights to be fundamental and inalienable, the latter has the merit of drawing attention to the morality of the rights by nature and conception. But both went astray and argued at cross-purposes in their respective claims of rights being primary in the one case and secondary in the other. When the 'strong rights' theories claimed rights to be primary, they meant this to imply that rights are absolute, inalienable and objective, that they can override all other considerations and cannot be overridden by any other consideration. While they are generally right on this, they are limited on two counts: firstly, they talked of natural human rights but seem to have taken them to be the model of (all) rights, and secondly, they seem to have overlooked the fact that even the most fundamental of the natural human rights are not absolute and inalienable in the strict sense of the terms. To be sure, the most fundamental of the human rights, like the rights to life, liberty or freedom and property, are inalienable and no one has the right to take away these rights from men and citizens, nor is anybody (any right holder) morally allowed renouncing them voluntarily. To take just one of these rights, it is an undeniable fact that we are free and purposive beings, and if someone tries to deny this he is engaging in a free and purposive activity. This is a transcendental argument, which Alan Gewirth adduced[18] in support of the said right as inalienable and absolute. This right, as also the rights to life and property, are not concerned with

17. *Ibid*, p. 202.
18. *Reason and Morality* (University of Chicago Press, Chicago, 1978).

some peripheral or incidental human needs like desiring to have a colour television or a computer; they are concerned with *the core conditions* of being human, and it would be grossly irrational to deny that we have the right to be the sort of beings we most fundamentally are. However, while these rights are what they are, they do not and cannot constitute *all* the rights men have. Some other rights, like the right to marry and choose a profession, are also *human* rights, but they are not absolute and inalienable, but fairly renounceable, for a person is free to choose not to marry and not to go in for any profession. These rights are not only voluntarily renounceable by the right holder, but can sometimes be overridden by other considerations. For while criminal offence and proven dishonesty may justify depriving a person from entering into a profession, severe physical and mental disability may stand in the way of someone wanting to marry. These rights, compared to the rights to freedom, life and property, are secondary but nevertheless recognized rights of men and citizens. Thus the 'strong rights' theorists' claim that rights are absolute and inalienable is exclusive and one sided. Besides, their claim of absoluteness and inalienability, even for the fundamental human rights, is also not borne out by facts. For it is a well-known fact about our political, social and legal systems that such rights may be lost or forfeited for misuse when someone commits a serious crime like murder, thereby losing his right to life which he would otherwise have been enjoying *equally* with his fellow humans. Rights to liberty and freedom of speech can be taken away or temporarily suspended in the greater interest of the nation, as it happens during the declaration of a national emergency. The right to property and religious beliefs can also be forfeited in the greater interest of the nation and society. These are compelling circumstances, which justify the violation of even the most fundamental of human rights. Naturalness of human rights does not *suo motto* make them primary and overriding, nor does the rights being primarily moral make them secondary and overridable. It is rather to some extent amusing that the "moral nature" theorists, who plead for rights to be principally *moral,* should treat them indiscriminately as secondary to and derivative from other moral considerations like duty, utility or contract. We have cited some reasons against the claims of the utilitarians and the deontologists to show that superiority of utility and duty over rights is neither borne out by facts nor by logic; for some rights cannot be superseded by considerations of utility, even if maximum, and some duties even do not admit of the corresponding rights to be claimed by anyone. The contractualists' claim that rights are the results of, and so are dependent upon, agreed contracts has also been shown to be untenable. The claim that these *other* moral considerations justify and override rights cannot be absolute; hence the theory that moral rights are secondary *simplicitor* cannot be sustained. The fact rather is that, contrary to the exclusive claims of the two opposite theories discussed above, rights, like other moral concepts and rules, are objective but *defeasible.* Which rights are sustainable and which ones are defeasible will depend on the context and the demands of the situation. Just like moral principles, objective and universal though they are, nevertheless admitting of justified violations under the demands of compelling situations (see ch.1), all rights, including the natural rights, as shown above, can, in some situations, be overridden by other rights (of other people or of oneself) and also by other moral considerations. As in the case of the moral principles in general, so also in the case of rights, the violation or supersession must take proper account of the spirit behind (holding of) the right in question and of the urgency of the situation.

Conflicts of Rights with Rights and Duties

Defeasibility and overridability of rights become pronounced and demanding in situations involving conflicts: rights may conflict with rights or with duties; one's right may conflict with somebody else's right or with another of one's own right, or with one's own duty. Current discussions in practical ethics abound with cases of such conflicts. Indeed these situations make the study of rights more engaging and call for clarity of the concept of rights and status thereof. The controversy on abortion has often been, and still continues to be, a case of conflict of rights: the fetus's right to life and the woman's rights to privacy. With spectacular advancement in both medical science and bio-medical ethics, debates are on as to whether a person has the right to die and whether a doctor has the right or duty to terminate the life of a patient suffering from a disease with terminal incurability. A scientist's right to use animals for research and testing is often threatened by the protagonists of animal rights. Such conflicts of rival rights (as well as of rights and duties) call for closer scrutiny of the concept of right and of the moral status of different rights, a review of rights being absolute or relative (overriding or defeasible).

I have already indicated that such conflicts are largely because of extreme and exclusive views on the notions of 'absolute' and 'relative' as applied to rights—indeed to anything. Such theories do not take the situations into consideration at all. What is to be done when a right conflicts with a duty and a duty with another duty? About the last conflict, we have argued in the first chapter (Arjuna's *svadharma* versus his *sādhāraṇa dharma*) that the nature and peculiarity of the situation will make one duty (*svadharma* of fighting in the interest of winning a righteous war) override another, rival duty (*sādhāraṇa dharma* of non-killing), which becomes in this case *defeasible* but not, as we have argued, degraded below its normal status as a cardinal moral duty. As we have argued, defeasibility of a virtue under a demanding situation does not turn this virtue into a vice. Likewise, morally inviolable the rights are, and so they remain, despite their being defeasible under circumstances. Some rights, generally inalienable and absolute, may be overridden by rival rights, which may stand out as stronger and more compelling in particular situations, but it could not for that matter be denigrated as relative and secondary *simplicitor*. Termination of a pregnancy may be absolutely necessary to save the life of an expectant mother. But even then the fetus's right to life, though defeated in this case by the expectant woman's right to life, still remains absolutely justified and morally inviolable. This sort of defeasibility may also depend on which properties would be considered right-making properties—not definitionally but contextually. For the resolutions of conflicts, where other things do not remain the same, no hard and fast rules are available at hand. Each case must be taken in its concrete setting and every situation must be carefully weighed. To know which rights are weightier and stronger in comparison to their rival rights and obligations under particular situations, we (especially those of us who are interested and engaged in applied ethics) must do some thinking, apply some critical power we all are capable of. What I mean by saying this is that applied ethics, like any philosophical activity, must not be blandly reportive, but analytic and reconstructive to some (required) extent. (Again, *to what extent* it has to be so cannot be determined by any rule of the thumb). Perhaps reason and experience can be of help in some situations and moral intuition can help in some, perhaps most, others. Austin Fagothey has suggestions to this effect in his *Right and Reason*:

> Both reason and experience prescribe that we shall set up such means for determining just which right or duty prevails, and in most of the matters that come under their jurisdiction the decision of the courts, *unless manifestly unjust*, are binding in conscience (p. 206, emphasis mine*).

And he continues,

> But not all matters are subject to civil laws and its courts; often the decision must be made *on the basis of natural ethics*. (p. 206, emphasis added*)

Perhaps, as he also suggests, commonsense "which is another name for the cardinal virtue of prudence" can have no substitute in these matters (*ibid,* p. 206). But what is undeniable is that:

> Most cases are settled by working out some proportion or compromise between the various factors and claims, *except that the negative duty of never doing anything inherently evil prevails over everything else.*
>
> (*Ibid,* pp. 206-7, emphasis added*)

The compromise and apportionment is necessary by situational conditions in working out a solution. And rights and obligations being primarily moral in nature, the compromise required for conflict resolution has to be a moral compromise proportionate to the spirit behind the rights/obligations and the demand of the situation. It is in this sense perhaps that Brandt, with an obvious utilitarian undertone, speaks of an "optimal moral conscience" as the guide in the conflict ridden moral predicaments. Thus Brandt:

> ... the notion of an *optimal* moral conscience [is that] where "conscience" is construed as motivation not to do certain types of thing, plus a disposition to feel guilty if one acts contrariwise, plus a disposition to be indignant with those who do and a disposition to believe that the foregoing attitudes can be justified in some appropriate way.[19]

---

* The emphasized portions in the above three quotations point to the significant fact of the primacy of the ethical, which we have seen to be an important precondition of applied ethics. Rights, which are morally grounded, will be absolute and inalienable, but any right,—political, civil or legal,—if it could be shown not to be moral, will lose importance and will not be claimable by all. No amount of civil sanction and legal force can create a right to do what there is a moral duty not to do.

19. Richard Brandt, *Facts, Values and Morality* (Cambridge University Press, 1996), p. 156.

Although Brandt prescribed this as a criterion for determining wrong and right actions, the relevance of this "optimal" criterion to conflict resolution is more than apparent. For he goes on to say a little later, "Rights are not fixed by actual moral codes but rather by a code's being optimal. And to determine which moral code is optimal for a given society may not be obvious", which means there are no hard and fast rules, as we said, and for this Brandt recommends us to "do some thinking" in order that we may come to know "how weighty they [the moral rights] are *in comparison with each other and with other obligations*"[20]. Brandt cites Scanlon's view for confirmation of his own that an "optimal moral code is one that could be reasonably agreed to, as having moral force in the society, by everyone", (*ibid*, p. 160) and "by any system of rules for the general regulation of behaviour *which no one could reasonably reject* as a basis for informed, unforced, general agreement".(Scanlon quoted on pp.159-60, *ibid;* emphasis added). I find here a clear reflection of Nagel's concept of "objective tolerance" discussed in chapter 3, which prescribes in effect a secondary, non-absolute form of objectivity applicable in, and available to, the case of moral rules; "optimal moral code" likewise envisages a non-absolute form of moral standard, suitable to specific social situations, for determining wrong and right actions as well as defeasible and sustainable rights.

The conclusion, to which we are drawn from the foregoing, including our foregoing analysis of conflict situations, may be summed up thus: Rights are normally inviolable and can be claimed absolutely. But they cannot be defined as absolutely inviolable and overriding *in all circumstances*; for some of them, perhaps each of them, may be superseded by other rights and obligations as well as by other moral considerations. Like all moral principles, which have been shown to be objective but defeasible, rights are also defeasible, though inalienable and

20. *Ibid*, pp. 158-59. (Emphasis added).

inviolable generally. The key to a proper understanding of the nature and status of rights lies in abstaining from exclusive views on the nature of rights and on the notion of 'absolute' and 'relative' as applied to the rights, since literal adherence to exclusive views would result in presenting distorted picture of moral life as it is. Conflicts of rights can be resolved in the same way as conflicts between competing duties are dealt with, i.e. by taking into consideration the peculiarities and specificities of particular situations in which such conflicts are encountered. Such situations call for closer and critical review of the conventional theories and bring to light the inevitable fact of defeasibility of rights and duties under demanding circumstances. This fact we have seen to be a recognized aspect of the tradition, though not a conspicuous and pronounced one; the Indian concepts like *āpad dharma* consider violations of celebrated moral principles (performance of a non-duty and abstaining from a duty as well as renunciation and infringement of rights under demanding situations) not only permissible but also justifiable and morally commendable. However, defeasibility of rights and duties, as of any moral principle, has nothing to make them relative and secondary. Rights, therefore, are inviolable and inalienable, which they are supposed to be, despite being defeasible under circumstances, which they have to be. Inviolability and inalienability, call it absoluteness if you like, of rights has thus to be of a weaker form like "objective tolerance" in Nagel's sense.

With the proviso that rights are defeasible, the most fundamental of the natural human rights, such as the right to liberty, life and property, can be said to be basic and absolute, but they can never be overriding *by definition*. In view of this, the attempt to deny that animal rights are rights at all on the putative ground that they can never override human rights is deeply irrational; rights are, by nature and conception, overriding as well as overridable.

Right to Equality

All rights, thus conceived, are equally claimable by the right holders and equally to be respected and promoted by the right promoters, irrespective of whether the right promoters happen to be individuals or the society or the government in authority. This brings us to the right to equality, which has a special logical status among all forms of rights. From the most fundamental of natural rights to the relatively less important (because alienable and renounceable) ones like the right to marry and the right to hold a profession, the common theme is *equal treatment and equality of opportunity*. The right to equality is thus a very special sort of right, which guarantees how people hold these other rights. It is in this sense a "meta-right" that ensures that we all have *the same rights*, that some of us are not allowed any unfair advantage over others and that no discrimination is allowed on considerations of race, birth and blood.

In view of this, particularly the last, the right to equality is taken to involve two explicit aspects: while it clearly imposes negative obligations not to deprive some people or a section of the society of opportunities discriminatingly, it also calls for positive action for ensuring or creating equal opportunities for all. Consider the issues of minorities' admission to technical courses. It is not enough that the minorities or the so called backward classes are not denied this opportunity, it has to be ensured that such opportunity *exists* or is created, if non-existent, for them. Creation of opportunities become particularly imperative if social conditions happen to provide far fewer opportunities to the minority and backward classes to be able to compete equally, with equal competence, with others—perhaps because of acts of discrimination and repression perpetrated on them earlier in life. Factors like these have often been thought to justify the view that the right to equality entails positive obligations to provide and create conditions to overcome previous discriminations. (The "affirmative action" in America and the policy of reservation in post-independent India are cases in point: we will have occasion to consider this later in this chapter). This will give real force and significance to the principle that to treat people justly is to treat them equally. The right to equality is thus closely and meaningfully related to the principle of justice. We will now proceed to analyse this in what follows.

JUSTICE, EQUALITY AND JUST-MAKING CONSIDERATIONS

Justice and Equality: The Close Tie

If much of human history has been an incessant quest for justice, the same history has witnessed an almost inseparable link between justice and equality. For the struggles against slavery, racial discrimination, economic exploitation, political subjugation and discrimination of classes and castes have all been centering around one demand—the demand for equality or equal rights for all men. Besides the testimony of history, the close tie between justice and equality is manifest in language and general usage, so much so that even those who meant to break the conceptual link by pleading for unequal apportionment of benefits and burdens on grounds of differing merits did, nonetheless, stick to the verbal link. This is evident from the fact that "...the meritarian view of justice paid reluctant homage to the equalitarian one by using the vocabulary of equality to assert the justice of inequality."[21] Even Popper, holding on to "general usage", becomes intolerant of Plato's account of justice in terms of unequal allotment: "Why did Plato claim that justice meant inequality if, *in general usage,* it meant equality?", he asks in his *Open Society*, [22] and goes on to say, "To me the only

21. Gregory Vlastos, "Justice and Equality" in *Social Justice,* ed. Richard Brandt (Prentice Hall, Englewood Cliffs, N.J., 1962), p. 32.
22. K.R. Popper, *The Open Society and Its Enemies* (Rutledge and Kegan Paul, London, 1949), pp. 79-80.Emphasis added.

likely reply seems to be that he wanted to make propaganda for his totalitarian state by persuading the people that it was the 'just' state...His attack on equalitarianism was not an honest attack." Thus, from common usage to definition of justice and from Plato to Rawls, the conceptual closeness of justice to equality is more than manifest. If Plato said that justice is rendering to every one his due (*Republic*) and Rawls said that everybody has equal right to the basic liberties unless an inequal distribution of any social value is to the advantage of every one (*A Theory of Justice*), then the notion of justice—be it individual or social—bears clear stamp of equality on it and the familiar formula of social justice—treating similars, similarly and dissimilars differently—stands solidly on the foundation of equality and equitable distribution. The principle of equality can, therefore, be dubbed not only as a part of justice but the distinctive feature thereof. "The principles of justice are distinguished from other principles of morality by being governed by the ideal of equality."[23]

It follows, therefore, that any plausible theory of justice largely depends on the correct analysis of the concept of equality. In other words, much depends on a proper understanding of what 'equality' means. It is not that we do not understand the meaning of equality in common conversation, nor that this is a very hard word to be understood easily. But taking the word in its etymological sense—in the sense in which it is the antonym of 'inequality' and is incompatible with 'difference', for example—might lead one to, as indeed it actually has (we shall soon be able to see), mistaken theories of justice and an unreal opposition between the justice theories based on such superficial grammatical understanding of the word. It is necessary, therefore, to distinguish between this understanding of 'equality' and knowing the correct analysis of its meaning. What I have in mind is reminiscent of that salutary distinction made by G.E. Moore between knowing what a word means and knowing the

23. "The Concept of Social Justice" in Brandt ed,, *Social Justice*, p. 17.

correct analysis of its meaning.[24] To know the latter, one has to delve deep into what Wittgenstein would call its depth grammar—what the word means in a specific context and in the light of the surrounding circumstances. In default of that, a superficial grammatical understanding of the word would create fixed pictures and obscure understanding. Such type of understanding of equality is likely to leave one wondering as to how can a theory of justice, based on merit and desert, be a theory of *justice* at all and even make sense since people obviously differ in respect of merit and worth, and justice is inseparable from equality! We have seen this sort of perplexity in the case of many a philosophical problems, like how a person can be the same person over a period of time if nothing about him remains unchanged, or how can an arrow move at all if, at each moment during its motion, it *is* at one particular point of space! Similarly we are perplexed about the controversy between equalitarianism and meritarianism as theories of justice: If equality is built into the concept of justice then there is no controversy here, it would be said, since equalitarianism is the only theory of justice that *should* be there; and yet the other theory seems to make a lot of sense! So there must be something seriously wrong somewhere. Yes, it is our grammatical habit of understanding 'equality' torn out of its use in the specific contexts and configurations. What is to be considered here is that if justice requires equality—equal treatment to all—then what kind of equal treatment is meant here? Does it rule out all types of unequal treatment—e.g., treating people differently on the basis of their differing merits, worth and need—as *unjust*? An appeal to the common usage regarding justice will verily show that not all types of equality is required to make our actions, individual and social, just. Granting of equal liberty, equal opportunities and equality of the fundamental rights to all is

24. "*A Defense of Commonsense*" in *Contemporary British Philosophy*, 2nd series, ed. J.H. Muirhead (Allen and Unwin, U.S.A.,1925). Reprinted in *Philosophy of G.E. Moore*, ed. Schillp.

just, since each individual has equal human worth; but granting of exactly equal status to a judge and a criminal, for example, is certainly not in keeping with the spirit, principles and procedures of social justice. Differential treatment and unequal distribution of the benefits and burdens of the society in certain circumstances are very much in tune with the principles of justice. What is more to the point, some such differences and unequal treatments are *required* in the interest of equality in the long run.

Just-making Conditions

So, not all forms of equalities and all sorts of differences are just-making conditions; which ones are will depend on their reference to the specific situations. The ethics of justice requires that all should be given equal opportunity to promote their good life in the sense of their happy life. But the good life and its conditions differ from person to person because of their needs and the situations in which they happen to be placed. Equal distributions in such cases will necessarily require and mean differential treatments, viz, to give food to the hungry, books to a student, musical instrument to a musician and a car to a business executive and so on. Even *different* musical instruments *need* to be given to different categories of musicians, even though they form one class by themselves. In all these cases people are treated *differently yet equally*. Indeed, in such types of situations, equality means and requires differential treatment. Thus, though equality is the *prima facie* requirement of justice, a just society must also respect some *differences* as just-making conditions. Considerations of merit, potentialities and needs are some of the prominent just-making considerations in justicising differences, just as considerations of human worth and natural rights are some of the just-making considerations in justicising equality. Considerations of the former type give content and sense and justification to the meritarian view of justice. I shall shortly argue that the controversy between meritarianism and egalitarianism is only apparent, since the claims of both boil down to the demand for equality in the long run, as would be revealed by a correct analysis of the concept of equality.

Sticking to the just-making considerations for the moment, it should by now be clear that these are related to and contingent upon what I have been indicating as the proper understanding of the meaning of 'equality' *vis-à-vis* 'inequality' or 'difference' and similar *vis-à-vis* differential (or even preferential) treatments. Once again, though the primary condition of justice is to treat similars similarly and dissimilars differently, yet not all similarities and not all types of differences are just-making considerations. It would not be unjust to treat some similars differently and some dissimilars equally. For example, debaring a Veerappan from holding any public office and nominating a Deve Gowda to the Rajya Sabha will not be unjust, though both of them are citizens of India; nor was it unjust on the part of the Queen of England to confer knighthood on Bertrand Russell and Alfred Ayer, though they differed in respect of race and blood. Sameness of nationality is not just-making consideration in all cases, nor is difference in blood, race and colour. Indeed, as we have argued, Drona did a great act of injustice by refusing to teach the art of archery to Eklavya whereas Duryodhana, notwithstanding his motive, committed an act of justice by conferring the status of a king on Karna. Consideration of birth and caste is by no means just-making conditions in the context of learning while that of valour, heroism and personality most certainly is in the context of kingship.

It should be pretty clear from the above discussion that what is a just-making condition is not a matter of definition, nor is it something absolute or even amenable to general agreement. All that can be said is that there must be some just-making considerations on the basis of which actions and conducts of individuals and societies could be judged as just or unjust. What they are will depend on the context and a proper understanding of the meaning and implications of 'equal' (and 'unequal' and 'different'). We may quote William Frankena to substantiate this contention: "Justice", he says, "is treating persons equally except as unequal treatment is required by just-making considerations *of substantial weight in the circumstances*."[25]

Meaning of Equality vis-à-vis Just-making Conditions

In what follows, I shall concentrate on what I think to be a proper analysis of the meaning of equality in the context of justice—what sorts of inequalities are compatible with the ideal of equality and what sorts of departure from equality are allowable and pertinent. Our analysis will naturally have reflections on the egalitarian/meritarian controversy as well as on differential or preferential treatment, both of which figure prominently in considerations of the ethics of justice. And I hope to show that both the meritarian view of justice and preferential treatment are required by the ideal of equality and are, hence, subservient to it in the long run.

In this endeavour, I shall have to address to two crucial questions: (1) whether there are (or can be) principles of justice or just-making considerations, which overrule equality? (2) if there are, can they render the principle of equality otiose? As would be quite evident from the foregoing, my answer to the first question is in the affirmative while that to the second, negative. To this purpose, let me begin with that crucial remark by Aristotle in his *Nicomachian Ethics*,[26] that is at once simplistic in verbiage but cryptic in implications. Aristotle says, "Justice is equality, as all men believe it to be, quite apart from any argument." It is quite natural for a Greek to say this, since the Greek word for equality, to *ison* or *isotes*, is closer to being the right word for justice than the Greek word *dikaiosyne,* which is a usual translation of the word 'justice'. Thus, for a Greek speaking person it is quite plausible to say 'equality' and mean 'justice'.[27] But a closer scrutiny of the use of the word 'isotes'

25. William K. Frankena in Brandt (ed.) *Social Justice*, p. 10. Emphasis added.
26. *Nicomachian Ethics*, Book V, 1131a 13.
27. I owe this formulation to Gregory Vlastos, *op.cit,* p. 31.

shows that it means 'geometrical equality', i.e., proportionality; hence the 'equal' (or just) distribution of the benefits and burdens of the society to persons will have to be *proportionate to their merits and capacities*. This is what equality or equitable distribution *means.* In a society of different types of people with different needs, for example, giving the same one thing to everybody, an expensive guitar or a motor car each, will not only be a parody of equitable distribution, but will neither be just nor equal treatment. For some would need a house, some others clothing, and still some others two meals a day. Equal treatment, therefore, will have to be differential and even preferential treatment, proportionate to the needs, merits and capabilities of people. This explains what would otherwise appear to most of us as a startling revelation that Aristotle, like Plato, propounded the view that a just distribution is, in effect, an unequal one.[28] What would look to be more startling is that, if 'equal' is one's word for just, as it is for a Greek speaking person, one would have to say that an *equal* distribution is indeed an *unequal* one!

But far from expressing a self-contradiction, this only brings home the point that some inequalities, though not all, are built into the concept of just and equitable distribution. When merit, or need or capability and so on are the just-making considerations, an equal (just or fair) distribution to persons of unequal merit, etc., will have to be inevitably unequal. Unless one chooses to take an extremely literal view of equalitarianism, one can speak in a perfectly matter of fact way of 'equitable inequalities' and 'inequitable equalities'. In fact Plato was more emphatic on the logic of *just inequalities* justified on grounds of merit and worth. He had not only made his equalitarian rivals—the democrats in particular—intellectually defenseless by his cryptic quip that democracy distributes a very odd sort of

---

28. Plato, *Georgias,* 508a, *Republic,* 558c and *Laws,* 744bc. Also Aristotle, *ibid,* 1131a 15ff.

equality to equals and unequals alike,[29] but also challenged them to say if they really meant to universalise equality, say if there are no just inequalities, no rights in respect of which men are unequal? Understandably, the equalitarians have never come up with a clear answer to this and Plato's question has gone by default. We have come across profound declarations like 'Men are born and remain free and equal in rights'.[30] But in actual practice and application of the concepts, men have remained neither free nor equal in respect of all rights unconditionally and without exceptions. One of the most obvious departures (justified departure, I should say) from the ideal of equal rights can be illustrated as follows. The holding of a unique public office, like the office of the President of India, is not a matter of equal right to all men; for no other man has a right to this office except Dr. A.P.J. Abdul Kalam (who holds the office as this book goes to press), though every Indian has equal right of *eligibility to this office*. To be sure, the equalitarian, the democrat in particular, can draw comfort from the last, but he should not fight shy of conceding that men are (born and remain) equal in respect of *some* rights, but not in respect of a great many others. Further, as we have seen above, there not only can be but are justified exceptions to fundamental rights and even to our natural rights as human beings, when equality is denied and freedom is curtailed under compelling circumstances. Contrary to the claims of equalitarianism—literal equalitarianism, as I have indicated above—even natural human rights, in respect of which all men are supposed to be equal, are not absolute and unexceptionable. If I have natural right to a certain benefit, it does not follow that I ought to be granted that benefit in *all* circumstances, no matter how it affects the rights of others and even some of *my* other rights. John Rawls, quite to the point, has prescribed his two principles of justice[31] with exceptional pertinence, the first of

29. Republic, 558c.
30. Article I of the *Declaration of Rights of Man and Citizen* (enacted by the Constituent Assembly of the First French Republic in 1971).
31. *A Theory of Justice*, (Cambridge, Mass: The Balkan Press of Harvard University, 1971).

which (of the second, shortly later) says that every person has equal rights to the basic freedom compatible with *similar freedom* for all. This clearly envisions the fact that one can enjoy equal natural rights (e.g. right to life, liberty, property, security etc.) only so long as they—some of them, or any of them—do not adversely affect those of others and, we may add, some others of one's own. Even John Locke who, some claim, is known for his advocacy for the view that natural rights are absolute,[32] allows justified exceptions to natural rights in approving imprisonment as a punishment for crime and detention of beggars in corrective homes.[33] Natural rights, I repeat, can be construed as *prima facie* rights, which are *defeasible*, i.e., can be overruled in special circumstances, the speciality and the exceptionally demanding nature of which provide the just-making conditions in these contexts. All we need, perhaps, is to find *reasons for our natural rights, which will be the moral reasons for just exceptions.* Reasons can be many in specific circumstances. John Rawls provides one important reason in his second principle of justice (which he calls "the difference principle"): all social and economic inequalities are to be so arranged as to be (a) reasonably expected to be to everyone's advantage and (b) attached to positions and offices open to all. Here differences and inequalities are justicised on the same ground on which equality (i.e., equal basic liberties) is also justicised, namely, equity or equitable distribution that is to *everyone's advantage*. This is what I wish to call 'liberal equalitarianism' (as distinct from what I have described as 'literal equalitarianism'), which construes equality as *compatible with* unequal treatment in some respects as shown above. This view which, I think, is perfectly in keeping with our normal intuitions on justice, not only recognizes meritarianism as a respectable theory of justice but

---

32. See for example, E.F. Carritt, *Ethical and Political Thinking* (Oxford Univ. Press, 1947), p. 154ff, and R.B. Brandt, *Ethical Theory*, (Prentice Hall, Englewood Cliffs, N.J.) 1959, p. 442.
33. See H. R. Foxbourne, *Life of Locke* (London, 1976, Vol.2), pp.371-81.

also shortens the gap between this theory and the equalitarian theory of justice. Thus, with unequal treatment in meritarianism seen as a requirement for the principle of equitable distribution, the gap becomes almost nonexistent (i.e., there is seen to be virtually no conflict between the two theories), unless one wants obstinately to hold on literally to an extreme form of equalitarianism.[34] Indeed, the differences and inequalities justified in meritarianism and other non-equalitarian theories of justice are not only compatible with, but are subservient to, the ideal of equality in the long run. In the rest of this chapter, I shall try to supplement this contention by considering differences and preferences (in justified treatment of people), which are either required by (hence built into) the concept of equality or are intended, as we shall see, to restore equality in society that had been disturbed by actions of individuals or the state.

Justice as Preferential Treatment

It is a well-known fact about penal procedures that, notwithstanding the equal liberties of individuals, a criminal has to be treated differently from his victim and also from other persons, for by committing the crime he has harmed some others and has disturbed equality (i.e., equal right of people not to be harmed and deprived of one's property) and so has to be punished in order that the equality disturbed by his action can be restored; in the process, the criminal has justifiably lost his right not to be harmed or not to be deprived of his property. Yet, as a human person, he retains the basic natural right not to be treated unequally before the law. Even though the criminal is a cruel

34. The extreme form of equalitarianism issues from taking a literal view of equality. Such a tendency is displayed even by a very discriminating philosopher, William Frankena, perhaps in one of his unguarded moments, when he says: "In opposition to the classical meritarian view of social justice I accepted as part of my own view the principle that all men are to be treated as equals, not because they are equal in any respect but simply because they are human", *op.cit.*, p.19. (My emphasis)

person, it will be unjust to treat him equally cruelly; for although he has broken the law, *he is still within the purview of the law* and deserves equal protection from it except the punishment as required by his desert and in the interest of equality which he has disturbed. The extreme retributive policy of punishment, followed in some fundamentalist Islamic countries, does not care to take this into account and therefore fall short of a justice-theory. Similarly, in the case of our taxation policies. The unequal concentration of wealth in the society is usually sought to be rectified by progressive taxation so that an equitable distribution of wealth can be effected. Marx's maxim "from each according to his capacity" is an eminent pointer and this, together with the principle "to each according to his need", sought to restore some sort of [economic] equality in the society.

If justice is giving everyone his due, then to deprive someone or some group of men of what is his or their due is denial of justice, i.e., injustice. The struggle for social justice has been to undo this wrong by compensating the victims of such denials and deprivations—the Blacks in America, the Jews in Germany and the so-called lower castes in India, for example. With a view to restoring equality of rights (to opportunities and liberties) that has been disturbed by the denial of justice, a just society has to make provisions for *preferential treatments* to the members of the wronged class. For the right to equality, as we have said, entails a positive obligation to provide or create opportunities to overcome, and compensate for, previous discriminations in order that an earlier wrong can be righted. This would of course mean that in the process of dispensation of preferential justice some members of the non-preferred class would suffer injustice. For example, taking the case of the reservation policy followed in post independence India,[35] a

35. This example and the arguments that follow owe their source largely to Professor Rajendra Prasad, "Social Justice, Retribution and Revenge" in *Social Justice: Philosophical Perspectives* ed. P.K. Mohapatra, (D.K. Print world, New Delhi, 1999).

candidate belonging to the P-caste, despite securing 75 per cent marks, may have to lose his chance of admission to a professional course because an R-caste candidate* with only 35 per cent marks got the seat, since it was *reserved* for the R-caste candidates. This is inevitable, because the provision of this concession to the R-caste candidates is the only way available to the society for correcting the social and moral imbalance and restoring equality of rights and opportunities; and the particular student of the P-caste can take his non-admission to the course as *his* share of the cost of social development or restoration of social justice. Thus preferential treatment, though unequal distribution, is only a means to the ideal of equality (or equitable distribution) in the long run and is subservient to this ideal.

Why, then, is there so much of controversy and resentment over the reservation policy, if preferential treatment is an essential element of social justice and subservient to the ideal of equality? The reason, I reckon, is a misunderstanding (I hope it is not a wilful misunderstanding). The misunderstanding relates to the 'reason' for the P-caste candidate being denied what he deserved on merit. I have said that this candidate has been *wronged* and so his resentment is genuine. But instead of admitting this, the general trend of thinking, thanks to excessive politicization of the issue, has been to consider his resentment and frustration as unjustified and as an expression of "undue" attachment of the privileged class to the powers and privileges it has wrongfully acquired and has been enjoying for ages. What is unfortunate is that, not only some reservation enthusiasts and its beneficiaries, but the people in power, the politicians in particular, seem to think that the P-student's *caste* is a good enough reason for his non-admission to the course and that there is nothing for him to complain against or to have a feeling of having made a sacrifice! This is a blatant misunderstanding of the just-making considerations for preferential treatment in this

* P and R may be taken to mean the so called *privileged* castes and the *repressed* castes respectively.

context. The fact that one belongs to a particular caste cannot, *by itself,* justicise granting to, or withholding from, him anything whatsoever. It is counterintuitive to our moral common sense to make one's caste (for which one is not responsible) the *reason* for giving him something, which he does not deserve on merit, or for denying something he does deserve. The right reason, as we have seen, is restoration of social balance and the P-caste student has to be made to see that his non-admission to the course is his share of the burden, nonetheless recognizing, and sympathizing for, the sacrifice he makes and injustice he suffers. (Compare the case of a child who must, nonetheless, be praised for decent manners despite the fact that his manners are largely due to decent upbringing or constant and careful conditioning by his parents). And since, I argue, this is an injustice, it should not go on forever. Considering the fact that we are about to cross the 60th year of our country's independence, the government and the society must start working for a healthy social order in which such injustice to deserving persons become uncalled for and the occasion for depriving a deserving candidate in order to accommodate a less deserving one—on grounds of a concession, *al beit* justified otherwise—does not arise at all. The so-called weaker section too has an onerous role in making this possible. They must realize the important truth that it is more dignified and self-respecting for the young people to earn something on merit than to get it under the protection of a concession, and they must work earnestly towards realization of this truth. It is deplorable that neither our government nor our educational planners nor even the national media is making any effort in this direction. But social justice will be a far cry unless such conditions are created in which everyone *deserves* what he earns or what benefit he gets.

5

Ethics in Business

We have argued that applicability to practical situations is a theoretical requirement of moral principles; for given the required application conditions detailed in chapter I (p. 19 above), if an ethical theory is found to be not applicable, it must suffer from some theoretical defect. In tune with this feature of ethical theories, their supposed objectivity and universality has been interpreted and understood not in the conventional form of absolute abstraction but as of a secondary form, somewhat in Nagel's sense of 'objective tolerance' we have vindicated in chapter 3 (especially p. 85); for that is what 'objectivity' means in moral matters and that is how ethical theories can be universally applied to varying cases without yielding to ethical relativism. But while applied ethics in general makes ethical theories applicable to practical situations with little or no variations, its role in the area of business is sometimes thought to be slightly different and difficult, since the area of business—complicated as it is—is often supposed to be a problem area for ethical principles to be applied there with equal ease and generality. Of the supposed reasons for this, the most important seems to be the apparent opposition between ethics and business—the latter, being primarily profit-oriented and money minded, is thought to be incompatible with the former, which is predominantly ideal-minded and often altruistically oriented.

In what follows, I want to show that, while the speciality of business ethics is generally justified, the supposed opposition between ethics and business rests on a grossly improper understanding of what is involved in both ethics and business. To this purpose a careful consideration of what exactly is the problem that arises or is supposed to arise if applied ethics is extended to the area of business will be helpful and illuminating.

Business Ethics: The Concept and the Problem

A common enough tendency among a sizeable number of thinkers and business persons has long been to treat the idea of 'business ethics' as involving some kind of a contradiction, a tendency to believe that business and ethics cannot go together. This is reflected in the equally common dilemma that almost every manager and business owner happens to face: *If something is good for business can it be ethical? And if it is ethical can it be good business?* The supposed conflict is largely due to business's purpose being profiteering and maximization of owner value; for this being so, the commercial concern that is the core feature of business would reject the social concern or welfare concern, which primarily constitutes the ethical objective. The business of business, it is usually thought, is to make profit, and people who work for business organizations must concern themselves with producing goods and services at a profit and to maximize the owner value. To this purpose, their interest must lie in buying and selling, developing new products, increasing market shares and such other commercial concerns rather than in morality. Indeed, ethics or morality is considered by many as not only irrelevant to business but as *anti-business* in spirit and intent and many a business people are often contemptuous of the idea of business ethics and tend to resist conventional applications of ethical standards to business. Unlike the aggressive critics of business ethics, the more moderates among them, presumably apprehensive of their activities being branded as outright unethical or immoral, become defensive about business's supposedly inferior ethical conduct; some for this reason, though acknowledging the role of ethics in business activities, regard the ethical considerations as an "optional extra", to be viewed in conjunction with, and perhaps subservient to, the main purpose of business,—which is maximizing long term owner value by producing and selling goods and services. A large part of this resistance is due to the belief, common among businessmen, that value considerations are separate from, and less important than, the other aspects of business—these other aspects being the more essential ones like its commercial concern and profit motive. If the described belief and dismissive attitude towards business ethics has often seemed justified, that is because, besides treating ethics as separate from, if not opposed to, business many have taken 'business ethics' to mean a separate set of ethical rules that apply exclusively to business matters and to nowhere else. A variant of such supposed business ethics is the demand, often sanctimoniously made, for the so-called "social responsibility", which business must promote besides maximizing owner value. Sometimes the ethical values governing such business ethics are wishfully thought to be less stringent and more liberal, purportedly suiting the business's commercial objective. We shall show that there can be no such thing as business ethics in this sense. Indeed, much of this and similar stuff that masquerade as business ethics have nothing to do with either business or ethics. Such travesties must be carefully discerned from business ethics proper, which I shall try to sketch and defend in what follows. This is a vitally important philosophical requirement, for otherwise there is the danger that "bad expositions of business ethics [may] tend to drive the good ones out of circulation"—a most unwelcome variant of Gresham's Law—and "the resistance that is justified in respect of counterfeits of business ethics [may] often extend[s] inappropriately to the real thing."[1]

1. As Elaine Sternberg points out in her excellent work, *Just Business* (Warner Books, U.K., 1994), p. 21.

Why and What is Business Ethics

In order to vindicate the claim, indicated above, that a proper understanding of business ethics would remove this supposed opposition between business and ethics as unreal and dissolve the consequent problem as non-existent, I must address to two questions: how is ethics related to and important for business and why need business be ethical? In fact the answer to the second question will answer a large part of the first, for to provide reasons for business to be ethical would be to say something, often a great deal, about the nature of the relation between business and ethics; showing how important is this relation would only be a matter of filling out details. Let me therefore begin by considering an answer to the second question, namely, why at all is business required to be ethical, despite apparent reasons to the contrary?

In view of the apparent opposition between business and ethics, it may appear to be quite in order to ask why should business (or a businessman) be ethical? But a little reflection into the nature of business would reveal that the question is hardly less than outrageous, because business is basically a human affair and man, I have shown, is a *naturally* moral being (see chapter 2 above); indeed I have argued that if man is a spiritual being as much as he is a rational being, his rationality and spirituality together imply morality as a necessary human faculty. It is only to the human person that morality can be meaningfully attributed, because man alone is gifted with freedom of choice by virtue of which he is held responsible for what he does. Further, if *per impossible* morality and humanity are torn apart, the life of man would be inevitably "solitary, poor, nasty, brutish and short". To be moral is therefore not only a necessary feature of man but also a necessity in the life of man. In as much as business is an essentially human activity, to be ethical is accordingly a necessary requirement for business. Since all the activities of man are more often moral than not, so must be his activities in business. Sternberg puts it rather more emphatically: "Ethical concerns permeate every aspect of business activity because ethical concerns permeate all human activities."[2] The other reason for business to be ethical stems from societal considerations. The most obvious societal reason is that since business operates in the society and benefits from the social structure that provides all its stakeholders, it naturally owes some moral responsibilities to the society in return. If reciprocal personal stance is what makes an essential aspect of moral personhood (see chapter 2 above for details), a like stance is essential to obtain between the corporation and the society. As A.B. Carroll expressed it, one fundamental aspect of management ethics is that managers should be responsive to the expectations of society and stakeholders if they wish to maintain their legitimacy as agents in society."[3] In general, the social responsibility of business means that a private corporation has responsibilities to society that go far beyond the production of goods and services. For corporations are more than economic institutions. However, what is more crucial and compelling a societal reason is that in the process of producing and selling goods and services the business organizations also create social hazards in the form of major industrial accidents and business scandals as well as industrial wastes which affect the lives of people, not only of the present generation but also of the future generations at times. The Bhopal Gas Tragedy of December 1984, the worst industrial disaster of the 20th century, is still alive in public memory and creating moral flutters in international business circles. Leakage of 40 tonnes of methyl isocynate and other lethal gases on the fateful day not only resulted in the death of over 4,000 people on the day of this disaster, casualty figure swelled to 16,000 over the year and lakhs of people continued to suffer from after effects. Several lakhs of people in Bhopal, including unborn children, suffered

2. *Just Business,* p. 17.
3. "Ethics in Management", in *A Companion to Business Ethics,* ed. Robert E. Frederick, (Blackwell Publishing Co. U.K., 1999, 2002), p. 142.

from multiple systemic injuries. (*Civil Service Chronicle*, September 2004, p. 42). There is also the undeniable factor of environmental pollution and health hazards through creation of industrial waste. No business can sensibly evade responsibility towards the people and their environs who/which are affected directly or indirectly. It is for this reason that those who are concerned with the so called social responsibilities of business also treat business as a moral institution having impact on society that goes beyond the production and sale of goods and services to make a profit.[4]

I now come to the third reason for business to be ethical, which serves as much as a reason for this as it does as an explication of the crucial connection between business and ethics. This being so, our discussion here will inevitably involve some elaborate analysis of the nature of both ethics and business as we proceed. But a terse statement of this third reason is that it is in the best interest of business that it be ethical. The very purpose of business requires that the conduct of business must be ethical, for that will lead to maximization of long term owner value.

James Fieser[5] points out two versions of the profit oriented view of business, which work upon the maxim that there is a symbiotic connection between business and ethics in such a way that business in its best interest would need to be ethical. The implication is that ethical business is good business. The weaker version of this theory, championed eminently by Robert Hartley (*Business Ethics*, 1993), which states that good ethics results in good business, contends that ethics naturally emerges in the profit-oriented business. This view simply means that moral business practices are profitable. If the purpose of business is maximization of long term owner value, or, narrowly put,

4. See Rosene A. Buchholz, *Fundamental Concepts and Problems in Business Ethics* (Prentice Hall, Englewood Cliffs, New Jersey, 1989), p. 1.
5. *Business Ethics*, Ch. 1 (website,http://www.utm.edu/jfieser/vita/research/busbook.htm).

maximizing the company's profit, then moral business is more suited for achieving this objective. For although a morally responsible company, because of its emphasis on product safety, environmental concern, truthful advertising, scrupulous marketing and humane working conditions, may lag behind in a competitive market where short termism is likely to dictate business decisions, it is bound to succeed and thrive in the long run. For if customers demand safe products and workers demand conducive working conditions, they will certainly buy from and work for companies, which meet these demands. Businesses ignoring these demands have lesser chance of survival. Thus, the drive for profit will create morality and necessitate moral business practice. This is the strong version of the profit-oriented business ethics theory, addressed to by Milton Freidman, among others, which states that *good business results in good ethics*, and contends that, in a competitive free market, profit motive will bring about a proper moral environment which, in turn, will lead to profit making and maximization of owner value in the long run. It is hardly disputed that a business's reputation for trustworthiness and ethical conduct commands strong customer loyalty; what promotes sales and long term owner value is not short term profiteering by means of untruthfulness and conceited business practices but by "paying attention to customer needs and attending to them promptly, knowledgeably and helpfully"(Sternberg, *Just Business*, pp. 86-7). Customers, who are cheated and let down, are unlikely to return. Honesty therefore is not just proverbially but practically the best policy. A good business must have the strength of moral courage and conviction displayed in steadfast adherence to the fundamental values of fairness and honesty even at short-term risks and losses. Carroll cites a couple of illustrative cases[6] of moral management, which I consider worth citing here. A U.S. company, McCullough Corporation, who were makers of chain saws, withdrew from the National Chain Saw Manufacturers

6. A.B. Carroll, *op cit*, p. 147.

Association in protest of the latter's fight against the mandatory safety standards for dangerous saws. Besides showing their allegiance to the country's legal system, the company had displayed exemplary business conduct by putting chain brakes on its saws years before this incident even though it was not required to do so by law; they had done so for they knew their products were dangerous, and took preventive steps within reasonable limits of cost. Another case of model moral management cited by Carroll is that of M/s Merck and Co., a pharmaceutical firm which invested millions of dollars and developed a treatment for river blindness affecting 8 million people in the third world; not only that, when no government or aid organizations came forward to buy this drug, the company, on humanitarian grounds, pledged to supply the drug free of cost for ever, not minding the considerable financial loss it involved. We in Orissa are aware of an exemplary business conduct by Utkal Gaurav Madhusudan Das, one of the prominent architects of modern Orissa, who ordered the entire stock of shoes in his Utkal Tannery to be burnt and destroyed on detection of a single defective product in the workshop. It is of course a different matter that the business was closed down thereafter, which may be because of an imbalanced (adherence to and) application of ethics (honesty and fairness) to business by an extremely ideal minded proprietor. (I shall in due course deal with the application of moral principles to tackle business crises); but Madhusudan's action remains a paradigm of moral business—which may be emulated to greater or lesser degree—glorifying the principle that immoral actions like 'managing' to sell out defective products can never serve the interest of good business. For good business is distinguished from a bad one mainly by being ethical. This illustration may, however, point in the opposite direction that moral business can be costly and counterproductive, and strengthen the popular view that ethics has nothing to do with business (and *vice versa*) and the corresponding modern 'separatist view', championed by Adam

Smith and Milton Friedman, that business should be left alone to operate as per prevalent market conditions and that the introduction of ethics to business would create an imbalance in the market dynamics. Such a view highlights the supposed tension between the commercial concern and the welfare concern or social concern giving force to plausibility of the managers' dilemma mentioned above. But this tension is not insuperable, for such supposed dilemma that is based on improper understanding of the ethics-business relation, can be refuted within the confines of logic and practical wisdom. To be able to tackle the dilemma and alleviate the described tension between the commercial concern of business and the welfare concern of ethics, we have to bear in mind that business ethics is applied ethics in the sphere of business, that it is application of ethical principles in this sphere. And in the light of the reasons adduced above for business to be ethical, this may serve as an important beginning in the proper understanding of business ethics.

As we have seen, two factors are of crucial importance in applied ethics—and so it must be in the case of business ethics as well. These are: (a) relevance of the context and (b) justified violation of moral principles to suit concrete situations. That means the principles must be applied in such a way as to strike a reasonable balance between the demands of the situation and the spirit of the principle. Accordingly, in the realm of business, the principles must be applied in such a way as to achieve an effective trade off between the economic objectives and the social obligations of business. To be able to see how this can be possible, we may put some pressure on the concept of applied ethics and its application in business.

Applied ethics, we have seen, works upon the assumption that every good ethical theory has a built-in applicability to practical life. Ethics in this sense was shown to be not only a condition of the world, like logic, but also a necessary condition of a desirable world (see ch.1). Applied ethics can help in the making of a desirable world by trying to increase the number of what we have called the ethically desirables (permissible and recommended actions or conducts in Rajendra Prasad's scheme) and minimize the ethically forbidden or the ethically impermissible ones. On this model, we can say of business ethics, which is a variant of applied ethics, that it can create, as it must, a proper ethical environment in business by keeping the morally impermissible business practices to the minimum and increasing the desirable business conduct and behaviour. Elaine Sternberg stressed on two key principles of ethical business conduct (*ibid*, p. 7 and ch. 3), which are bound to strike a balance between the commercial concern and the social concern. The principles, which she calls distributive justice and ordinary decency, are the values without which maximizing long term owner value would be impossible and the very purpose of business would be frustrated. Distributive justice requires that the benefits and rewards of business be distributed in proportion to the contributions made to the organizational goals; and ordinary decency is the condition of trust necessary for a long term view of the business and its survival over time. What follows from both these principles taken together is: *good ethics is good business.* These principles, together with the basic purpose of the business, i.e., maximizing long-term owner value, we can consider as the 'ethically desirable' in business. In other words, the desirable business practice is maximizing long-term owner value by just and decent means. As Sternberg says, "...the specific performance which business emphasises is that of (retributively) just and (ordinarily) decent business behaviour—all of the time, to all those involved in the business, and by them all".[7]

The forbiddens in business, which must be kept to the minimum, can be many, prominent among them being maximizing profit by immoral means like selling or 'managing' to sell defective and dangerous products, adopting deceitful

7. *Just Business*, p. 88.

advertising and unscrupulous marketing, disregarding employees' rights and stakeholders' interests and so on. Short-term profit might easily accrue from such practices, but when weighed against both present and future consequences they are detrimental to the long-term interest of the business. They are not only contrary to the inherent moral sense of everyone involved, but are positively harmful to the business itself in the sense that they often lead to increasing law suit costs and loss of goodwill and credibility. A business with dubious ethics is sure to find it hard to attract employees, suppliers and finance. Shortsighted commercial concern must be weighed against long-term consequences. Business's best interest lies in a proper balance between the two conflicting concerns; they conflict when viewed with one-sided perspectives. The managers dilemma, which rests on the latter, will stand refuted if applied ethics works in the described way, balancing between the conflicting (one-sided) concerns, and the resulting truth "good ethics is good business" gets a firm foothold in the corporate psyche.

Ethics and Business

Milton Friedman, an eminent political economist and a leading expert on business ethics, speaks of the purpose and function of business thus:

> "In [a free] economy that is the one and only social responsibility of business—to use its resources and engage in activities designed to increase its profits *so long as it stays within the rules of the game,* which is to say, engages in open and free competition, *without deception or fraud.*"[8]

One can see in this a telling indication not only of the purpose of business but also of the crucial role of ethics in the conduct of business—a virtual balance of the commercial concern and

8. *Capitalism and Freedom*, (The University of Chicago Press, 1962), p. 133. Emphasis added.

the social concern so very essential in removing the apparent discord between the two and in exposing the unreality of the supposed opposition between business and ethics endemic not only in popular conceptions but also in some modern theories like the Separatist View, adduced ironically by Friedman, among others. Ironically, because Friedman who steadfastly maintained that social responsibility of business is to maximize profit[9] and [that] most of the social responsibilities concerning the moral and social obligations thrust now a days on modern business are extraneous goals only, nonetheless cared to emphasize (e.g., in this above quoted view) that the profits to be generated and increased must be made so *within the rules of the game* and *without deception and fraud.* The emphasis on ethical conduct in business is loud and clear. Maximizing profits by fraudulent means is neither proper business nor is conducive to the very purpose of business, which is maximizing long-term owner value. A business known for deceitful conduct can never make profit, much less maximize it, in the long run. A just business must be willing and able to work upon the guiding principle that one man's gain need not be another man's loss. This is the minimum moral sense, applicable as much universally as it applies specially in the domain of business. Sternberg's exhortation to distributive justice and ordinary decency is a couth composition of this basic moral sense. Thus, business ethics is the application of ethical principles and ethical reasoning to specifically business situations and activities. Ethical principles, by their very nature and conception, are universal and unvarying and supposed to apply to real life situations in like manner. Accordingly, in their application to business, these principles help delineate right business behaviour irrespective of the nature of the business concerned. For the point of principles, including moral principles, is that it must be applied consistently to all relevant situations and in this lies the point and efficacy of

9. "The Social Responsibility of Business is to Increase its Profits," *New York Times Magazine*, Sept. 13, 1970.

applied ethics. As a variant of applied ethics "business ethics applies general principles [of ethics] in an attempt to identify what is right in business...everywhere and always."[10] "Moral principles, therefore", the argument continues, "provide criteria for right and reasonable business behaviour which can be justifiably applied consistently to a wide range of people, places and times".[11]

In the writings on business ethics it is worth noticing two discernible models of this feature of universality of ethical principles and their consistent application in the realm of business. While one model dates back to Kant in the eighteenth century, another model is offered in recent times by Elaine Sternberg, among others, prominently in her book cited above. On the former model, the universality of ethical principles is categorical and deontic, grounded on pure reason and sense of duty, while the later model, being expressedly teleological—especially in its approach to business[12]— is hypothetical and consequentialist in approach. But despite this difference in approach of these two models, their agreement on *ethics being universal and consistently applicable as such* to business is interesting and instructive. In what follows is a detailed and critical analysis of the two models, which is not only in order, but would be fruitful and enlightening regarding the nature of ethics and of business and of their relationship.

The Kantian Model

Kant's ethics, especially the categorical imperative, is predominantly theoretical and had little explicit reference to business ethics or the application of his ethical theories to business. No books have been published on the specific impact

10. Sternberg, *Just Business*, p. 76, emphasis added.
11. *Ibid.*
12. Elaine Sternberg, (*ibid*), pleads for an expressedly teleological approach to business ethics, claiming nonetheless that the universal moral principles must be consistently applied to business everywhere and always, since it is in the interest of the very purpose of the business.

of Kant on business ethics until recently in the work of Norman Bowie,[13] which systematically applies the Kantian ethical theory to business. But the impact of his moral philosophy on the area of business is too compelling to be ignored or overlooked. As Bowie rightly remarks, "even the most cursory foray to business ethics will bring one face to face with Kantianism."[14] The categorical imperative, which for Kant is the fundamental principle of ethics, determines the morality/immorality of actions, including business activities in a simple and straightforward way. Commentators on the categorical imperative highlight three formulations of this principle, which are distinct but interconnected and which together epitomize the moral philosophy of Kant. These formulations are[15]:

(1) Act only on maxims, which you can will to be universal laws.
(2) Always treat the humanity in a person as an end, never as a mere means.
(3) So act as if you were a member of the ideal kingdom of ends in which you are both the subject and the sovereign.

All these three formulations of the categorical imperative, collectively and distributively, have important bearings on business actions and hence on business ethics.

The most obvious and straightforward impact issues from the first formulation. Your actions, including business actions, must be based on that maxim, which you can will as a universal law. Conversely, if you act on a maxim which can't be willed universally, your action will be immoral or what we have called morally impermissible, which applied ethics requires avoided

13. *Business Ethics: A Kantian Perspective* (Blackwell, Oxford, 1999).
14. "A Kantian Approach to Business Ethics", in *A Companion to Business Ethics,* ed. Robert Frederick, (Blackwell, 1999).
15. Courtesy Norman Bowie, *op cit*, p. 4.

or at least kept to the minimum* (of that, some more later on). Such an action would be immoral and bad, not because it leads to bad and unacceptable consequences but because it would be an action that is self-defeating because the principles underlying it is incoherent. (Note that Kant's ethics is grounded on reason and not on consequential, hypothetical considerations). In order to know of an action if it is moral or morally acceptable, one has to ask whether the principle behind the action can be universally willed, whether it can be a universal law that everyone can act upon. What would happen if everyone acted on it? These questions can be asked of all human actions, including business actions and decisions. Kant asked this question, by way of illustration, regarding a conduct that pertains more to business ethics: that of making a promise with no intention of keeping it. Just because one is desperately in need of money, should one borrow it from someone promising to pay it back without the intention of doing so? Does or can one's extreme desperation justify this false promise? Can this principle of action be universalized? And would such a universalized maxim be logically coherent? Kant's answer to this is categorically in the negative, because this principle, if universalized, would be incoherent and hence the action (of making false promises) would be self-defeating. Thus Kant:

> And could I say to myself that everyone may make a false promise then he is in a difficulty from which he cannot escape? Immediately I see that *I could will the lie but not a universal law to lie*. For with such a law there could be no promises at all, in as much as it would be futile to make a pretense of my intentions in regard to future actions to those who would not believe this pretense or—if they ever hastily did so—would pay me back in my own coin. Thus *my maxim*

* Though Kant would have totally avoided it without 'ifs' and 'buts'. Other approaches to business ethics, including the one adopted in this work, are more catholic without of course yielding to ethical relativism.

> *would necessarily destroy itself as soon as it was made a universal law.*[16]

Thus as a matter of logic and conceptual condition, a promise that is made to be broken always would be no promise but a pretense and would not interest any financer or promoter, just as a business contract made to be broken or violated always would not attract financers and stakeholders. A universalized maxim that permitted false promises would be self-defeating, just as a universalized maxim that permitted contract breaking would be self-defeating. The concept of making false promises, if everyone made such promises always, would be bad—morally bad—not because the consequences would be bad, but because the concept is incoherent. Such concepts and principles, therefore, cannot be universalized and cannot be consistently applied in practice. Most naturally, actions based on such principles would be self-defeating. The categorical imperative thus provides a test, which every action of man must pass in order to be morally acceptable. On Kantian morality, every action, every business decision, must be such that the maxim on which it is based can be willed universally and coherently, i.e. without involving self-contradiction, for only on this condition the maxim can be applied consistently. Principles, which cannot be so willed, will make the actions based on them morally forbidden both in business as well as in the larger context of life. Kant's moral philosophy and [the resulting] business ethics thus provide the generating insight what nowadays is fashionably called 'ethics check', which managers are recommended to take resort to before making business decisions. This ethics check, recommended by Blanchard and Peale[17] as aid to ethical decision-making, consists of three crucial

---

16. *Foundations of the Metaphysics of Morals* (1785). Trans by L. Beck (Macmillan, New York, 1990), p. 19, Emphasis added.
17. K. Blanchard and N.V. Peale, *The Power of Ethical Management*, (Fawcett Crest, New York, 1988).

questions, the discussion of which I prefer to deter to a later stage in this chapter. But one of the questions that is relevant here and reflects the spirit of Kantian ethics, especially the first formulation of his categorical imperative under discussion, is the question that every manager must ask of his intended action or proposed decision, and the question is this:

> "How will it make me feel about myself? Will it make me proud? Would I feel good if my decision was published in the newspaper? Would I feel good if my family know about it?"[18]

This, one can easily see, is quite in the spirit of the Kantian dictate that any action/decision that (the principle of which) cannot be universalized must be morally forbidden. This is also in keeping with our moral common sense that anything that cannot be made public must never be thought in private. Could be the moral variant of the Wittgensteinean injunction that whereof one cannot speak thereof one must be silent! The conceptual point of Kant's ethics is that if a maxim for an action becomes self-defeating, when universalized, the contemplated action has to be unethical. Indeed the test of the categorical imperative is the principle of fairness in as much as the ethical principles (and by implication, principles guiding business actions) are meant to apply equally to all, including oneself. Kant emphasised on this by holding that one couldn't, without contradiction, make an exception of moral rules for (i.e., in the case of) oneself:

> When we observe ourselves in any transgression of a duty, we find that we do not actually will that our maxim should become a universal law. That is impossible for us; rather the contrary of the maxim should remain as the law generally and we only take the liberty of making an exception to it for ourselves or for the sake of inclination, and for this one

18. Archie B. Carroll, "Ethics in Management", *ibid*, p. 150.

> occasion. Consequently, if we weighed everything from one and the same standpoint, namely reason, *we would come upon a contradiction in our own will*, viz, that a certain principle is objectively necessary as a universal law and yet subjectively does not hold universally but rather admits of exceptions.[19]

Moral principles therefore cannot be discriminative. In fact this is the general spirit underlying the claim for universalisability and objectivity of moral principles, as we have discussed in chapter 3 above. In the eyes of the universal law, which for Kant is what a moral principle is, every body is equal and is equally a member of the moral community. Kant is best known for his firm defense of a version of the "respect for persons" principle, which we have shown to be an important variant of the principle of justice and fairness (ch. 4 above). The second formulation of the categorical imperative enjoins us to treat the humanity in a person as an end, and never as a mere means. And the third formulation, which follows from the second, envisions persons as members of an ideal kingdom of ends, in which you are both a subject and the sovereign at the same time. The idea is that, in a moral community there is no discrimination between the sovereign and the subjects, for the universal moral law applies consistently to all, always and everywhere. Because of their freedom and rationality human beings are able to act from laws required by reason and this confers on them a unique sort of dignity; so they must be respected and treated as ends, not as means merely. It is in recognizing this freedom in persons and the resulting dignity of persons that respect for persons can be effected.

Quite analogous to the negative rights and positive rights of man, discussed above in ch. 4, freedom of the person may be construed as both negative and positive. Negative freedom is the freedom *not to be* coerced and deceived. For coercion and

19. Kant, *Foundations of Metaphysics of Morals*, p. 41.

deception are "the most fundamental forms of wrong doings" to persons. "Physical coercion treats someone's person as a tool, and lying treats someone's reason as a tool"[20]. Kant finds it naturally "horrifying", for while forcing a person to do what he does not want to do is the worst disrespect to his humanity, making him do such a thing through deceitful means is a gross misuse of one's reasoning power, besides being mistreatment and disrespect of the other person. It is therefore vitally important for the "respect for persons" principle that people should refrain from coercive and deceptive actions and behaviour towards others. However, this is not enough. Respecting the person as an end requires the exercise of his positive freedom to develop his human capacities, which for Kant means developing his rational and moral capacities. Put in the language of rights, as used in the previous chapter, the right-promoters (members of the society, i.e.) not only must not prevent or interfere with the natural rights of the right holder, they must positively try to create conducive conditions for the exercise of these rights by the right holder.

Viewed from this perspective, the business firm is a moral community in which the stakeholders are the members of a kingdom of ends, where there is no distinction of substance between the owner/employer and the employees in respect of the rules that govern the business. The business must respect the humanity in its employees so that they are not treated as instruments or tools through coercion and deception. Treating the humanity in a person as an end, in a business, means two things; first, negatively, people in a business relationship must not be *used,* i.e, not be coerced or deceived, and second, positively, business organizations and business practices must be such that they create conducive conditions for the development and exercise of the rational and moral reasoning by all concerned. This will provide a kind of organizational

20. Christine Korsgaard, *Creating the Kingdom of Ends* (Cambridge Univ. Press, New York, 1996) pp. 140-41.

legitimacy.[21] It will ensure that all involved in the business receive some minimum benefits from being a part of it. Besides, treating the humanity in the person as the end invokes the principle of reciprocal personal stance, which we have shown to be the constitutive condition of moral personhood (see ch. 2 above). Even in terms of consequence, the Kantian principle of business ethics is in the best interest of the business itself. For people will tend to behave as they are treated; and if they are treated well, i.e. fairly respectfully and as per the principles of justice and decency, they will tend to reciprocate and behave responsibly. Besides creating a desirable ethical atmosphere, this will promote organized and disciplined business activities by all concerned and help maximize owner value in the long run.

One major implication of Kant's ethics is that it acts as an effective moral critique of authoritarian hierarchical organizational structure and helps promote democratisation of the workplace. For, on the third formulation of the categorical imperative, coupled with the first, the rules that govern an organization/business are those that are universally endorsed by everyone in the organization, irrespective of whether they are owners/employers or the employees, who participate in the process of decision-making and determination of these rules before they are given effect to. This has the merit of getting the interest of all the stakeholders, especially the stockholders and the employees, focused on responsible participatory business conduct which, in turn, will lead to maximum of profit and owner value.

However, the Kantian model of business ethics has its limitations and challenges too, the most conspicuous for the present work being that it is a bit too demanding. It has been argued in the first chapter that principles of ethics, which are meant to provide guidance in practical life, must be such that it should be empirically (not just logically) possible to apply them

21. See Norman Bowie, *op. cit.*, pp. 7-9.

to solve real life problems. But certain elements in Kantian ethics, e.g. its emphasis on the respect for persons principle and on purity of motive as condition of truly moral actions, if taken literally to the exclusion of contextual considerations, may make it difficult to be applied in practice. Especially it may appear too austere to apply to business. For it is a well-known fact about business that the business's good acts are almost always justified, *al beit* in part, if such actions results in profit. But though in the best interest of the recognized purpose of business, such actions of corporate houses and business organizations would not be considered truly moral by Kantian parameters. It is a common saying that no business can be done without committing some act of immorality in earning some minimum profit. The Islamic religious belief that charging interest and, by implication, making profit is immoral is irrelevant here, since on this belief business would not be a permissible activity just as banking would not be a permissible business. It may thus be construed a necessity—a necessary evil, it may be called—to affect or harm the interest of some (e.g. your business competitors); and in these cases one will be well advised to keep the harm or acts of immorality to the minimum. We are aware of the 'dirty hand' theory in business: since one can't avoid dirtying one's hands while staying in business, one can only try to keep the dirt in one's hands as thin as possible.[22] The *Mahabharata* war was fought on this principle in which some minimum act of immorality was taken resort to in the greater interest of winning a righteous war. Yudhisthira's telling the half-truth about the death of Aswasthama can be taken as an illustration. The philosophy of the *Bhagavad-Gita* offers us several such illustrations where, rather than following moral principles purely literally, violating them in sufficiently demanding situations would be morally justified. But the Kantian test would make such justified violations, particularly

22. See R.Prasad, *Varnadharma, Niskama Karma and Practical Morality*, p. 254.

Yudhistira's making exception to the moral principle of truth telling, immoral and impermissible *simplicitor*. For such actions, both in business and in war, were not performed out of "purity of motive", which constitutes the central tenet of Kantian ethics. At least Yudhisthira did not have the 'purity of motive' while declaring: "*Aswasthama hataḥ—naré vā gunjaré*". Justifying violation of moral principles, which we have shown to be an essential aspect of applied ethics, would apparently stand to fail the test of the categorical imperative and of the "respect for persons" principle. To be sure, making exception to morality in the interest of making profit cannot be universalized as a principle of action, nor would it be in conformity with the principle of respect for all persons, since the person harmed in this process would not be treated with respect—to say the least. But it must be borne in mind that the described exception and the consequent business action is an *exception* to the general rule that one should not act immorally, and the question of it being universalized does not arise. It would only be a violation of the general rule justified in the interest of the very purpose of business, just as violation of a moral principle under demanding circumstances, as we have seen, would be justified in the interest of the very purpose of morality. For the concept of morality has the concept of general well-being as an essential part of its purpose and the described violation would serve precisely *that* purpose. Likewise, the concept of business has the concept of profit as an integral aspect, an essential ingredient of the rules of the business language game, and in order to serve this purpose of business reasonably, business ethics would warrant a relevant moderation of the moral principle(s) concerned. And in this game the "respect for persons" principle may need to be violated; the reasoning that no one's interest, including even that of one's business competitors, should be harmed or affected in anyway would not only be impractical but virtually inappropriate to the concept of business. Protecting the interest of the adversary at the cost of the business objective would be no more justified than loosing deliberately in a game. For loosing deliberately in a game is as much undesirable as winning by unfair means. As Sternberg makes the point:

> Playing a game means playing to win; throwing a game deprives the other side of the chance to win fairly. A player may have all sorts of reasons for not winning; he may be trying to encourage a child to learn the game or flattering the boss or cheering up an invalid. Whatever the motive, however, within the game all behaviour, which is not devoted to winning, is either not seriously playing the game or is cheating. Much of what is ordinarily regarded as moral activity is therefore ruled out within a game: *however much kindness and generousity may be virtues, exercising them in helping the opposite side to win is incompatible with playing properly.*[23]

Likewise, Sternberg goes on to say, many ostensibly moral acts are inappropriate in business, for in both games and business the objectives determine what to count as the proper act or conduct. As a result, all behaviours that are not directed towards the objective in question are to be excluded as inappropriate. The inclusion of maximizing profit/owner value in business objective excludes all behaviours, including some moral behaviours, which are not directed towards this objective. The Kantian principle of "respect for persons" may thus not strictly apply in business. However, limitations like these not withstanding, the merits of Kantian ethics far outweigh in its impact on shaping up a sound business ethics theory and what is to count as ethical conduct in business remains reasonably undisputed.

The Teleological Model

While the Kantian model of business ethics is centrally concerned with the rightness or wrongness of business actions

23. *Just Business*, p. 65. Emphasis added.

themselves, the teleological model is primarily concerned with the purpose and consequences of such actions. More importantly, the thrust of emphasis in this approach is the very purpose of business, which is maximizing long-term owner value by selling goods and services. And any actions which, or whose consequences, lead to promoting this purpose will be considered good and desirable in business. A teleological ethical theory contends that an action is right if and only if it, or the rule underlying it, produces or is intended to produce, at least as great a balance of good over evil as any other alternative. If the good and the right be the fundamental concept of morality, the teleological theory first defines what is good and goes on to define the right in terms of this good. And since for business the good is maximization of owner value in the long run, the right business action is naturally held to be that which is intended to realize this objective. Defining the good in terms of business purpose is neither arbitrary nor anything contrary to principles. This is rather quite in keeping with the basic spirit of morality, which is universal: it is the universal ethical rule that the aim of ethics (ethical actions) is to attain the good; but what is not universal is what is the good, and what is good is determined by the context or the area of operation. (Compare my analysis of equality and justice in the last chapter). Bereft of contextual considerations, the idea of good would be vacuous, and to picture the good as the one thing in all cases would be an abstraction. Both in moral and non-moral senses, the model of good is subject to variations. Cold water is good to drink, but cold food is not good for health and cold behaviour is not good in social interactions. Sharp edge is good for a kitchen knife but sharp tongue is bad for a person in his social interactions. Speaking from the teleological point of view, what counts as the right action—including business activities—depends on the purpose of the action, in much the same way as the goodness of an object is determined by reference to the object's purpose. Investigative journalism and imaginative fiction writing have inevitably different criteria of goodness. And what counts as a morally right action also depends on objectives: cutting a man's throat is generally wrong, but as per the standards of morality and medical ethics such action is right and justified in the event of a life-saving tracheotomy. More in the moral context, speaking the truth is good in normal cases, but not so when an innocent life is in danger. We have therefore argued that in certain tricky cases of crisis/conflict of values one value may be defeasible and the other preferred to it under demanding circumstances though the value defeated does not turn into a disvalue. Speaking the truth may be justifiably overridden by the expediency of saving innocent lives, but that would never undermine the virtue of truth telling in all cases. Thus, though the different goods are instances of the idea of good in the Platonic sense, they are different nonetheless. It is therefore the specialty of business ethics that what is good here is subservient to the *purpose* of business i.e., that sort of action that helps maximizing owner value in the long run. The teleologist, therefore, shows no hesitation in emphasizing the primacy of this purpose of business and making it largely determine what is ethical in business and what is not. Milton Friedman, we have seen, tersely makes the point by saying that the social responsibility of business—whatever it may be said to have—is to increase its profits. By implication I take it to mean that any socio-moral responsibility that a business may be said to have would be justified only in so far as it leads to or is intended to lead to maximization of profits and/or owner values. In other words, business's being ethical, according to this view, is subservient to the said purpose of business. This brings us straight on to the tension between the "stock holders theory" and the "stakeholders theory" in business. The latter, which I suspect has been a main source of [the need for] business ethics, strongly pleads for business's social and moral responsibilities which it owes to all concerned,—and not only to the stockholders or the shareholders and the owners of business—, including the society at large. This responsibility it owes to the society (or the stakeholders) not only because business operates in the society and with at least indirect social support but also because, side by side and in the process of producing goods a service for maximizing owner value/profit, business organizations also create major industrial hazards and accidents which affect the environment and the lives of people, not only of the present generations but also of many future generations to come.

But social responsibility, if not pursued rationally in keeping with the business purpose, will affect the business itself and may threaten its very existence. For what distinguishes business from other social activities is its purpose, which is to maximize long-term owner value. And a business organization that puts prime emphasis on social responsibility *independent of its consequences for long-term owner value* will cease to operate as a business. It must be borne in mind that the purpose of business is not to promote public good. Though in course of its operation business may happen to be a prime contributor to the good of the stakeholders, yet this cannot constitute the distinctive business objective. For if it were, business would be substantially no different from medicine and education, both of which also normally contribute to public good in a significant way. (Courtesy Sternberg, *ibid,* p. 36). Any zealous extension of social responsibility would result in the use of business time and resources for non-profitable, *al beit* otherwise moral, purpose, and would be detrimental to the business. If business is not to be construed as a profitable hobby, it is not to be confused with charity either. There is no place for 'industrial democracy' in business ethics; for even if they are all equal in law as citizens, participants in a business—especially the employees and the stock holders—are not at all to be construed as equals. Democratization in the name of socialization would be likely to frustrate the business purpose, which is the prominent determinant of desirable business conduct. Friedman's critique of the social responsibility theory in business is therefore terse and steadfast: the social responsibility of business, he said, is to increase profit. (Courtesy: the *New York Times Magazine*, 13 September,1970.)

This might seem to be a bit too harsh on the stakeholders view and the commonly laudable social responsibilities perspective of business. But Elaine Sternberg could not agree with it more. She vindicates the Friedman theory thus:

> Far from being too harsh, that characterization is in fact too polite. What using business resources for non-business purposes actually is, is theft: an unjustified appropriation of the owner's property. Managers who employ business funds for anything other than the legitimate business objective are simply embezzling.....
>
> That the diverted resources are applied to ends which are commonly regarded as laudable as 'social responsibilities' does not make the act of diverting them any less larcenous. However worthy the charity being helped, if the employee uses company time and telephone to solicit contributions rather than business, he is cheating the business's owners. Despite what might be called the 'Robin Hood Syndrome', stealing from the rich to give to the poor is still stealing; so is all embezzling from business owners to give to others. Crimes are not annulled by worthy motives...[24]

Sternberg's penchant for the primacy of the business purpose leads her to adduce the argument that using business funds for non-business purposes makes a manager commit the logical offence of teleopathy. For given the significance of ends in judging and defining rightness and wrongness of business actions, misunderstanding the ends in question or pursuing the wrong end and even pursuing the right end in a wrong way are all examples of teleopathy, says Sternberg. And teleopathy is a serious offence, the generic form of prostitution.

24. *Ibid*, p. 41.

> Just as prostitution occurs when sex is proferred for money rather than love, so it exists when business pursues love—or 'social responsibility'—rather than money. Business managers, who eschew maximising long-term owner value and direct their firms resources to any other goal, are as much prostitutes as artists or sportsmen who sell out for financial gain. In each case, the activity is perverted, and the 'right, true end' is neglected in favour of some other extraneous objective.[25]

Making maximization of long-term owner value the definitive and primary purpose of business not only explains the speciality of business and business ethics, it makes the definition of business precise and significant. Fervent proponents of the social responsibility theory might try to brand this as a less noble objective than social responsibility. They may undermine it as paltry and too insignificant, because business is supposedly too important to be restricted to this narrow commercial end. But this would be mistaking the very purpose of defining a term and distorting the concept of business. For the purpose of definition is "not glorification but clarification", and clarity lies in the fact that "maximizing long-term owner value may be a less noble objective than curing the ills of the world,—but if it is then so is business".[26] In the interest of clarity and precision, a concept must be analysed as what it is, not as what it ought to be. The purpose of business is to maximize owner value, and to include anything else into the definition of business simply because they are perceived as good, laudable and noble would be to distort the truth[27]. A concept that is defined to include everything is useless. A definition, which tries to incorporate all social goals into the purpose of business, risks rendering business insignificant. Because of these considerations, teleological theories, in their account of business

25. *Ibid*, p. 42.
26. Sternberg, *ibid*, p. 33.
27. *Ibid*.

ethics, not only pinpoint the purpose of business as maximizing profit/owner value, but also define the rightness/wrongness of business actions in terms of compliance or otherwise of this purpose. The utilitarian approach to business ethics, which is an important variant of the teleological ethical theory, has similar approach too to business ethics. The idea behind utilitarianism is that we should act to bring about the best consequences, the minimum, i.e. the least disputed sense of which is the best balance of benefit over harm. One version of utilitarianism, which goes by the name of act-utilitarianism, holds that an act is morally right if and only if it *maximizes utility.* And that means the balance of benefit over harm, calculated by taking into consideration everyone affected by the act, is greater than such balance resulting from any other alternative act. However, act-utilitarianism would not take maximization of utility (MU) to be maximization of total benefits. (This rules out unethical means of maximizing profit and emphasizes the importance of ethics in business. I will have more to say of this later.) And secondly, it is not concerned solely with short-term consequences in terms of benefit-to-harm ratios; long-term consequences are more important[28], in the interest of MU. This requirement is in consonance with good business practices, where research and capital expenditures are aimed at long-term benefits. Thus, utilitarianism too specifies the business purpose and 'good' business actions are defined in its terms. Analogous to long-term owner value, long-term benefits defines maximized utility (MU). Utilitarianism in this sense holds great attraction for business, because it provides a foundation for cost-benefit analysis which calculates benefits and costs in terms of money. "Maximisation of profits", therefore, is a rule of the thumb for business which is to be violated only in the interest of maximizing utility. Having set the latter as the exclusive business objective, utilitarian thinkers make that the measure of efficiency

28. See Milton Snoeyenbos and James Humber, "Utilitarianism and Business Ethics" in Robert Frederick (ed.) A Compnion to Business Ethics, p. 19.

in business. Celebrated economists like Adam Smith and Milton Friedman, for example, provided distinctively utilitarian justifications for the free market by expressedly making the claim that the market is the most efficient means to maximize utility[29]. Even our most common understanding of the basic principle of business efficiency takes important note of utility. Messers Snoeyenbos and Humber pointedly emphasized the importance of the utilitarian consideration in achieving the business objective (profit, that is) efficiently by maximizing benefits and minimizing costs:

> However, the ordinary notion of business efficiency as applied to the individual firm also has a utilitarian basis. The efficient firm maximizes outputs in relation to inputs which squares with the utilitarian's argument that one should act to maximize benefits and minimize costs. Profit, which in one sense is just a measure of efficiency, thereby has a utilitarian justification.[30]

The utilitarian cost-benefit analysis is considered by many business analysts as the best way of evaluating the ethical propriety of a business decision. In all fairness, concern for consequences and the 'best consequences' measured in terms of largest total benefits and lowest total costs is something a good business boss has to take account of. With the proviso that this principle of maximizing utility is pursued [or applied] reasonably objectively and altruistically, this will be more in the interest of the business in the long run.

Universality and Consistency

Stressing on the primacy of the purpose of business and deciding the ethicality of business actions by reference to this purpose and the consequences of the actions leading to fulfilment of the purpose is thus the distinctive mark of the teleological model in

29. Courtesy: Snoeyenbos and Humber, *ibid*, p. 23.
30. *Ibid*, p. 23.

general and the utilitarian approach in particular. But this has the danger of leading to a misunderstanding or rather a couple, though connected, of misunderstandings: one, the apparent bias in favour of the business's purpose—maximizing long-term owner value (Sternberg)/maximizing utility in the long run (Act-utilitarianism)—might strengthen the "separatist theory" and undermine the role of ethics in business. And secondly, in expressedly defining rightness of business actions and decisions by reference to the business purpose and thus making it subservient to the latter might make it appear that business ethics is a separate ethics where perhaps the moral standards are [to be] applied with somewhat lesser stringency in order to suit the purpose of the business; and once this misgiving gets a foothold the inevitable result would be ethical relativism. A similar misgiving with separatist underpinnings can be found to be implicit in a view expresses by Rajendra Prasad in his *Karma, Causation and Retributive Morality* (p. 253). While questioning the wisdom and logicality of Krishna's advice to Arjuna to perform his *svadharma* and stop worrying about his *sāmānya dharma* of non-killing, Prasad argued that the former, being the duty of a particular *varṇa*, is a professional duty specific to the members of that particular *varṇa* and hence cannot override a *sāmānya dharma,* which is a universal duty. The implication is clear in this view that professional ethics (of which business ethics is one form) is of a separate status, inferior to universal duties and presumably defeasible and overridable by the latter. I have given reasons, in the first chapter, for exposing a weakness of this view in the light of my interpretation of the defeasibility of ethical principles that is compatible with their universality and that places the universal duties and the specific duties alike on the same footing. In what follows I shall try further to quell such misgivings about professional ethics and business ethics in particular and argue to the effect that ethical principles are universal and applied as universal rules consistently *wherever they are applied,* including their application in business; I shall show that this view is shared implicitly and explicitly by the protagonists of the teleological approach themselves.

Friedman's observations quoted in the beginning of the section on Ethics and Business above may be taken as a useful pointer in dislodging/subverting the first of the misgivings. For far from undermining, much less dissociating, ethics from business conducts, Friedman stressed the need for realizing the purpose of business through ethical means: to be sure, increasing profit or maximizing owner value is the defining purpose of business and the primary function of business is to work towards realizing this objective; but business must do so by "staying within the rules of the game" and by engaging in "open and free competition, without deception and fraud". If the purpose of business is to maximize profit or owner value in the long run, and if this purpose is of prime significance for the teleologist, this purpose will not be served by non-ethical means. For a business that is prone to and known for deceit and fraudulence will never make profit/have owner value, much less maximize the same; we have shown already that even if short-term profit may result through unhealthy competition, the business is bound to suffer in the long run if short-termism dictates its *modus operandi.* That is the reason, despite their differences in emphasis (on the action itself and on the consequences and purpose of the action), "bad ethics is bad business" marks the motto of the teleologists as much as it does of the Kantians. To be sure, the teleologist takes considerable pain to emphasise and specify, very rightly in my opinion, the domain and purpose of business. And in doing so the purpose of business is rightly distinguished as not being ethical but commercial. But this has nothing to contribute to the theory, popularly maintained, that the ethical concern is alien to the commercial concern of business,—unless 'commercial' and 'ethical' are taken to be antithetical. It is no more the case that profit is immoral than it is that property is theft. Properties and profits acquired through unfair means is certainly bad in the ethical sense; but to draw from this anything like a conclusion that all properties are theft and all profits are bad is to fall an easy prey to the fallacy of illicit generalization. On the other side, maximizing profit or owner value may be held to be suspect from the ethical point of view because of a basic confusion about what is ethical. The domain of ethics is the whole of life; it is much wider in scope. But business occupies a very small aspect of human life and actions, as do the various other professions like medicine, animal husbandry, legal practices and philanthropy. Each of these professions is distinguished by its specific purpose, and there are distinctively different ethical ways of pursuing and realizing these purposes. But the ethics of one profession may be inappropriate in the case of another. What is right in medicine or jurisprudence is inappropriate in, and perhaps irrelevant to, business. Medical ethics studies ethical problems confronted by the medical professionals, which (problems) will not arise in business. Similarly, what is legal need not strictly suit the business objective. That is why many otherwise ethical actions and objectives are inappropriate in business. For example, philanthropy and working for the public good is inappropriate in business and cannot be included in the business objective. Philanthropy is ethical but anything (e.g., the business purpose) that is not philanthropy need not be considered unethical,—unless philanthropy is taken as co-extensive with ethics. Ethical pursuits of professional objectives vary from profession to profession and are determined by the objective of the profession concerned, but the one variety of professional ethics (e.g. ethics of one particular profession) cannot provide the paradigm of the ethical to be followed in all other professions. Specific instances are poor surrogates for the generic concept, though the spirit of the later is the guiding principle of the former.

The social responsibility enthusiasts and the protagonists of the 'stakeholders' philosophy fail to see the point while insisting on including social work and public good (good of all concerned) in the business objective. For social work and working for the good of all concerned is no doubt eminently ethical; but considering the limited focus of business, it cannot constitute the essential purpose, not even an important one, of business. The teleologists rightly maintain that social responsibility is to be taken up and fulfilled by business only to the extent of and only in so far as it contributes to the maximization of long-term owner value,—only if the former is a means to the latter. But not taking this (ethical responsibility, though it eminently is) as an end in business does not make business unethical. Quite to the contrary, eminent teleologists like Elaine Sternberg claim it with emphasis that, although the proper purpose of business is not to promote morality but to maximize long-term owner value, this (latter) purpose must be pursued in the ethical way; rather the proper concern of business is to pursue this objective in an ethical way.[31] Earlier we have noted her argument to the effect that unethical business conduct is detrimental to the very purpose of business,—that it is in the best interest of business that it be ethical. "The challenge", she says, "is thus to set up systems and structures within the business that encourage its members to do the (morally) right (business) thing."[32] Whatever limited interest a business is to pursue, it has to do it in an ethical way. Not all ethical actions are business ethical actions, nor is business to be considered unethical because of this. Many otherwise ethical actions would not be business ethical actions simply because they fall outside the limited ambit of the business objective. But "ethical" is such an adjective, which is meant to qualify variegated actions and conducts belonging to varieties of aspects of human life. Rather it must qualify actions in all spheres of life; no action in business or education or medicine or law would be considered genuine if it is not ethically conducted. This is what I have called the primacy of the ethical, which I claimed to be an imperative for applied ethics. The idea behind the claim of primacy of the ethical is

31. See Sternberg, *ibid*, p. 67 especially.
32. Sternberg, *ibid*, p. 67.

that actions in every sphere of life be ethically right in order to be considered right in that sphere. Business being an important sphere of human actions needs to follow the *relevant* principles of ethics and conduct its action of pursuing the goal of maximization of long-term owner value accordingly. And whatever relevant rule is followed in this case is followed universally and consistently. Sternberg makes the point as follows:

> ....putting the word 'business' before the word 'ethics' merely provides a focus. *It reduces the range of problems to be addressed, not the stringency of the moral standards to be applied.* Although ethical queries are only questions of business ethics if they relate to the activity of maximizing long-term owner value, the principles which apply in solving them are the same ethical principles which apply everywhere and always.[33]

This takes us straight to grips with the second misgiving I mentioned above: Because business's defining purpose is maximizing owner value and because this purpose determines the right business action, it has been argued by some, "business ethics" must be a separate sort of ethics meant to guide business actions for maximizing owner value and, in the interest of that, is beyond the clutches of stringent standards of ordinary conventional ethics. In view of the intense competitiveness of modern business, some even have claimed that ordinary ethics is a luxury which business can ill afford. In the interest of increasing profit (Friedman) and in the struggle for survival, somewhat less rigorous ethical rules are thought to be appropriate in business. The view of Rajendra Prasad too, which we questioned above, has implications to this effect.

Such construal of business ethics—and for that matter any particular form of professional ethics—is symptomatic of a gross misunderstanding about the nature and concept of ethics. For

33. *Ibid.* p. 68. Emphasis added.

ethics, like logic, is an all-or-nothing concept in the sense that being ethical is an absolute feature of an action or a conduct; there cannot be *more* or *less* in an action's being ethical. Either it is an ethical action or it is not. I suppose this is because ethics is a normative science with clearly defined standards, which either apply to a particular case or don't. Fuzziness and considerations of *more* or *less* is normally alien to things ethical. To be sure, as we have seen, not all actions or all conducts are ethical, some actions are amoral in the sense that they need neither be called moral action nor immoral ones. But whatever actions are described as ethical or moral at all, they are said to be so *simplicitor*. An action is done in an ethical way if and only if it is done in accordance with a principle of ethics. And any other action that is done in accordance with this ethical principle is ethical in like manner. Ethics thus defines a *class* of actions, and ethical principles identify the unvarying essential features of these diverse actions. Ethical principles, which make these actions ethical, are universal. And when we call a business action ethical, if at all, it is because the principle underlying this is ethical. Therefore business ethics cannot be a separate ethics with laxer standards of value. Because of the limited nature of its purpose or objective (maximizing long-term owner value), what is reduced is the range of problems it addresses to—not the stringency of the moral standards applied to solve them. It is true that certain categories of moral strictures are inappropriate in business, but it is because they typically apply to situations outside the limited scope of business. And this sort of limitation *also* applies to other professions like medicine and law. The codes of conduct that guide the business persons to do (the morally) right things, like the ones guiding doctors and practicing lawyers to do the right things in medicine and jurisprudence, are as much binding and as much stringent as any general ethical code of conduct applied elsewhere to human actions and conducts. There is therefore no justification whatsoever for a separate ethics for business with less stringent standards of application any more than there is for a separate ethics for other professions like medicine and law. Moral principles that are indefensible elsewhere cannot be acceptable in business. The ban on cheating, fraudulence and promise- (or contract-) breaking are as much to be observed in business as they are observed elsewhere. Such conducts cannot be made right in business if they would not be right otherwise.

The argument from competition and the plea for survival, which are sometimes invoked to justify laxer ethical standards in business, are palpably weak and indefensible. For competition is certainly not war, and survival of business is also at stake if a company is known for its laxer ethical conducts. Short-termism, buttressed with moral laxity, is detrimental to maximizing utility and owner value in the long run. With zealous attempt to tackle business problems by this means, it is not the problems but the business that goes away.

With the plea for a separate business ethics with lesser stringent standards thus dismissed, the related danger of relativism also loses ground. Sternberg therefore trenchantly makes the point that "business ethics is universal, because the principles underlying it are. And these principles being universal by their very nature,...provide criterion of acceptable business behaviour which can be argued for and applied consistently over a wide range of actual people, places and times."[34] Thus the teleological approach, spearheaded eminently by her, shares this common ground with the deontological approach of Kant—that *ethics is (ethical principles are) universal and consistently applicable to all human actions, including business actions.* As it is clear to the common understanding of morality, ethical values are normally expected to transcend specific interests, and business ethics likewise is supposed to provide a common basis for assessing and guiding all sorts of business conducts; and the principles of business ethics, by providing this common standard,

34. *Ibid*, p. 76. Emphasis added.

makes decision-making possible across the widely differing business situations.[35]

However, universality of the principles of ethics—including those of business ethics—has not been construed as a rule of the thumb, as easy as our common moral sense makes it out to be. In the complexities of the actual human situations, conflicts of principles pose serious threats. In the pluralist perspective of the modern society, there seem to be as many values as there are proponents thereof with no generally acceptable way of choosing among them. But despite their competing claims it cannot be the case that all of them are equally right. And given (given due discounts to) the peculiarities of the nature of man and his situations, it *is* possible to "abstract out" ethical principles that are genuinely unvarying and generally acceptable as making sense of the moral universe. "Lying, cheating and stealing are simply wrong. So are killing, cowardice, irresponsibility, breaking promises and betrayal." Justice and fairness, in contrast, are always right; "...these values hold good everywhere, be it in love or war, business or pleasure."[36]

To be sure, the universality of such principles are not to be taken literally and no ethical principle is applicable literally to all cases. Conflicts of principles often lead to moral crises; but the crises are overcome by adopting one principle in preference to another, or by making a justified violation of an ethical principle. In the Indian ethical thoughts reflected in her scriptural tradition, *dharma shankata* is tackled with *āpad dharma.* But these are done by keeping in view the spirit of the principle and the demand of the situation properly in balance. (We have had a long discussion on this in chapter one above.) Principles of ethics, including those of business ethics, are thus universal but *defeasible* under sufficiently demanding situations. But this is no concession to ethical relativism; for a value defeated in favour

35. Sternberg spells out the meaning of the universality of ethics and of business ethics in this way; see especially *ibid* p. 77.

36. *Ibid.*

of another, more relevant one under the circumstances does not cease to be a value. We have therefore argued that ethical values are applicable to all *relevant* situations—not to *all* situations indiscriminatingly. This is the proper spirit of ethics being universal and objective. Elaine Sternberg's endorsement of this analysis appears in her work cited, especially in pp. 77-78.

It is now necessary to specify the universal ethical principles that apply in business. For in view of the limited nature of business's purpose, not all ethical principles are relevant to business, and many of the ethical principles, not related to this purpose, would not be appropriate in business. The principles, which are relevant to business and must guide business activities, are what Sternberg calls ordinary decency and distributive justice.[37] We have dealt at length with what are involved in these principles of distributive justice and ordinary decency earlier above.These principles constitute the basic values of business ethics and guide business activities towards maximizing long-term owner value; but this is not what makes them *ethical*, though this is what makes them the *relevant* principles in business ethics. What makes them ethical principles is their moral rightness, which is universal and which is prior to and independent of their business application. This is an interesting convergence of the teleological model and the deontological model of business ethics. The principles' ethicality lies in their rightness and their universality lies in their independence of the definitive purpose of business: what makes them specifically relevant and applicable to business is their role in helping realize the particular purpose of the business; but even if they fail to maximize owner value, the principles would still be ethically correct and would continue to be the guiding principles of good business, and a business's violating these principles would be considered bad, even if it chances to maximize long-term owner value. This explains the fact that the business, for example, of contract killing is morally wrong even if it happens to maximize

37. See *ibid*, pp. 79-86 for a detailed discussion on this.

profit and owner value; and so is promise-breaking and so also is deceitful business transactions.

A reasonable and acceptable account of business ethics, based on the principles of ordinary decency and distributive justice, may be stated thus:

(1) Maximising long-term owner value (profit or utility, if you like) must be the aim of business, but not at the cost of (distributive) justice and (ordinary) decency.
(2) Business behaviour must be (distributively) just and (ordinarily) decent, but only to the extent that its maximization of owner value is not affected adversely.

On this construal of the concept of business ethics, business must pursue its objective of maximizing owner value through just and decent means.

The first of these above characterizations, (1) emphasises on the primacy of the business purpose, which is to be achieved or pursued within the limitations of basic ethical principles. And the second characterization, (2) stresses on the primacy of ethical conducts in business though [the realization of] the business purpose is a limiting condition of the primacy of the ethical. This is what makes business a problem area; but what is interesting is the fact that (1) and (2) together provide a happy confluence of deontology and teleology/consequentialism in the explanation of business ethics. However, the ethical being subject to a limiting condition does not make business ethics (so much) problematic any more than ethical rules being subject to defeasibility or what we have called justified violations makes ethics relative. On the contrary, if our account of applied ethics adduced in this work—especially in chapters 1 and 3 above—holds ground, this only puts the concept of ethics and the nature of ethical principles in their proper perspective. For ethics or ethical values and principles, we have shown, are objective and universal but defeasible under specific demanding situations.

We have illustrated a few cases of justified violations of moral principles in the interest of a desirable balance between the spirit of the principles and the demands of the situations, neither of which should be totally ignored if ethics is to help solving real life problems. Business ethics (i.e., ethical principles applied in business), it has been similarly shown, must strike a reasonable balance between its commercial concern and the social (or welfare) concern, both of which are equally important in the operation of good business. And for this purpose ethical principles applied to business situations must be naturally [business] purpose-specific and context-specific. Once again this is not to concede to ethical relativism, since (a) the ethical value or principle that is foregone in preference to another, more appropriate, value does not become a disvalue thereby and (b) the ethical principle that is applied to business in consonance with the latter's purpose is right and universal prior to its application to the business and independent of it. Such analysis of ethics and ethical principles applied to business is quite in keeping with our common understanding of ethics and with the spirit of the ethical principles. The remainder of this chapter will be concerned with a few illustrations of this feature of ethics as applied to business situations.

Consider justice and fairness as well as honesty, which are the ingredients of ordinary decency and distributive justice. It is generally agreed that justice and fairness require treating people equally. But as I have shown in chapter 4 part 2 above, neither 'justice' nor 'equality', in terms of which it is often defined, is a blanket term to be applied and understood with absolute abstraction.[38] What is to count as 'equal treatment' must be determined by the context. To use one of my earlier examples

38. In analyzing justice, fairness and honesty in business, I have used materials from a special lecture on "Ethics and Business", which I delivered at the 13th annual conference of the Orissa Philosophy Association held under the auspices of the Xavier's Institute of Management, Bhubaneswar in January, 2001. The lecture is published in the Proceedings of the Orissa Philosophy Association, 2002.

given in chapter 4, a judge and a criminal are equal as persons, but it would be unjust to treat them alike and give them equal status in society, as much as it would be a parody of equalitarianism if, for example, a musical instrument (an electric guitar, say) is given to or demanded by everybody irrespective of whether they are musicians, factory workers, management trainees or business executives. When we consider application of ethical principles in the realm of business, the importance and relevance of contexts is even more fairly obvious. Let us consider honesty, for another example, which is an essential ingredient of ordinary decency. Although it will be generally agreed that honest business is good business, it is very important to determine *what* is honesty in business. What would count as 'honest information' and 'dishonest disclosure' very much depends on the purpose of the business and also on the audience addressed to. A manager, who does not speak the (whole) truth in a business meeting or a press conference, is not being dishonest but is only being tactful, which is expected of him. For not all business statements are meant to convey accurate factual information and those which do have to be assessed in specific contexts.[39] A news headline is not considered false or dishonest for not conveying an information in exact detail, nor would it be charged with suppression of facts because of this. "The everyday standard of disclosure in life, and thus in business, varies considerably, but is almost always less than 'the truth, the whole truth and nothing but the truth'".[40] Indeed, ordinary business conventions are strong enough to serve the business objectives like promoting sales, but not providing general consumer guidance; adopting a stronger, non-standard level of honesty, e.g. speaking the whole truth and not telling a lie at all—come what may—may be counter-productive to the business concerned. This is what happened in the case of the Utkal Tannery of Mdhusudan Das, which was closed down

39. See Sternberg, *Just Business*, especially p. 85.

40. Sternberg, *ibid*, p. 86.

because of absolute honesty and an extreme form of commitment to truthfulness on the part of its ideal minded proprictor.

It is interesting to note that the importance of and the emphasis on the context (which includes the business purpose and audience addressed to) in business is not in variance with common usage. To say “Fine !”in response to a formal greeting “How are you?”is not at all dishonest, which it would certainly be in reply to the very same question by one’s attending physician. A conventional greeting does not call for the same *medical* evaluation that a physician’s query does. Likewise, just and decent behaviour in business must be assessed in view of the context and the purpose of the business. This is also true of international trade, which has its own business ethics questions that call for context- or purpose-specific answers. For example, is it ethical to sell in another country the products which fail to meet the home standards? It depends. If the target market is too poor to afford color televisions then it is not immoral, but good business, to supply black and white sets instead. But what about selling products that are “unsafe” in the home market? Again, I suspect, it depends. If the danger is small or negligible, it is then a matter of trade off. For example, cars without seat belts still have good market in the third world countries and there is nothing immoral in this business. However, if the products are seriously unsafe, then selling them *anywhere* is wrong.

Far from giving in to ethical relativism, as it would appear to some, the aforesaid view of business ethics is a pithy reminder that to reject absolutism is not necessarily to espouse relativism in ethics. For what is rejected is the tendency to understand a moral principle in its absolute, literal sense and to say this is not to make the principle ad hoc and relative. Justice and decency, the two conditional principles of busincss ethics, are universal principlcs though, as should be clear by now, what is to count as just and decent is context-specific, quite in the same sense, as, in general ethical enterprise, it is a virtue to be good, though what is good will vary from context to context. Business ethics, therefore, is not something fundamentally different from ethics in general; what is true of the latter is, *mutatis mutandis*, also true of the former. To repeat, far from being relative, business ethics is universal in its application to all sorts of activities called business; because the ethical principles that underlie it are universal. And universal they remain despite admitting of defeasibility and violations, which nonetheless are morally justified.

6

Environmental Ethics

Duties to and Rights of Animals, Plants and the Environment

On several counts this chapter is a continuation of my contention on rights and duties put forward in chapters 4 and 5. In chapter four, I pleaded for man as the primary right holder and human right as right in the primary sense of the term. For only in the case of man as person that the all important reciprocal correlation between rights and duties can be meaningfully talked about and the right holder–right promoter conceptual link can be properly operational. Consequently, it was indicated, our talk of rights in the case of animals and inanimate objects of nature does make good but a secondary sense,—a sense that is an extension of its (the concept of right's) use in the human context. And still in the realm of human rights and duties of men, and in keeping with our above contention on them, the fifth chapter analyzed the role of ethics in business and other professions—the former elaborately and the latter rather perfunctorily in as much as such analysis (of them) helped buttress the mainstream of my contention on the former. However, pleading for primacy of human rights is not to undermine altogether the use of rights in the case of animals, plants and other non-human inanimate things. Indeed, far from this, the talk of animal rights in particular and of rights of the environment in general not only makes a lot of sense, but issues regarding such rights give rise to profound ethical concerns and do comprise a sizable interest of contemporary moral philosophers and social scientists. As we have said, (in chapter four), the idea of rights presupposes the idea of duties or obligations. The talk of (ascription of) rights of (to) **X** is to imply that **Y** has the corresponding duties, positive and negative, to promote **X**'s rights to be exercised and not to interfere with it. To talk of animals, plants and other inanimate things having rights, if at all, is to commit ourselves to the corresponding obligations to promote such rights,—whether or not these supposed right holders can reciprocate with parallel obligations to promote any of *our* rights. What is important is just that these right holders have some sort of moral standing in order to have the right to be treated with respect by us. It is thus all a question of what we owe, not only to members of our species but also to others—animals, plants and other inanimate things—who/which are the major constituents of our environment along with our relations to them. If ethics is the study of goodness and rightness, of our reasons for acting in one way rather than another, the foregoing considerations lead us on to issues in environmental ethics. We shall address to these issues in what follows.

Special Features of Environmental Ethics

Environmental ethics is one of the prominent areas of applied ethics, like business ethics and other professional ethics such as medical ethics; and this is in the sense that it is application of the results of normative ethics to the sphere of the environment, i.e. to the broad world of humans, animals, plants and the other inanimate things of nature. But there is an important asymmetry that spells out the distinctive features of environmental ethics vis-à-vis these other areas of applied ethics. The first point to be noted is that business ethics and medical ethics are forms of professional ethics which environmental ethics is not. This is simply because environment is not a profession and environmental ethics is neither the study of ethical issues specific to any particular profession nor is it the application of ethical theories to any specific occupational area. It is much too wider in scope and application, for while it applies normative ethics to a particular set of practical issues, it is also a new way of doing normative ethics in general. It is not confined to what we owe to each other as human beings and what we can claim against each other. That is, it is not confined to questions of rights and duties of men; it tries to figure out what rights, if at all, animals, plants and the non-living items of nature can be said to have and what we, the humans, owe to them. In this sense, environmental ethics is the study not only of the value of human life but of life in general and the value of the objects of nature, *albeit*, in the opinion of many, as related to that of life in general. Thus, unlike business ethics and other forms of professional ethics, environmental ethics transcends human ethics. And if ethics is supposed to seek respect for life in general, environmental ethics can claim to be somewhat coextensive with ethics in general. It is perhaps in this sense that environmental ethics is said not only to *apply* normative ethics but also to *encompass* normative ethics.[1] This brings us to the second point of the asymmetry mentioned above, which is that it is not just a human ethics that is needed to be applied to the environment, as is the case with business ethics and medical ethics—indeed with all forms of professional ethics like law, technology and international development. To be sure, human welfare does figure prominently in an ethics that seeks respect for life; but what concerns the environmental ethicists is more than human well-being. "...[E]nvironmental ethics in a deeper sense stands on a frontier, as radically theoretical as it is applied. *It alone asks whether there can be non-human objects of duty.*"[2] No other ethics seeks to study values outside human values. In its

1. Elizabeth Willott and David Schmidtz in *Environmental Ethics* (eds. both), Oxford, 2002, p. xii.
2. Holmes Rolston III, "Values in and Duties to the Natural World" in *ibid*, p. 33 (Emphasis added).

'biologically objective'[3] spirit and non-anthropocentric approach to values, environmental ethics seeks to bring science and ethics closer together. In an environmental ethical framework, nature can never be considered value free, as conventional science takes it to be, nor can humans be considered the only subjects of moral concern, as the mainstream ethics tends to reckon. This is perhaps the only area where science and philosophy expressedly seek to work together and need each other,—where science seeks to outgrow its factuality and shades into normativity and valuationality, where ethics seeks to expand its horizon beyond human affairs to encompass the biosphere and indeed the entire ecosphere. And for the latter purpose, ethics badly needs the support of science's rich storehouse of pertinent facts to know how the real world actually works. For this reason some would consider it "unethical" to engage in environmental ethical pronouncements without having had adequate access to the pertinent facts.[4] Away from armchair philosophizing and abstract speculation, environmental ethics is rational appreciation of the world around us and of our relation to the community of life and other non-living constituents of this world. In this role of world-directed evaluation, environmental ethics eminently figures as applied ethics in the sense in which this concept has been enunciated in this work. As in the case of applied ethics in general, so also in this case, certain moral principles are invoked to guide our conduct with regard to the natural ecosystem and the community of life therein. Environmental ethics attempts to provide the rational grounds for such a system of moral principles. In this sense, as a form of applied ethics, environmental ethics seeks to determine how human beings are to live with the right relations to the natural world. In this endeavour, environmental ethics cannot be simply content with the principle of preserving the balance of nature and living in

3. *Op cit.*
4. As Willot and Schmidtz do in their Introduction to *Environmental Ethics*, edited by them, p. xiii.

accord with the design "built into the very nature of things"; the role of us, the moral agents, is of inevitable importance in rationally devising the required standard of character and rules of conduct. We shall see that this has a considerable impact on the theory of environmental ethics that we maintain in this chapter. But whatever theory one wants to adopt will necessarily address to some moral issues in order for it to count as a systematic theory of environmental ethics. Do we have duties towards non-human living things and other non-living things? And if we do, are these duties independent of our duties towards human beings? And if the latter, how are our duties and responsibilities towards the natural world to be considered vis-à-vis our human interest and values? Secondly there is also the further question of whether there can be valid principles of environmental ethics which are binding on everyone.[5] The second question, which relates to the wider issue of objectivity of moral principles, I am inclined to answer in the very same light in which the latter concept has been analysed in chapter 3 above, and the inevitable *defeasibility* of environmental ethical principles will be illustrated in appropriate contexts as we move on. And as we move on, more light will be shed on the kind of objectivity attributable to principles of environmental ethics. (It may be recalled that, instead of pursuing an absolute standard of objectivity, we are committed to laying bare the kind of objectivity applicable to different areas of discourse, viz. the kind of objectivity attributable to moral values as distinct from the kind attributed to the sciences. This we dealt in as a methodological principle in the third chapter above.) For the present let us analyse the implications of the first question raised above. This question has clear indication that our duties to the environment are different from and hardly independent of our duties to the fellow humans, and the difference between environmental ethics and human ethics, as maintained above,

5. See Paul W. Taylor, *Respect for Nature* (Princeton University Press, New Jersey), pp. 9-10.

is also explainable in reference to this difference. What kind of duties it is that we owe to the environment and why do we owe them to it? Two types of theories have been suggested by way of rational justification of our environmental obligations: in the writings on environmental ethics the two theories are familiarly famous by the name of anthropocentric theory of environment and the bio-centric theory. Analysis and assessment of these theories will help clarify the nature of environmental ethics and of our obligations to the natural world of living and non-living things.

Forms of Environmental Ethics: Anthropocentric and Biocentric

While agreeing upon the fact that we owe certain moral duties to the natural world, the above named two theories differ sharply with regard to the nature and justification of such duties, which, in turn, spells out a corresponding difference of approach to the moral status of the natural things. For whether we accept the one or the other of these theories makes a practical difference in the way we treat the natural world.

On the first theory, familiar among environmentalists as the anthropocentric or human-centered theory, the moral duties we owe to the natural world are because of, or rather derived from[6], the duties we owe to one another as human beings. Things of nature, on this view, are supposed to be primarily for serving human ends and interests. By contrast, the second theory of environmental ethics, which goes by the name of bio-centric or life-centered view, holds that our duties to the natural world are independent of the duties we owe to human beings and arise directly from our moral relations to the natural world. Things of nature*—animals, plants and perhaps the non-living things

6. As Taylor puts it in *Ibid*, p. 11.

* There is no agreement among environmentalists on including the non-living things in the objects of moral concern. The protagonists of deep ecology though, as we shall see, take them to be of intrinsic worth as members of the ecosphere.

of nature—are considered not as instrumental or subservient to human ends but as having inherent worth and intrinsic value.

The anthropocentric theory of environment may be traced to the ancient western tradition especially as reflected in the Judaic-Christian theology as well as in ancient Greek philosophy. Both these traditions together expressedly made man the centre of the moral universe. While the former projected anthropocentrism as the result of divine design, the latter, especially Aristotle, projected man as genetically and generically superior to the rest of the species.

In *Genesis* it is maintained that man is made in the image of God, who blesses him to be "fruitful and multiply and replenish the earth and subdue it". Even though contemporary Christian approach to this grant of dominion to men is largely one of caution and moderation—treating human superiority not as a license to exploit other living beings and things but rather as an ordainment to promote their well-being on God's behalf—the textual authority continues to remain dominantly anthropocentric. For not only the Old Testament enjoins treatment of animals for the benefit to humans[7], the New Testament also shares this view, which is evident from the story of Jesus destroying a fig tree and causing a herd of pigs to drown—a story that St. Augustine explained as meant to tell us that to refrain from killing of animals and destroying of plants is the height of superstition[8]! Medieval Christian philosophy substantiated its human-centric approach to nature by incorporating the thoughts of Aristotle whose definition of man as a (apparently meant as *the)* rational animal virtually elevated man to the apex of creation. Aristotle's portrayal of man as the (only!) possessor of rational faculty and intellectual competence purportedly proclaimed that man has the dominion over nature,

7. In course of a discussion of an Old Testament command to rest one's ox, on the Sabbath, St. Paul asked, "Doth God care for oxen?" rhetorically implying that He does not. (see Peter Singer, *Practical Ethics* (Cambridge Univ. Press, 1993), p. 266.
8. See *ibid*, p. 267.

which is but a hierarchy, where species with less reasoning power exist for the sake of those with more. As Aristotle himself put it:

> Plants exists for the sake of animals and brute beasts for the sake of man—domestic animals for his use and food, wild ones (or at any rate most of them) for food and other accessories of life, such as clothing and various tools. Since nature makes nothing purposeless or in vain, it is undeniably true that she has made all the animals for the sake of man.[9]

This view of Aristotle was literally adopted by St. Thomas Aquinas in his *Summa Theologica* with the additional plea that it is in accord with God's command. The primacy of human interest and values was so much stressed that Aquinas did not even recognize the possibility of sinning against non-human animals and things of nature—there could be sins only against God and man. Barring the very few moderate reformists like St. Francis, this view represented the dominant Christian thinking up to the 18th century (courtesy Singer), which also constitute the major trend of the western approach to the environment. Accordingly the western ethical tradition has treated men as the only morally important members of the global community. The natural world of plants and animals exist only to benefit the human beings; it has at best an instrumental value, meant to serve human ends and purposes. And since on this view, nature has no intrinsic value—value in itself or value for its own sake—it naturally seemed to follow that the exploitation and destruction of plants and animals cannot be considered sinful, except when this (destruction) is harmful to human beings and detrimental to human interests.

To be sure, this is not to say that this view does not take nature and environment seriously, that it is not concerned for the preservation of nature that constitutes the central feature of

9. As quoted by Singer, *ibid*, p. 267

environmental ethics. Aforestation and protection of environment is as much the concern of this view as it is of any alternative socio-moral point of view. But this is pleaded on the ground that human welfare is to be protected and harm to it prevented thereby. Uranium that is hazardous to human health and life is better left in the ground rather than being used for production of nuclear power, which may be otherwise (economically) gainful and (strategically) honourable. Likewise consideration of human health and welfare—and this alone—induces the anthropocentrist against pollution, use of gases that are harmful to the ozone layer, burning of fossil fuels and destruction of natural ecosystem. Thus even within the human-centric moral framework, preservation of the environment is a crucially important value and objective.

Preservation of wilderness and pristine nature assumes even greater importance in a human-centered ethics if, as is increasingly the case in recent day industrial–technocratic society, the natural ecosystem gets distorted and scarce. For not only the present mankind is thrown into the danger of losing the benefit derived from useful plants and organisms. What is more important, the future generations are also deprived of their fair share of benefit and enjoyment of the natural ecology. If not for any other reason, wilderness is the source of profound feeling of aesthetic enjoyment that becomes more and more sought after the more it becomes scarce and truncated in the artificiality of modern living. It may well be the case that future generation a century after will have neither the time nor the interest to enjoy and appreciate nature; *but it may not be the case as well.* And if the wilderness is destroyed, "the choice is gone for ever", as Singer quite rightly said (*ibid.* p. 272), in case the future generation continues in our way. Future generations of people have as much right to live a life of secure physical health and sound aesthetic enjoyment as people of the present generation. We are therefore under obligation not to allow the natural environment to deteriorate to an extent that would jeopardize their survival and well-being.[10] But the obligations we thus owe to nature, as already noted, is derived from our duty to fellow human beings. And man nurtures nature for the benefit of man.

However, if we take the other different approach to the environment, i.e. the life-centered environmental ethics, that would necessitate a profound reordering of our moral point of view, and the whole of the ecosystem and the community of life would make its claim upon us in place of the limited world of human beings. Things will appear in an entirely new light. The obligations we owe to nature become of a different kind if our approach to nature becomes different in this way. If, that is, the natural environment is seen to have value in itself and not as instrumental to human values. That is why, as we noted above, in a bio-centric environmental ethic the obligations and responsibilities we owe to the animals and plants in nature are seen to follow from the moral relations holding between ourselves and this natural world, and these are independent of the duties we have towards our fellow humans; in fact these obligations are independent of the fact that the plants and animals may happen to be of use and benefit to us. They have not only to be cared for but also respected as having values in themselves. In other words, the other living beings and things of the natural world have intrinsic values as much as we humans do. Because of this, some[11] have pleaded for what they describe as respect for nature, which essentially characterizes the bio-centric environmental ethics.

This view as outlined above is in direct conflict with the anthropocentric ethics, which prides itself with the supposed fact that humans alone have intrinsic value. And this is usually backed up by the further supposition that humans alone have inherent worth. But in all fairness, this supposition is open to question. Why should humans be supposed to have inherent

---

10. See Paul W. Taylor, *Respect for Nature*, p. 11.
11. Taylor, for an example; see *ibid.* I shall have more to say on this, which will have an important bearing on my view on environmental ethics.

worth and intrinsic value and why should the non-human beings and things (the living non-human things) be supposed to lack this? The most obvious point against this supposition is species bias or what some have called "speciesism"[12]. For apparently no good reason, we tend to regard the interests of our own species, the interests of human beings, as weightier and more worthwhile than that of other species like animals and plants. As cited earlier, one of the major sources of this supposed superiority of the human species has been Christian theology. But there is nothing either logically binding or factually compelling about this. For what if one is not a theist? What if someone is not a believer in Christian theology but an ardent follower of the Hindu Vedic and Upanishadic belief systems, which expressedly plead for value and worth of all things living,—animals and plants? Given these possibilities, how would it be fair to sacrifice the most important interests of other beings like pigs, hens, deers and rabbits in order to satisfy trivial interests of man like eating tasty food and enjoying poaching? Perhaps the same questions can be raised about using animals in laboratory experiments. The other major source of the described speciesism, as also noted above, is the Greek philosophical tradition, especially Aristotle's definition of man as a rational animal or even the Cartesian-Lockean theory of man as a 'thinking intelligent being' capable of 'reason and reflection'. But that does not work as a ground for discrimination even within the sphere of human beings. More intelligent people are not entitled to subdue the less intelligent and use them for their own ends. The struggle for equality and social justice, endemic in human history, is glaring testimony to this. The inequality displayed in the discriminations based on race, colour, and caste—supposedly ordained by divine design and/or division of natural kinds—has been considered worldwide as paradigms

12. E.g., Richard Ryder and Peter Singer. See Singer's "All Animals are Equal" in Schmidtz and Willott (ed.) *Environmental Ethics* pp.17-27 esp. pp. 21 and 27.

of natural injustice. This essential principle of moral equality forms the basis of Bentham's dictum: "Each to count for one and none for more than one". Henry Sidgwick makes the same point by saying: "The good of any one individual is of no more importance, from the point of view of the universe, than the good of any other"[13]. Moral equality is inevitably based on the principle of equal consideration for everyone's interests, irrespective of their intelligence, reasoning power or such other capacities. For whereas the latter are matters of empirical fact, equality is a moral matter. Rather than intelligence, merit and rational capacity, it is worth that is inherent to and equal among men that matters for moral consideration. On the basis of reasoning like this, Peter Singer points at a powerful argument against speciesism. "If possessing a higher degree of intelligence does not entitle one human to use another for his own ends", he argued, "How can it entitle humans to exploit non-humans?"[14]

Species partiality, which underlies the anthropocentric attitude to environment, is a clear violation of the principles of equality and justice (both of which we have shown to be virtually one and the same principle in Ch. 4 above). In this respect it is no different from racism of medieval west and classism or casteism *(varṇavaisamya)* of ancient India. For while the racist and the casteist violate the principle of equality by displaying implicit preference for members of their own race and caste, the speciesist in a similar manner allows the interest of his own species to override even greater interests of the members of the other species. "The pattern is the same in each case", as Singer rightly draws our attention to[15]. The pattern is a pattern of a tendencious mindset that embodies class-consciousness and category preference. The racist and the casteist not only work in the interest of their own class, but subject the other class to contemptuous subversion. The speciesist likewise exploits the

13. *Methods of Ethics,* 7th edition, p. 382.
14. "All Animals are Equal", in *Environmental Ethics,* Schmidtz and Willott (eds), p. 20.
15. *Ibid.*, p. 21

members of other species in the interest of the members of his own species. The worst exploitation of animals by the human speciesits is eating them for pleasure and good taste, not even for nutrition, for which recognized vegetarian alternatives are easily at hand. In doing so we not only treat them as mere means to our ends, we regard their life and well-being as subordinate to our pleasure and taste. How much does it differ from treating human slaves as possessions and properties to be treated as usable and even exploitable to serve the trivial ends of the master (slave owner)? And why should we consider it horribly unjust and inhumanly tyrannous but take animal exploitation with relative ease and apparent normalcy of attitude? If the basis of moral principle is the principle of equal consideration of interests, why do we, even some philosophers (I suspect many of them), fail to see this principle applicable to members of the other species as well? Being moved at the black slaves being treated as animals and properties in British dominions of his time, Jeremy Bentham expressed the hope that:

> The day may come when rest of the animal creation may acquire these rights which never could have been withholden from them but by the hand of tyranny. The French have already discovered that the blackness of the skin is no reason why a human being should be abandoned without redress to the caprice of a tormentor. It may one day come to be recognized that the number of the legs, the villosity of the skin or the termination of *os sacrum* are reasons equally insufficient for abandoning a sensitive being to the same fate. *What else is it that should trace the inseparable line*? Is it the faculty of reason or perhaps the faculty of discourse? But a full-grown horse or dog is beyond comparison a more rational, as well as a more conversable animal, than an infant of a day, or a week or even a month old. But suppose they were otherwise, what would it avail? The question is not, can they reason? nor can they talk?,but can they suffer? [16]

16. *Introduction to the Principles of Morals and Legislation*, Ch. XVII. Emphasis added.

In the last part of this passage, Bentham points to the capacity to suffer (and enjoy)—which some others call sentience[17]—that gives a being (hence a non-human animal too) the right to equal consideration. I shall come to this point in some detail when I consider the question of rights of animals and plants *vis à vis* their status as moral subjects or as objects of our moral concern—and in fact the broader question of the possibility of a rights-based environmental ethics. But the more important points raised here are on the limitations of speciesism or species partiality in favour of human beings and a question of a rationale for this partiality or bias. Why should the members of the *homo sapiens* enjoy this privilege if neither logic nor factual compulsions entitle them to do so? If, as is familiarly claimed, humans alone have inherent worth and intrinsic value, why must this be so and why should the animals and plants be supposed to lack *this?* To this question we turn in what follows.

Inherent Worth, Intrinsic Value and Good of a Being

To return to the question raised above few moments ago, why do we feel terribly bad about slavery and do not feel that bad about cruelty to animals and even about animal slaughter?.Why do we consider the former as utterly unjust but the latter is passed on without much of a moral flutter or at best accepted with a rationalisation? In order not to beg the question at issue, the answer must not be, "Because the slaves are human beings", and so it is not. The usual answer, from the moral point of view, has often been that human beings have inherent worth that makes them worthy of respect. They are worthy of respect not because they are rational beings* or thinking intelligent beings they are supposed to be since all men are not equally reasonable or

17. William Frankena, for example. "Ethics and the Environment" in K.E. Goodpaster and K.M. Sayre (eds), *Ethics and Problems of 21st Century* (University of Notre Dame Press, 1979).

* Nor because men are "made in the image of God" since, as we have shown, non-belief in theology or belief in a non-Christian theology would rule out respect for men on that account.

equally intelligent and some of them are either temporarily or permanently incapable of thinking and reasoning. Rationality and intelligence are not only present in varying degrees in different men, but may not be present at all in some of them. Yet, intelligent people and idiots and insane adults alike, all men are treated as equal and equally worthy of respect and moral consideration. In the light of Vlastos's famous distinction[18], these capacities like rationality and intelligence are *gradable traits* as distinct from what he calls the *valuable traits*, i.e. human worth that is inherent to human beings as persons. Kant would call it the inherent dignity that entitles humans to be treated as ends and never as means. This valuable trait, which is the touchstone of contemporary egalitarianism and the principle of universal human rights, is also the basis of equal respect and equality of considerations for all men. Right and justice are thus equally due to all of them. We have seen (in Ch.4 above) that right and justice, and even equality itself, attributed to men are attributed to them in *some* respects, depending on situations and the point at issue. Accordingly, all humans command equal respect in *some* sense, but not in every sense. This equality attributed to all human beings is, therefore, not based on any actual equality between them in respect of merits, talents, race and colour (in respect of which they differ more than they agree), but *despite* these considerations. This equality, which means equality of moral considerations, is not based on any factual considerations of the above mentioned gradable features of men, but on a deeper aspect independent of them, even in respect of which men may happen to agree. For if it were so, then their difference in these respects would imply difference in the amount of consideration we give/have for men and their interests and well-being. Peter Singer puts this as follows:

> Equality is a moral ideal, not a simple assertion of fact. There is no logically compelling reason for assuming that factual

18. Gregory Vlastos, "Justice and Equality" in Richard Brandt (ed), *Social Justice* (Prentice Hall, New Jersey, 1962).

> difference in ability between two people justifies any difference in the amount of consideration we give to satisfying their needs and interests. The principle of the equality of human beings is not a description of an alleged actual equality among humans: *it is a prescription of how we should treat humans.*[19]

Thus, underneath the actual differences manifested in men's ability, merits and intelligence etc. there is something inherent in them that qualifies them for equal consideration. This is the *inherent worth* that makes men worthy of respect and moral considerations. The anthropocentric theory of environmental ethics, and the species partiality which it implicitly displays, leans heavily on this concept of *inherent worth*, which it takes as the distinctively human trait, analysis and reconstruction of which is crucial to the understanding of environmental ethics.

In his excellently illuminating paper "All Animals are Equal", Paul Taylor offers a sort of definition of "inherent worth" by saying:

> To say that it [a living thing] possess inherent worth is to say that its good is deserving of the concern and consideration of all moral agents, and that the realization of its good has intrinsic value, to be pursued as an end in itself and for the sake of the entity whose good it is.

And he goes on to say a few lines later:

> When rational autonomous agents regard such entities as possessing inherent worth, they place intrinsic value on the realization of their good and so hold themselves responsible for performing actions that will have this effect and for refraining from the actions having the contrary effect.[20]

---

19. In Schimdtz and Willott (eds.), *Environmental Ethics*, p. 19.(Emphasis added).
20. "The Ethics of Respect for Nature" in *ibid,* p. 86.

The first part of the quotation specifies two important aspects of someone's (or something's) possessing inherent worth: (1) that the being (or thing) has a good of its own and (2) that the realization of this good is of *intrinsic value.* The second part of the quotation I understand as speculating that, because of the above aspects of inherent worth, the possession of inherent worth earns its possessors the status of *moral subjects* worthy of respect and responsibility, for which the *moral agents* are obligated. The distinction as well as interconnection between moral subjects and moral agents has far reaching implications on a broader understanding of environmental ethics, consideration of which will be deferred for a while. My present concern is the good of a being and its supposed intrinsic value which, I think, will help explicate the implications of inherent worth that seems to hold a key to environmental rights and responsibilities.

The good of a being involves its life and well-being, which can be preserved and enhanced or can be harmed and damaged by the actions of moral agents. To say that a being has good of its own is to say that it can be *benefited* or *harmed.* We can do good to it or cause harm to it, in which case its good is affected this way or that. And what is furthered or what is harmed in this process is the being's *interest*. Thus to say that a being has good of its own is to say that it has interests to be preserved and protected by all rational moral agents. In view of this, a being's having a good of its own makes it worthy of our moral concern and consideration. The good of each being, whoever has it, is to be accorded some value—the same for each being—and must have some weight in rational deliberations.

If the good of a being thus makes it worthy of moral consideration, and if in virtue of this (good) all beings deserve equal moral considerations despite their manifest differences in respect of merit, talent and intelligence etc., then this must be because of something about such beings which is deeply intrinsic to them, and it follows therefore that the realization of this good of beings is something *intrinsically valuable.* What it means is that the good of a being is worthy of being protected and furthered *as an end in itself* and never as a means to further some other being's interests and ends. In other words, the good of a being is to be preserved and promoted for the sake of the being whose good it is. Thus, taking together the results of the above analysis of the concepts of *good* and *intrinsic value* leads to the conclusion that a being's having inherent worth—i.e. it's having a good of its own, the realisation of which has intrinsic value—implies that it should never be treated as instrumental to the good of some other being or entity, but rather that the good or well-being of each such being has a value in itself.

Now, Human beings, for sure, are thought to have inherent worth in the described sense—in the sense of having good of their own, which is of intrinsic value. This presumably is why human beings are treated as ends in themselves—eminently by Immanuel Kant, who treated the world of human persons as the kingdom of ends—and in contrast to this, animals and plants are often thought to exist for the sake of human beings, as of benefit and use to them. Quite aside from the validity of this presumption, human beings surely have good of their own, independent of the good and value of any other beings or things. Humans have interest, which are furthered by our actions, and ought to be furthered (and ought not to be deterred or harmed) by the actions of us, the moral agents. If we did not have any interest to be served or preserved, we would not be having any good of our own. In contrast to the human beings, it has been argued, animals, plants and mere non-living things like artifacts and historical monuments, do not have interests of their own and, as such, do not have good of their own. At least this would be the case in accordance with the anthropocentric view of environment.

But wait, we need not move that fast. For there is quite a familiar sense in which we speak of these non-human beings and things, which fairly suggests that they also have good of their own. We say, for example, watering is good for the plants, manures are good for them, though fertilizers are not as good. Similarly, we say of cattle and sheep that fodder and grass is good for them; even we say of pet dogs that walking and running is good for them. It is good for the birds to fly around, we say, and build nests for shelter that keeps them 'safe' from rain and the Sun.

As we speak and plead for preservation of, and prevention of cruelty to, animals, we also speak of preserving and preventing damage to the ancient monuments, most of which are not only precious but also adorably valuable. All this *prima facie* suggests that humans are not alone in having good of their own. If this makes good sense, then we seem to have a case for species egalitarianism and perhaps a strong case for the bio-centric,—nay eco-centric—environmental ethics. Speaking of their good also suggests their having interests, preservation and protection of which should constitute their good. So animals, plants and mere things having good of their own and interests to be protected appears to be pretty plausible and coherent an idea.

However, the idea has not found easy, if not universal acceptance. H.J. McCloskey[21], for example, argued that animals cannot have good of their own on the ground that they cannot have interests, in the preservation of which would lie their good, and this would apply more strongly to the case of plants and mere things. For a being's having interests involves conscious wishes, desires and drives, urges and impulses, hopes and goals. We desire and hope that our interests be protected, our natural impulse is to safeguard our own interests, and promoting one's interests is what one aims at in all his actions, plans and projects. Interests thus must be "compounded" out of conative faculties, which animals eminently lack. On similar grounds living and non-living things, viz. plants and other material things, cannot have good of their own, for most surely they do not have conative life at all.

21. "Rights", *Philosophical Quarterly*, Vol. 15 (1965): 124.

An important counter to this argument is the obvious fact of experience that many (what we call higher) animals are found to display remarkable conative faculties, which are naturally present in them in a rudimentary form and which are found to be improved and enhanced by means of training and conditioning. Desire for food and shelter as well as the urge to preserve and protect the young is characteristic of the wild animals. Pets and tamed ones are observed to be capable of even more; they are found to have fairly manifest, though determinate, conative life. The fact that many others of the animals and birds do not seem to have the conative faculties does not mean that they do not have them. All that this may prove is that we do not know that they have them, but our ignorance of the presence of any conative faculty in these animals does not imply their non-existence in them. To exist may of course be to be perceived for some people, but even for these people non-perception does not imply non-existence. God's knowledge would have to be invoked to explain the existence of unperceived things. (Though it was perhaps the other way round for Berkeley; the Bishop wanted to prove the existence of God on the basis of the obvious continuous existence of things even when no finite being perceives them). If this argument holds, the animals having interests of their own, and so good of their own, is a fairly coherent idea that makes pretty good sense. McCloskey's argument may hold in the case of *mere* things which are not the loci of value but whose value rather consists in their being the objects of our interests—aesthetic and economic interests, if we are considering historical monuments and things that are of tourists' attraction. We agree with him, as Feinberg does,[22] because when these monuments are preserved and protected, they are protected not "for their own sake" nor for their "own true welfare", but "for the sake of a nation's pride and art lovers' fancy". But McCloskey's 'no conation—

22. As Feinberg does; see his "The Rights of Animals" in Schmidtz and Willott, *Environmental Ethics*, p. 54

no interest' theory does not hold against animals. We have given an important counter to this above. To add to that, we have laws to prevent cruelty to animals; and this is intended not merely to protect the animals themselves but to protect and safeguard their interests and well-being,—or so we believe. Kindness to animals, which has long been a prominent feature of the oriental value system, has become an important aspect of modern thinking. But this kindness is not just a tender feeling that some of us have towards the suffering of animals; it presupposes a positive *belief* that the animals deserve our protection in their own right in virtue of their interests and well-being, which is of intrinsic value. In the absence of such belief, it would be difficult to account for this kindness, which would remain a vacuous feeling only. Hence Feinberg:

> ...but one can quarrel with his [McCloskey's] denial that any animals but humans have interests. I should think that the trustees of funds willed to a dog or cat is more than a mere a custodian of the animals he protects. Rather his job is to *look out for the interests of the animal and make sure no one denies it its due.* The animal itself is the beneficiary of his dutiful services. Many of the higher animals at least have appetites, conative urges and rudimentary purposes, the integrated satisfaction of which constitutes their *welfare or good*[23].

It can be seen here that Feinberg pleads not only in favour of animals' interests and well-being, but for a stronger case for the rights of animals, which are "due" to them and which must not be denied to them. I shall discuss the question of rights of animals and plants in due course, as the chapter makes progress. What is of present importance is his "interest principle" that supposedly makes animals one with the humans. If, like the humans, animals also have interests then they clearly have good of their own, the realization of which has value of its own. And in the sense stipulated above, this means that animals too have

23. *Ibid*, p. 54 (Emphasis added).

inherent worth. As a result of this, they are objects of our moral concern and consideration. For a being's having inherent worth is ground enough for it's being worthy of respect.

It is sometimes argued that animals cannot have interests because they are neither interested in whether or not they have interests nor are they consciously aware, if they have any. Therefore, the argument goes, they cannot have any interests of their own or any good of their own. But this, I suspect, is the symptom of a myopic view of the matter. The authors of this view unduly overlook the obvious fact that many of the humans suffer from this limitation but do not, for that reason, cease to have interests and good of their own. We have the cases of the infants and the insane and also of the severely mentally retarded adult human beings. If we speak of and plead for their interests and well-being, and even of their rights, why should animals be said not to have interests and good of their own? Indeed it is true of both animals and the described handicapped human beings that favourable and unfavourable things happen to them, about which they may be totally unàware; but these things, nevertheless, are affecting their interest this way or that. Thus Paul W. Taylor:

> The idea of a being's having good of its own, as I understand it, does not entail that the being must have interest or *take an interest in what affects its life* for better or worse. We can act in a being's interest or contrary to its interest *without its being interested in what we are doing to it* in the sense of it wanting or not wanting us to do it[24].

What is to the point is that we can do good to a being or cause harm to it, whether or not it is aware of it, whether or not it wants us to do this to it. As long as a being can be benefited or harmed, it has a good of its own and so it is a moral subject and

24. "The Ethics of Respect for Nature" in Schmidtz and Willott (eds) *Environmental Ethics* p. 84. (Emphasis added).

worthy of our moral considerations. It is worthy of respect by all moral agents.

Good of the Plants and the Non-living Things

The foregoing arguments have the effect of leading us slowly but surely from the confines of the anthropocentric environmental ethics towards a bio-centric theory. But though the emphasis has thus shifted to the inherent worth of living beings, a complete life-centered ethics of the environment would be nowhere in sight unless the plants and the vegetative world is included within its fold. If, in addition, the non-living things are also considered as having interests and good of their own, that will lead to what is called eco-centric environmental ethics, which some in recent times have been arguing for. Proponents of the philosophy of deep ecology, who plead for biotic equality and species egalitarianism, not only ascribe inherent worth to all things living, but also extend this to classes of non-living things like the earth, the land, and rocks as well as species and the ecosystems considered as entities distinct from the members or items thereof[25]. In view of our stipulation of the inherent worth adduced above, it is difficult to be in the company of the deep ecologists in their latter claim, for in the obvious absence of conative abilities in them these mere things and entities cannot be said to have any interest and good of their own. The deep ecologist's argument from intrinsic value of these things would not only be problematic, as Peter Singer would like to hold,[26] it would entirely lose its ground because of its conceptual incoherence. A mere thing, however precious and valuable on other grounds—economic or aesthetic—cannot have good of

25. For example, Aldo Leopold, "Land Ethic" in *A Sand Country Almanac* (Oxford, Oxford University Press, 1981), Arne Naess, "The Shallow and the Deep: Long-Range Ecology Movements" in *Inquiry*,16 (Oslo, 1973) and Freya Mathews, "Letting the World Grow Old: An Ethos of Counter-modernity" in *Worldviews*, vol.3, no.2 (1999).
26. *Practical Ethics* (Cambridge University Press, 1993), p. 284.

its own to be protected and preserved for its own sake. For although they can be said to be preserved or damaged, it makes no sense to speak of them as being *benefited* or *harmed*; it would be conceptually odd to say that one can help them or hurt them. This does not, however, mean that the plea for preservation of wilderness, ecology and the historical monuments is not sustainable. But unless the plea for their supposed intrinsic value is placed on a ground that is stronger and *other* than the interest principle, preservation of these mere things would at best claim a value that is *instrumental* to human interests, and perhaps to the interests of other sentient beings as well. Hence Singer:

> .....in a society where no one needs to destroy wilderness in order to obtain food for survival or materials for shelter from the elements, the value of preserving the remaining significant areas of wilderness greatly exceeds the economic values gained by its destruction.[27]

I cannot agree with him more. Food and shelter signify the importance of animals' interest; economic gain, with which the value of preserving wilderness is compared, emphasizes human interests. The value of preserving wilderness, which is thus better than the economic gain from destruction thereof, is nevertheless overridable by human (and animal) interest, for which food and shelter has a priority value.

The case of human beings and other animals and the case of mere things belong to the extremes in the application of the interest principle. For while human beings and other animals have been clearly seen to have interests and good of their own, the inanimate non-living things and entities have been shown not to have any. Now, in between these clear cases at the opposite extremes, there is the somewhat dubious case of the plants and the vegetable world—*dubious* because plants, unlike the mere things, have life but unlike the humans and other animals, lack

---

27. *Ibid*, p. 284

sentience, i.e. feeling of pleasure and pain and the capacity to suffer. The advocates of the bio-centric view of environment would include the plants in the class of things as objects of moral concern solely on the ground that they have life, and are living things beyond doubt. But the interest principle, strictly speaking, would consider only those as having good of their own, who or which can be benefited or harmed, helped or hurt; and it hardly makes any plausible sense to speak of helping or hurting plants that do not have the capacity to feel pleasure or pain in being helped or hurt. (That is, it would not make any sense to say *that*). We have noted earlier that Bentham considered the capacity to suffer, as an essential requirement for something's being an object of our moral concern (as having right to equal consideration). And Frankena considered *sentience* as essential for something to have a moral standing. A further example of this is Peter Singer again, who argued that "only a being with subjective experience of pleasure or the experience of pain, can have interest in the full sense of the term[28], and can put us humans under moral obligation to protect their interest and safeguard their well-being[29]. The crucial question, therefore, is: should trees have a moral standing? Which, in turn, involves addressing to the question, can trees suffer (pain) in being "harmed' and enjoy (pleasure) in being 'benefited'? Can trees and plants have good of their own?

We have already noted that a compelling reason for saying that plants and trees are capable of having a good of their own is strongly suggested by the fact that we often say with no artificiality in the use of our language and thinking that certain conditions are "good" or "bad", "useful" or "harmful" for plants and vegetables. There are now-a-days laws and legislations to

28. "Not for Humans Only: The Place of Non-humans in Environmental Issues", in Goddpaster and Sayre (eds), *Ethics and the Problems of Twenty First Century*, p. 194.
29. See also Singer, "All Animals are Equal" in *Philosophical Exchange*, Vol. I (1974) pp. 103-16.

"protect" rare plant species and preserve wilderness and the natural eco-system, which also suggest, though not as strongly, that the plants have "interest" and a "good" which humans as moral agents are obligated to protect and preserve.

However, what is thus suggested by discourse or manner of speaking as well as by laws and legislations is neither implied by them nor is a matter of general agreement among environmentalists and ethicists. Modern writings on these subjects are widely divided. It would be worthwhile, therefore, to put some pressure on the sense or senses of 'good' as the concept has been used to signify inherent worth and intrinsic value of beings and things. To this purpose we may consider facts of common usage, which may or may not develop into technical or quasi-technical philosophical language. Now there are at least two ways of understanding the meaning of 'good' as it occurs in the descriptions 'the good of *X*': 'the good of *X*' may be used as opposed to 'the harm of *X*' *and* as signifying 'the value of *X*'. There is also a third sense in which 'good' can be understood, namely, when 'the good of *X* ' is used in the sense of "the (or a) use of *X*". In which of these senses is 'good' to be understood when we speak of a being or thing having a good of its own in order to be of intrinsic value and so to have inherent worth? If a thing or being is said to have good in the third sense of its having a use or being useful, it clearly has value, if at all, that is instrumental to the interest or value of some other being or thing or sort of beings or sort of things, and as such an *X* having a good in this sense cannot be said to have a good of its own. This is the sense in which an anthropocentric environmentalist would consider the good of the plants and animals being of instrumental value in relation to human ends and interests. A bio-centrist, who pleads for respect for life and sentience and whom I would like to call a weak bio-centrist as he stops at sentience but leaves out living things like plants and trees, would spare the animals but not the plants from the clutches of instrumentalism. For while recognizing the need of plants for their natural growth and survival they would perhaps unflinchingly argue that, unless the growth and survival of trees are matters of human concern or at least of concern for the survival of some sentient beings, their need would be value-neutral and cannot be said to be the basis for what is "due" to them in their own right[30]. Pursuing our analysis in the ascending order of the distinction (of senses of 'good') made above, we may contrast this (third) sense with the second, i.e. good as *value*. If we do not take it in the trivial sense of 'price', 'cost' or 'exchange value', the good of ***X*** will mean that ***X*** has to be valued for its own sake, not for the sake of anything else. In this sense the value of ***X*** is independent of the value of anything else; it will therefore have a good of its own, the realization of which will be of intrinsic value and the frustration of which a gross disvalue. Clearly enough, this sense of good is what is meant when a being is said to have a good of its own. Such sense of good makes its owner a special sort of being from the moral point of view—a definite subject of moral concern, the realization of whose good is of intrinsic value, and we would consider the being whose good it is as having inherent worth. The first sense of 'the good of ***X***' is a little ambivalent between "***X*** is not to be physically harmed" and "***X***'s desires and interests are not to be frustrated". We speak of a man or an animal as being in good condition or good health and we also speak of a car or a tree as being in good condition with no damage or harm done to it physically, and we take care to preserve and protect their 'good' in the sense of protecting them from such harm or damage. In this sense we do not speak of an ***X*** having a good of its own, since its physical good is not of much consequence in the matter of its inherent worth, if it has any. A person, by contrast, has inherent worth and good of his own despite being physically (even psychologically) harmed or hurt. The other sense of good as not being harmed relate to the desires and

30. This, at any rate, is my reading of Feinberg's remark on trees on p. 56 of Schmidtz and Willott (eds), *Environmental Ethics*.

interests of ***X*** not being frustrated. Good in this sense is the realization of one's desires[31]. Only in this interpretation of our first sense of 'good' mentioned above, it would mean the good of a being's or thing's own; for it conforms to the interest principle we discussed above (following Feinberg) as constituting the basis of inherent worth. I agree with Feinberg that "desires or wants are the material interests are made of" and hence that "mindless creatures have no interests of their own"[32], (with which Attfield has his own differences). For as I have maintained, when a being is said to have a good of its own, what is meant is that the realization of its good lies in the realization or satisfaction of its own interest. A being without interest, we have maintained, cannot have any good of its own.

On this reading of the concept of good (of a being), which I subscribe to and for which the interest principle has been adduced as justification, trees and plants cannot be said to have good of their own. We have, however, taken note of the fact that we often quite naturally speak of plants and trees having good of their own when we say that there are things (water, sunlight and manure etc) that are good for them. We also speak of plants having needs like growing up in ways (in search of sunlight, for example) conducive to the satisfaction of this need, and it is even said that it is in the interest of the plants that such needs be satisfied. But it would only be indicative of a linguistic illusion to think, *because of this*, that plants have interests and needs of their own, the satisfaction of which is of intrinsic value. It is only a manner of speaking that something, **x** is in the interest of something else, **y**; but this does not imply that **y** has an interest of its own unless we take the language literally. It is surely one thing to say the former but an entirely different thing to claim the latter, for something's having an interest involves at least some rudimentary form of conative ability on the part of the

31. I owe this interpretation to Robin Attfield's illuminating paper "The Good of Trees" in Schmidtz and Willott (eds), *Environmental Ethics*. p. 59.
32. *Ibid.* p. 55.

thing in question, e.g. wants and desires and also in addition the cognitive capacity to be aware of these wants and desires. This is not the case with plants and so the talk of their having interests is at best derivative, if not metaphorical. And since desires and wants are (or are related to) needs, the same also is true of the "needs" of the plants. (We will have more to say of the needs of plants a little while later.)

Regarding the foregoing view of interest, it will perhaps be objected that a being's being aware of its interests is not binding for it's having the interests. I have indeed alluded to the case of infants and of insane adults being unaware of their interests. If this does not imply denial of their having interests, it may be pointed out, why should it do so in the case of plants? Robin Attfield, for example, who believes that trees have interests in the sense of fulfilment of their natural propensities, does not consider lack of cognitive capacity as a negative factor against the plants and trees having interests. "Truistically they [plants] are unaware of their interests", he argues, "but [then] even creatures with cognitive powers are often unaware of theirs…"[33]

This, I have found, is a stock argument against the anthropocentric theory and in favour of preservation of the interests, even rights, of animals and plants. But despite the general cogency of this argument, I suspect that it overlooks an important asymmetry between 'creatures with cognitive powers' and things without. For in the case of the former, in the case, i.e., of human beings, paradigmatically,* it is quite conceivable what it is like for them to be aware of their wants and desires. It is fairly conceivable *what it would be like* for an adult insane to be (suddenly) aware of his wants and desires, though as a matter of fact he is not able to do so. We are often told of very little children not only knowing much more than they are expected to—which include knowing their wants and desires—but also

33. "The Good of Trees" in *ibid*, p. 62.

* The same would hold in the case of animals, many of whom are plausibly endowed with cognitive abilities, *albeit* to a much lesser degree.

perhaps much more clearly than most normal adults. In the case of the mindless plants and trees, by contrasts, it does not make sense to talk of *what it would be like* for them to be aware of their interests. If they cannot be intelligibly said to *know* their interests, they cannot be said to have any.

It follows therefore that to speak of plants and trees having interests of their own is to speak naturally but derivatively; it is, if this be a permissible formulation, to speak anthropomorphically, to bring the language of interests from the human context, which is its original home, to the context of vegetative life in which, in the absence of conative life and cognitive capacity, it cannot signify independently. When we speak of trees "wanting" to realize or reach their goal, when for example we observe [interpret!] them grow and spread their branches and leaves in search of sunlight, we speak of this by analogical extension of the concept of wanting that primarily functions in the human context as a goal-directed cognitive state. But saying this neither proves the presence of (the conscious state of) wants and desires in the trees nor does it prove the *pursuit* of a goal any more than saying "water seeks its own level" proves the presence of (the conscious state of) *seeking* in water. To repeat, in the absence of wants and desires nothing can be said to have interests and good of its own. It has been argued already that the concept of interest involves benefit (or good) and harm that can be done to *who* have the interest. We cannot properly speak of benefit and harm of trees, because harm always turns on frustration of wants and desires and benefit or good on their realization. And "where we talk of good and harm which are unaccompanied by desires, we must be pretending that desires really are present, that desires, so to speak, grow on trees. Our usage, though inherited, must be derivative."[34] This is how Attfield alluded to Hare's prescriptivist view on the so-called good of trees. Though Attfield would not quite agree with this sort of interpretation of the talk of interest and good of plants

34. Robin Attfield, *ibid*, p. 59.

and trees, I am inclined to agree with this because of reasons and considerations adduced above.

Because of the foregoing considerations, prominent contemporary philosophers like R.M. Hare[35] and Joel Feinberg[36] have held the view that plants can only be harmed when some plant-related human desires and interests are frustrated, that their good lies in the realization of such desires, and that, strictly speaking, the needs and interests of trees and plants depend on the interests of humans. It is quite a familiar fact that we not only look upon the trees and plants from our own point of view and interests, we consider them as flourishing when they do so in keeping with *our* interests—physical, psychological or aesthetic—in them. As Feinberg points out, the interests that thrive when plants flourish are human interests, not plant-interests, and some of our talk about plants strongly suggest this.[37] It is not because of the often enough coincidence between human interests and plant nature that we say this, as Attfield seems to suggest. Indeed Attfield appears to attribute this view to Feinberg when he says: "It is probably the overlap between their [plants'] nature and our purposes which allows us to call this condition 'flourishing'; such talk does not however show that whether or not plants flourish turns on our interests rather than theirs".[38] Sure enough, the overlap between plants nature and human interests does not imply that human interests determine the condition of the plants,—their flourishing and their thriving. But neither Feinberg's nor our account of the plants' interests (flourishing and thriving) as instrumental to, and explainable in terms of, human interests involves saying this. Plants certainly do have a natural propensity to grow in a

35. *Essays on the Moral Concepts* (Macmillan, New York,1972), p. 98 ff.
36. "The Rights of Animals and Unborn Generations", originally published in William Blackstone (ed), *Philosophy and Environmental Crisis* (Athens, University of Georgia Press, 1974), pp. 51-55.
37. See his "Rights of Animals" reprinted in Schmidtz and Willott (eds), *Environmental Ethics*, p. 57.
38. "The Good of Trees", in *ibid*, p. 62.

particular manner, and such biological propensities—which are hardly any sort of conscious pursuits of goal realization—sometimes coincide with how *we* would like them to grow and flourish. But such coincidences, which are *mere* coincidences, do not and cannot form the basis for the described account of plants' "interest" and well-being. Nor is the growth of plants in accordance with their natural biological propensities to be considered as a plant's flourishing in all cases. For in many cases plants are *made to flourish* by frustrating their natural propensities. It is a common gardening experience that the first few buds of a flowering plant are pinched off to make the plant flourish with luxuriant and healthy flowers. And the interest that thrives here is thus not any interest of the plants but the aesthetic interest of the gardener and the spectator. The fact therefore is that it is not the coincidence of human interests and plant interests (their natural propensities, i.e.) but rather their *divergence* that provide the real clue to the understanding of a plant's good; and where the interests diverge, it is the human interest and/or the interest of animals that determines what constitutes the plants' well-being. Besides, frustrating the so called natural interest of some plants is to the general advantage of the entire garden. Unwanted (and harmful to the garden's plant population) weeds are cleared for a very good reason. We can imagine a harmful rare plant which, in course of its natural growth, emits dangerously poisonous gas that is dangerous for the plant population and harmful to the living beings. In such cases eliminating this harmful plant, or at least stunting its natural growth under controlled conditions, will be in conformity with the spirit of environmental ethics—indeed with the spirit of ethics. The ancient *niti sloka* "*Viṣa-brukṣyopi sambardhya swayam chhetumasāmpratam*" is in need of violation or modification in the interest of morally desirable consequences and to prevent consequences that would be morally disastrous. This will be justified violation both literally as well as metaphorically. It is said in the *Mahabharat* that when Duryodhana was born, apparently with alarmingly inauspicious stellar indications, the just and wise Vidura had suggested elimination of the baby in order to prevent ruinous calamities to the country and the subjects,—a suggestion Gandhari repented for not complying with after the ghastly immoral incident of attempted disrobing of the virtuous Draupadi. What a catastrophe was perpetrated that day and after on Hastinapura and the moral community at large is didactic history. Not only harmful plants but even pernicious humans may merit elimination in the interest of the good of the living world. So natural flourishing may sometimes need prevention and regulation.

It has been a pet contention of the life-centered environmental ethics that anything living has interest and good of its own characterized by recognized concepts of benefit and harm that can possibly be done to their good and interest. In the case of plants and trees, it is thought to be the realization of their natural propensities. Aristotle's principle that the good life of a living organism turns on the fulfilment of its nature is often invoked[39] to justify this contention. Besides having a good in the sense of use to humans and animals, plants and trees are said to have a good of their own, which is supposed to be independent of human interests, and this good is to freely grow and survive as per their nature or natural propensities. Environmentalists in recent times put increasing emphasis on this by arguing that humans are the latest entrants into the biotic community and that the ecosystem existed long before them, which means that plants and trees existed independently of them and, by implication, *can* exist independently of them. The ubiquitous meddling impact of the humans is often causing harm to the ecosystem's good, and interfering with the need of plants, which is the fulfilment of their nature. If trees have these needs before people existed, the argument goes, they cannot be said

---

39. See Stephen Cark, *The Moral Status of Animals* (Oxford, the Clarendon Press,1977), pp 57-58 and Robin Attfield, "The Good of Trees". While Clark defends Aristotle's principle in the interest of animals, Attfield used it to defend the interest of trees.

to have lost this after people came to the scene. In view of this, trees are claimed to have needs, interests and good of their own, which deserve our obligation to preserve and protect them. Among others, Robin Attfield specifically argues for this and provides ground for preservation. While agreeing with him in respect of preservation *in principle* of the plants and the vegetable world, our account of interest as involving a minimum of conative life and cognitive ability would lead to the denial of the interest and (hence) the good theory in their case. Besides, as has been made clear, the idea of interest and good is connected with the idea of inherent worth and intrinsic value. The question of plants having interests, therefore, is a question having inherent worth and intrinsic value, which are supposed to merit preservation. What sort of value the plants can be said to have? They cannot be said to have even instrumental value *before* the humans and the animals came into being and *after* they become possibly extinct. Will they have intrinsic value after the possible extinction of living beings, especially the human beings who judge them to be of any value whatsoever? In view of the fact that there would be none to judge them to be of value, the concept of their having any value in that possible state of affairs would be vacuous, to say the least. It would be vacuous to argue that trees had values before people existed and that they cannot be supposed to lose this after they go out of existence. For equally it could be argued the other way round: that trees did not have value before people existed and so cannot be said to lose this after their extinction. The concept of their coming into existence first only proves their being alive independently of the human beings, but it cannot *prove* their having any value of their own. Thus, the talk of their having value is, in effect, an unsupported supposition, and so the other talk of their not having value before humans came to the scene is also a supposition, equally unsupported ! It is interesting that Attfield, in the referred paper, admits that plants do not have a value of their own, though insisting that they have good, interests, needs and even a 'sake' of their own (*ibid*, p. 63). This is indeed a paradoxical situation to be in. For if interest and good are said to be there without there being any value, how much far it would be from saying that the supposed good and interest of the trees and plants are of no value?

The conclusion seems inevitable that our talk of interests and good and even of the needs of trees is only derivative and explainable in terms of *our* interest in and need for them, and that their good cannot be comprehended without reference to how good they are for us. Their good is promoted (they are said to flourish and thrive), not necessarily by letting them grow "naturally", but often by "pruning" them and "shaping them up" so as to be useful and/or enjoyable. Admittedly they cannot have interest and good of their own, the realization of which could be of intrinsic value. Their value, if at all they can be said to have any, would be instrumental to human values and human interests. Their pseudo needs and shammed interests that pose as real ones in our talk of them fall far short of ascribing inherent worth to them. We would, therefore, not be having a complete life-centered ethics of the environment granting inherent worth to plants as well as to men and animals. That is as far as the facts obtain. To look for a complete bio-centric explanation of the environment, if none is possible, would be as irrational as it would be to insist on certainty in the realm of matters of fact. In fact the demand for a complete bio-centric view as an explanation of everything in the environment would betray absolutism and a one-sided mind set as much as the demand for explaining everything in terms of the anthropocentric view does. None of the two theories is self-complete in itself, but they must not be thought to be incompatible; for I think they can jointly explain the nature of environment more effectively than either of them can by itself. As I have said in an earlier stage of this chapter, a sound environmental ethics can be very well developed out of the elements inherent in anthropocentricism. In fact we ought to preserve the natural ecosystem and refrain from causing unnecessary harm (read 'damage') to it if it is for the good of men and animals, who we have seen to be clear possessors of inherent worth and intrinsic value. This itself would justify preservation and protection of wilderness, and their lack of inherent worth and value would be no serious reason against.

This type of analysis of environmental ethics would not be termed as a case of speciesism in favour of anthropocentrism, because the good of trees are not being explained in terms of human good alone but also in terms of the good of the animals as well,—in fact in terms of the good of all living beings. What is denied is not our duty to preserve the plants but only their having any interest and good of their own, and what are asserted are not the interests of the humans alone but also those of all sentient beings. Clark's argument that it would be absurd to define creatures' good by an extrinsic teleology, e.g. by their use to man because it would then be taken to mean that it is to the benefit of deers and pigs to be killed and eaten[40], is certainly valid if animals are supposed to have good of their own; but a like argument for the supposed good of plants and trees would not be valid, since on our showing it is not absurd to define the good of trees in terms of an extrinsic teleology, i.e. in terms of their usefulness to men.

However, preservation of plants and trees—the wilderness, in effect—is still a moral duty even if they are shown to be bereft of good and interest and to be unworthy of having any rights, even the right to (their) preservation. There is nothing odd or improper in saying that plants need to be preserved, even ought to be preserved, but that they do not have any right to be preserved, and the latter is because they do not have any interest of their own to be preserved. Interests and rights, however, are closely connected concepts, though they are not synonymous. If my reading of Feinberg is correct, the main reason for his denying that plants have interests seems to be that interests and

40. See Stephen Clark, *ibid.*

rights are closely connected and that plants have no rights.[41] However I do not wish to preempt the theory that plants have no rights, though I am strongly inclined to believe that it is the right view, until it is argued on the basis of a closer analysis of the concept of right.

What it is to Have a Right? Reflections on a Right-Based Environmental Ethics

"To have a right", says Feinberg, "is to have a claim *to* something and *against* someone, the recognition of which is called for by legal rules or, in the case of moral rights, by the principles of an enlightened conscience."[42] If we look in retrospect, this could be the substance of what I have said about rights in chapter 4 above. Right, I have maintained, involves both a right holder and a right prompter, both together contributing to the meaning of 'right'. If someone has the right to something, **x**, this makes sense only if his claim to **x** is held against someone else—some individual or the society—whose duty it is not to obstruct the right holder from enjoying this right *as well as* to create conditions conducive to the enjoyment or exercise of this right. This is the substance of the platitude that rights and duties are correlatives. If the claim *to* something must go hand in hand with the claim *against* someone, it simply means that what is a right of someone is a duty for someone else and *vice versa*.* However, it is important to note that I cannot claim a right to *anything* and demand a corresponding duty from others to promote my right. In order for them to owe this to me, my claim must have moral legitimacy so that the claimees may acknowledge this legitimacy and feel obligated to promote my

41. "The Rights of Animals" in Schmidtz and Willott (eds), *Environmental Ethics*.
42. *Ibid*, p. 51.
* This relation of reciprocity has to be understood in the sense that someone's right is someone else's duty, though one of the latter's right need not be the duty of the former strictly, but of a third individual or group of individuals.

right both in the negative and in the positive sense. Assertion of a moral right, therefore, presupposes a valid ethical system, whose rules specify the (my) asserted right and the implied duties (of others). As we have shown it to be true of morality in general, so also in this specific case of the moral concept of rights, it is *reciprocity* that plays the crucial role. The person who offends against a right holder is answerable to him for his moral failing in not observing his corresponding duty to promote the right in question. These are the normative features of the assertion of rights, especially the two requirements mentioned above, namely *moral legitimacy* of the right claimed and *moral duty* of others to acknowledge this legitimacy.[43] The language of rights, thus, is normative, and "the assertion that someone has a right to something", Taylor puts it precisely, "is a normative statement, not a statement of fact." (*ibid,* p. 227).

This brings us to a review of the connection between rights and interests, which Feinberg considered crucial in denying that plants and trees have rights. Assertion of interests and assertion of rights fundamentally differ in the sense that the former is a statement of empirical fact while the latter is a normative statement. The assertion that someone has an interest in something can be known to be true or false by observing people's behaviour; but no such empirical evidence is relevant to tell us what is one's moral right. One's having the interest in, or need for, **x** is not a sufficient condition for one's claming the right to **x**. What more is needed is a valid moral principle justifying the putatively asserted right and the implied (corresponding) duty on the part of others to promote this right. Such distinction notwithstanding, it remains an undeniable fact that having interest is a necessary condition, though not sufficient, for having rights; for no one could claim a right to something if he/she did not have an interest in it or did not value it in some way. Indeed, to say that one did not have any interest in **x** but that one has the right to **x** would be self-stultifying, if not self-contradictory. It

43. See Paul W. Taylor, *Respect For Nature*, Ch. V., p. 227.

follows, therefore, that for someone to have a right to **x** is to have an interest in it. Interests do not entail rights, to be sure; but rights do presuppose interests, for sure. In order to be a logically proper subject of rights, one has to have interests. The crucial principle, says Feinberg, for resolution of riddles about rights is that "the sorts of beings who *can* have rights are precisely those who have (or can have) interests."[44]

The foregoing discussion brings into focus three specific features of (having a) right (to something), which are crucial in determining if animals and plants can be said to have rights. That the human beings are the paradigm holders of rights would be immediately evident from even a cursory look at these three features. Expressed schematically, those features relate to the notions of *reciprocity*, *claim* and *interest*. For a clear understanding of the concept of any one's having right to something and for considering the contentious question of animals and plants having rights at all, an elaborate analysis of these three concepts of reciprocity, claim and interest is in order.

When I say that rights involve reciprocity, it is meant that rights imply the corresponding duties on the part of whom I have described as the right promoters. This is what Feinberg meant when he said that to have a right is to have a claim *to* something and *against* someone. This 'someone', against whom one makes a claim to something, has a definite duty to ensure the exercise of this right by the right holder without constraints, hindrances or obstructions. There is also normally involved what may be called a "backward implication" in this talk of reciprocity, for the fact that an individual or institution or the society at large has a duty in the described sense implies that someone else has the corresponding right. However, a truism though it may seem to be, this converse implication does not obtain as strongly logically as the original principle that rights imply duties; for we will soon be able to see that duties in all cases do not imply the corresponding rights,—i.e., one may

44. *Environmental Ethics,* eds Schmidtz and Willott, p. 54.

simply have a duty towards some being or thing without the latter having to have any corresponding right, and without it having to have any sort of duty to reciprocate either. However, the strength of the converse implication (there being duties anywhere means that there are the corresponding rights somewhere) lies in the *general fact* that someone's duty normally points to someone else's right to something. This is not a matter of strict logical entailment, but the conceptual bond is almost a matter of necessity. To use a telling analogy, it is a *general fact of nature* that our first-person memory statements are normally made only when they are true, and likewise our sincere and confident memory claims are normally made only when they are true, i.e. only if the person claiming to remember is *really* remembering, i.e. has *really* done the thing he "remembers" having done. The fact that in neither case the statement is truistic is no reason against the conceptual bond holding between memory and personal identity—no reason, i.e., to suspect the conceptual truth that if one remembers having done something one must be the person who did that thing. Memory in this sense implies personal identity.[45] Likewise the strength of the conceptual bond between rights and duties is explained by the general fact not only that rights imply duties but also that duties imply the corresponding rights and also that one's duties necessitate reciprocal duties on the part of others in the society *against* whom the rights in question are claimed.

The second feature, which characterises rights and which emerges naturally from the first explained above, is the concept of *claim*. Feinberg's characterization of right as a *claim* to something and a *claim* against someone is, once again, the

45. This point has been argued fully in my *Personal Identity*, 2nd edition (Decent Books, New Delhi, 2000), p. 259 and elsewhere. I am inclined to believe that Wittgenstein's well known view of criterion as non-inductive evidence (and hence as non-contingently related to what it is a criterion of) relies heavily on this notion of "general fact of nature", which is evident from his account of pain behaviour vis-à-vis the concept of pain. (See *Philosophical Investigations*, Part I, esp. sec. 142.)

revelation of an important insight that to have a right is to claim what one has a right to. In other words, if someone has a right to something it is important that he *claims* this right, that he should be able to claim his right when it becomes appropriately necessary. In the standard situations of right explanation the right holder must be able to claim or assert his rights (to what he is entitled), which would not only indicate that he is aware of his right (*that* he is entitled to something by virtue of his being what he is), but which also would make others alive to what he has a right to and be obligated appropriately to promote this right of the right holder. This is one of those *general facts of nature* that gives meaning to the concept of right. With apology to Wittgenstein it can fairly be said that, if things were quite different from what they are—if no one claimed or asserted what he is entitled to and no one else ever recognized and felt obligated by what he is entitled to—that would make our normal language game in respect of the concept of right lose its point. It is because of this, because of the conceptual bond between having a right and being able to claim this right, that rights cannot be attributed to mere things. Even if some valuable mere things like the Taj Mahal or the Great Wall of China "deserve" our duty for their preservation and protection, they cannot be said to have this right—except in a figurative sense—to their preservation and protection simply on the ground that these mere things cannot ever be said to claim this right or any right whatsoever.

The third feature that is involved in the idea of right (having a right), which is linked with the second as discussed above, is the idea of *interest.* For it is very close to a truism that what is claimed, or is to be claimed, by a right holder is what he has an interest in; if one has no interest whatever (is not interested in any thing), and if having a right to any thing involves making a claim on what one has a right to, then it follows that there is nothing for him to claim. That is why, as Mark Sagoff points out, most writers in the Kantian tradition analyse rights as claims to something in which the claimant has an interest.[46] For to say that someone has no interest in **x** is to say that he has no reason to claim **x**, and yet to say that he has a right to **x** would be self-stultifying, to say the very least. Therefore only those things and beings can be said to have rights, or can have rights, who have or can have interests of their own.

Our analysis in the previous sections should have made it clear that interest and good or well-being are close conceptual causins. When demands are made for protection of the rights of the members of any species, what is demanded in effect is the protection and promotion of their interests and good. In the most obvious case of the plea for human rights—or what has been fashionably described as the rights of men and citizens—the protagonists plead for protection and promotion of the interests and well-being of all men. Rights of women as pleaded by the women's lib enthusiasts (liberation from the so called bondage under which several of their basic and important rights are allegedly denied to them) eminently include their right to equal treatment as human beings, denial and deprivation of which is against their interests and well-being. And what the protagonists of animal rights demand is solely the protection and promotion of the interests and good of all animals. Similar concept of right is also attributed to trees and the vegetable world by the preservationists. In all these cases, claims of rights are not only associated with, but are grounded on, the claims of interests. As we have seen, McCloskey, for this reason, denied that animals can have rights not only because animals cannot make claims of their rights but primarily (for him) because animals are incapable of having interests. To be a subject of rights, contends McCloskey, a being must have interests of its own. However, claims of rights by the members of a species, serious and

46. "Animal Liberation and Environmental Ethics: Bad Marriage and Quick Divorce" in Schmidtz and Willott (eds.) *Environmental Ethics*, p. 43. Sagoff cites the case of Joel Feinberg who analysed right in terms of interest in his "Duties, Rights and Claims", *American Philosophical Quarterly*, 137.

confident though they may be, would not *in themselves* justify reality of the rights in these cases.

We can use the foregoing analysis of the three features involved in right-claims to find out which species (members thereof) can be properly attributed rights. This is important in view of the third feature of rights discussed above, because a being having rights would be said to have interests that would straightaway entitle this being to our obligation to preserve and protect it; the case of beings having no interests would be somewhat dubious or at least stand in the need of some other grounds for such entitlement.

Now considering all the three features discussed above, members of the human species clearly qualify as the paradigm right holders. For as the unique owners of conative and cognitive faculties, human persons have interests and good of their own, the satisfaction or realization of which is of intrinsic value; and in virtue of having these faculties they are capable of claiming, directly and indirectly, protection of their interests. Further, it is uniquely true of human beings that they are not only thus capable of claiming their rights but also of reciprocating with corresponding obligations to ensure unhindered exercise of such rights of others. It is only of human beings that it can be properly said that they are both right holders and right promoters. Having right thus makes sense in their case full blooded and makes them moral agents in a unique sense. This can provide another dimension to my earlier claim, adduced in chapter 4, that human rights are the primary form of rights or rights in the primary sense of the term.

In sharp contrast to human beings, animals cannot strictly be said to have rights; firstly because, because of their intellectual incompetence,* they would be incapable of claiming their rights if they had any, and secondly because, as McCloskey has argued, animals cannot have interests of their own to be claimed or even

---

* A phrase I owe to Joel Feinberg.

to be indirectly represented by authorized agents or attorneys,[47] and thirdly because, with no conative or cognitive life of their own, animals cannot be said to have duties as correlative to their supposed rights. In view of the lacuna last mentioned, the rights ascribed to animals, if at all, would be devoid of full-blooded significance; rights without reciprocal duties in this case would, I suspect, be half as significant compared to its application in the case of the humans. "Quasi rights" would perhaps be their proper description and status.

It may be objected here that the supposed intellectual incompetence on the part of animals cannot be a conclusive ground for denial of rights to them. It will be said, that is, that failure to be conscious of their rights and failure to claim what they are entitled to cannot make animals unworthy of having any rights. For if it were the case then infants, adult idiots and the severely mentally disadvantaged among human beings would not have even legal rights and certainly not any moral rights.[48] But obviously they do; they can even 'claim' their rights by initiating legal proceedings through "actions of proxies or attorneys", though not on their own initiatives. "If there is no conceptual absurdity in this situation, why should there be in the case where a proxy makes a claim on behalf of an animal?"[49] Such an objection is plausible and has often been invoked as a stock argument in favour of animal rights. But I find it lacking in two important respects at least. As I have already said in the previous section, there is an important asymmetry between the intellectually incompetent humans and the animals in the sense that, even if the former are in fact incapable of claiming their rights, it is fairly conceivable *what it would be like* for them to

47. "Rights", *Philosophical Quarterly*, vol.15 (1965), p. 124.
48. See, for example, W.D.Lamont, *Principles of Moral Judgments* (Oxford, the Clarendon Press, 1946), pp. 80-85. We will have more to say on legal rights soon later on.
49. Feinberg, while making this objection plausible only to reject it, in "The Rights of Animals" reprinted in Schmidtz and Willott (eds) *Environmental Ethics*, p. 52.

make such claims, whereas this would not make any sense in the case of animals. Their being legally represented by attorneys and trustees perhaps does make sense; but as McCloskey has cogently shown, representation is always of interests that are claimed through representations, and since animals cannot have interests they cannot, strictly speaking, be represented. What I think to be the second limitation of the objection in question is concerned with the essential *reciprocal link* between rights and duties, which I have stressed above and which has been adopted as a methodological principle in chapter 4. If rights and duties are standardly reciprocal, and if the concept of right involves both the right holder and the right promoter, without which the concept of right would be useless and vacuous, if not senseless, then it follows that animals cannot have rights in as much as they cannot have duties. That they cannot have duties is evident from their being admittedly incapable of understanding, being reasoned with or being instructed about, duties and responsibilities; they cannot act as moral agents and so cannot act rightly or wrongly; they cannot be blamed for moral failings or for that matter praised for morally appreciable conducts. Therefore animals cannot have rights for this very same reason for which they cannot be said to have duties.

Nevertheless, for reasons other than right related considerations, animals are moral subjects in the sense that they are the objects of our moral concern and consideration. The very fact that they are living, sentient beings, capable of suffering pain and enjoying pleasure, makes them worthy of our moral consideration and respect. The notable fact about them is that we have duties towards them *without their having to have duties of any sort*. And more importantly, we have duties towards them despite their not having (being capable of having) the corresponding rights. It is because of this that, even if we talk of animal rights, as many would still be inclined to, the "right" in this case would be a sham—an extension of the concept that applies primarily to humans. Therefore the protagonists of animal rights in particular and life-centered environmentalism in general should be wary about the fact that respect for life and kindness to animals—profoundly moral ideals though they are—do not mean, much less imply, that animals have the right to claim kind treatment from us as their due any more than our careful and even reverential treatment of some 'valuable' mere things like rocks and monuments mean that these things can claim good treatment from us as their due. Legislations for prevention of cruelty to animals does not mean that animals have right to kind treatment any more than our "custodial duties" for historical monuments justify any correlative "thing rights" to be attributed to these monuments.[50]Animals cannot be the subjects of rights any more than mere things can be the locus of value. It is for this reason that a distinction may be made between one's having duties *to* something and one's having duties *regarding* something.[51] We may properly speak of having duties *regarding* animals and things rather than speaking of having duties *to* them. In the light of our contention in this section, we have duties *to* beings that have interests and good of their own and who are the subjects of rights, and we have duties *regarding* things and beings who cannot have interests and so cannot be genuine subjects of rights.

We are now in a position to assert that plants and the vegetable world, despite their being *living* things, cannot be said to have moral rights. For the arguments that applied against animals having rights would apply *mutatis mutandis* in this case too. Perhaps the arguments would apply in this case more strongly, since plants and trees can be arguably said to be morally inferior to animals in the sense that they (these) are totally devoid of conative life, while some of the higher animals do appear to

50. As tellingly argued by Feinberg, see *ibid*, p. 59.
51. Some recent writers do in fact prefer to make such distinction.

display signs of appetite and purposive behaviour*, *al beit* minimally. Because of this point of dissimilarity in principle I consider plants and trees as morally inferior to animals in the sense that, as moral subjects, they incite lesser moral concern in us than the animals do. There is, among some prominent environmentalists, a stronger reason for this, namely that animals deserve our greater moral concern because of their capacity to suffer. We have noted the views of Frankena and Bentham with this implication. Animal liberationists like Peter Singer also consider suffering of sentient beings as the basis of ethical concern.

The foregoing considerations inevitably lead to the conclusion that a right-based environmental ethics is an extremely difficult proposition to be sustained. It cannot, that is, be claimed that the environment, in respect of all its contents, has the moral right to be preserved and protected. On an anthropocentric view, this is impossible, since *ex hypothesi* rights are attributable exclusively to human beings. Even on a life-centered attitude towards the environment, attribution of rights to animals and plants being questionable, this becomes a questionable project too.

There is another point of view from which this project is thought to be indefensible. A right-based environmental ethics must not only take into consideration, but must be consistent with, the basic presupposition of the rights view, which is that the paradigm right holders are individuals, and even if *per impossible* the rights view is extended to animals and plants,

---

* Plants and trees, it may be claimed, also display purposive behaviour in the sense that they are 'systems of goal oriented activities', which are directed towards their preservation and well-being. E.g., they grow in search of sunlight and spread their branches and leaves accordingly; they also spread their roots in search of adequate water and minerals. In this sense they are "teleological centers of life" as Taylor describes them in his "The Ethics of Respects for Nature" (*Environmental Ethics,* vol.3,1981). But this description will mislead no one into believing that plants have purposes and intentions.

only the individuals, not the whole species, would be worthy of moral rights.[52] "That an individual animal is among the last remaining members of a species", says Regan, "confers no *further* right on that animal, and its right not to be harmed must be weighed *equitably* with the rights of any others [individual animals, PKM] who have this right."(*ibid*, p. 359; emphasis added). This is not to say that efforts should not be made to save endangered species because species do not have moral rights to be saved. They should be saved on the same ground as species that are not endangered and the ground is that "individual animals have valid claims and thus rights against those who would destroy their natural habitat,—or would make a living off their dead carcasses..." (*ibid*). On our analysis these individual animals, if they are not human beings, should be saved because of our attitude of respect for their life that makes them worthy of our moral concern. Sticking to the rights view for the moment, if this is taken in the described sense then a right-based environmental ethics cannot be developed, because the *individualistic* nature of moral rights would conflict with the holistic view of the environment as pleaded by most of the environmentalists. (See Reagan, *ibid,* p. 361). Because of this, Reagan points out, environmentalists are reluctant to take right seriously.

There is at least one prominent environmentalist who was expressedly disinclined from taking rights seriously in his account of environmental ethics. For reasons largely conducive to the contention of this work, Paul W.Taylor underplays the importance of a right-based environmental ethics and considers attempt to justify environmentalism on the basis of rights (of the biotic community) as needless. For, he points out, what we want to achieve by extending moral rights to the non-human

52. Such a view of rights has been elaborated and defended by Tom Reagan in his article "How to Worry about Endangered Species" that has formed a part of his book *The Case for Animal Rights* (University of California Press, Berkeley, 1983).

members of this community can be very well achieved by the attitude of respect for nature and the belief in the inherent worth of all living things.[53] It would be interesting and worth the while to analyze the implications of this telling remark. For although I do not see good reasons to agree with this remark in its entirety, I think nonetheless that here lies the key to what I consider a proper understanding of an environmental ethics.

Ethics of Respect for Nature and Blueprint for a Secular Environmentalism

It is interesting to examine why Taylor considered a right-based explanation of the environment as needless. Some explanation of ***X*** may be needless either because ***X*** may be self-explanatory or because a better explanation of ***X*** is available, though in either case the former explanation may be self-complete and may have its own justification. But Taylor's reason for considering the rights explanation of the environment as needless is not that environment does not need explaining nor that the respect-for-nature explanation is a better explanation than the rights-based explanation. It is rather that the latter explanation of the environment is not self-complete and cannot be sustained (and therefore the question of its being weaker than the other explanation does not arise). For admittedly, as we have argued, the concept of moral rights (as distinguished from legal rights) implies a relation of *reciprocity*, which makes it imperative that it be uniquely applicable to a system of human ethics based on respect for persons,[54] for only in the case of persons that assertable rights along with the implied duties can be meaningfully applied. And we have given reasons enough that in the case of lower animals and plants the *talk* of our obligations to them is not meant to imply the corresponding rights to be claimed by them. For animals and plants can't be said to owe

53. *Respect for Nature* (Princeton University Press, New Jersy, 1986), see especially p. 226.
54. As Taylor admits in *Respect for Nature*, p. 234.

any reciprocal duties towards us in any serious sense of the term. It follows therefore that any talk of rights ascribable to animals and plants would only have a secondary, extended sense. The concept of rights applied to them, if at all, would be a modified concept, says Taylor for this reason. (*ibid*, p. 251 ff). "Modified", I add, because no reciprocity is involved or required in this scheme of things. Legal rights may be ascribed to them by legislation from time to time, which can also be withdrawn from and restricted to specific groups. This has been illustrated and witnessed several times in the history of mankind. The most obvious case is the right to vote, which was denied to the blacks in the pre-civil rights America and which was restricted to the age group of 21 in independent India until recently till 1984. Christopher Stone cites a rather outrageous example of the first woman in Wisconsin, who was denied the right to practise law, because this was considered to be "inconsistent with the ...sacred duties of the fair sex [which was to nurture children and to look after homes, PKM] and a departure from the order of nature. Nature has tempered woman as little for the judicial conflicts of the court room as for the physical conflicts of the battle field" (*In re Goddell* 39, Wisc, 232, 245 [1875], quoted by Stone in his "Should Trees Have Standing? Towards Legal Rights of Natural Objects" in *University of California Law Review,* Vol. 45). Still in the 19th century the highest court in California had decreed that the Chinese had no right to testify against a white man; and earlier in the 13th century a Jew was legally treated as a being only to be protected by quasi-forest laws "like the roe and the deer." (See Stone, *op. cit*). But the status of such rights would be no better than that of a secondary modified from of right, which can be sanctioned and withdrawn by changing acts and legislations. Such rights would fall far short of the absolute and normally inalienable moral rights, which human persons have the paradigm claim to hold. Because of this, and presumably because of the danger of confusing the secondary sense of having moral rights applicable to animals and plants with the primary sense thereof, applicable to human persons, Taylor considers it "less misleading" to drop the language of rights in the case of animals and plants (*ibid*, pp. 253-55), and more appropriate to reserve it to apply in the case of human beings. Instead of speaking in terms of rights of the environment, Taylor's ground for preservation and protection of the environment is what he likes to call the ethics of respect for nature. This principle of respect for nature is based on a belief system called the bio-centric outlook that includes a belief and an attitude—the belief in the inherent worth of animals and plants and the attitude of respect for life.

This ethics of respect for nature, eminently pleaded in Taylor's *Respect for Nature* and in his article "The Ethics of Respect for Nature" (in *Environmental Ethics,* ed. Schmidtz and Willott), is a certain "ultimate moral attitude towards nature" that has a central place in the life-centered view on environment. This moral attitude is prominently marked by stressing on species egalitarianism and recognition of equal value of life. Man is seen not as the master but only as a member of the earth's community of life, all the members of which have equal worth as living organisms. Whether human or non-human, individual organisms are teleological centers of life, each striving to preserve itself and realize its own good. There is no place, in this scheme, for superiority of any species over any other, since life as such is supposed to be of equal intrinsic value. The natural world is conceived as an organic whole in which the various species are not only interrelated but are functionally interdependent. The good of the species lies in the ecological balance and equilibrium. This holds true of the good of plants and animals as well as of human beings

The foregoing characteristics of the ethics of respect for nature boils down to the two assumptions noted above, namely (a) the *belief in inherent worth* of the members of all species and (b) the *attitude of respect for life*. Although both these assumptions could ideally strengthen our moral attitude of respect for nature, I do not see any essential need for (a) in making nature a fit object of our moral concern. My reasons for saying this are two-fold. First I believe that (b) alone, i.e. the attitude of respect for life, is enough to arouse our moral concern for objects of nature and justify our obligations for plants and animals. My second reason for considering (a) to be needless for an ethic of respect for nature issues from my earlier analysis of inherent worth and good of a being or thing. If, as I have shown, plants cannot have interest and hence good of their own, they cannot be said to possess inherent worth in any strict sense. Our talk of interests in these cases, we have seen, is to be understood in terms of and as dependent on human interests at some point. The talk of inherent worth in these cases, therefore, will have to a secondary or a modified sense. With apologies to Paul Taylor, I would consider it "less misleading" to drop the language of inherent worth in the case of natural objects which, I repeat, would not affect our attitude of respect for them, since a genuine attitude of respect for life would *in itself* justify our moral concern and obligations for them. Objects of the natural world, by simply being *living* things, would qualify as objects of our moral concern and obligations. And this would be quite in keeping with a bio-centric environmental ethics.

However, it may be objected, the principle of respect for life cannot be reason enough for a comprehensive moral attitude of respect for nature. For nature includes much else besides the living beings and things. The things called wilderness and ecosystem include both the living and non-living items of the phenomenon called nature. Not only the flora and the fauna but also the mountains and springs, the rocks and the soil, the skies and the oceans incite in us a sense of reveling and even of respect, which justify our obligation for them and for their preservation and protection. Indeed environment means all of these, including ourselves and our relations to all these. But "respect for nature", if supposed to be grounded on the attitude of respect for life, would speak too narrowly of itself. And this excellent idea would suffer from self-defeat if made to be literally grounded on bio-centrism or a life-centered theoretical framework. Extension of "life" to include non-living things like rivers and landscapes and the ecosystems and the broader use of it in the epigram "let the river live", which is taken resort to by supporters of deep ecology[55], is a deceptive stratagem and a forced defense of the 'respect for life' principle being used as ground for the attitude of respect for nature. The objection therefore stands sustained.

The objection is plausible and can pose a threat to the 'respect for nature' principle by exposing the narrowness of its justification substructure. But this does not mean that the principle is flawed and without adequate support. The appearances of inadequate justification for the principle, I suspect, is because of an irrational preference for the life-centered theory and an implicit aversion for the human-centered considerations. Taylor's emphasis on the denial of human superiority[56] and the general stress on species egalitarianism in contempcrary writings on environment vouch for the described preference and aversion reflected in Taylor's offering of the respect-for-life principle as justification for the moral attitude of respect for nature. But while this counts on animals and plants as natural objects (can they constitute *all* that are objects of nature?), the described non-living mere things are left unexplained, though they constitute a sizable and significant part of nature as well. The 'Respect for nature' theory is thus in need of more support from something other than the 'respect for life' principle. I have shown, by illustrating the case of mere

55. As George Sessions and Anne Nass would like to do in their comments on the basic principles of deep ecology (reported by Bill Devall and George Sessions in "Deep Ecology" in Schmidtz and Willott eds. *Environmental Ethics*, p. 123.

56. "The basic connection is made through the denial of human superiority", says Taylor. (*Environmental Ethics*, eds Schimdtz and Willott, p. 94.)

things like historical monuments and aesthetic marvels, that we are obligated to preserve them, not for their own sake (since they cannot have a 'sake' of their own) but for the sake of serving *our* aesthetic or economic interests. Thus the attitude of respect, as far as these natural objects are concerned, is rooted in the bio-centric outlook on nature. One-sided emphasis on either perspective is bound to yield truncated views of the environment and inadequate justification for the attitude of respect for nature. Once we take the environment seriously, i.e., seriously value the need to preserve and protect the environment, justification for this should be welcome, irrespective of whether it comes from bio-centric consideration or from anthropocentric consideration. There is indeed no serious conflict between the two views; the two can jointly help buttress a better understanding of the natural environment. Certain aspects of nature, which cannot be explained by one, can very well be explained in terms of the other, and that which needs to be explained in one way must be explained in that way rather than in another per force. Even if one does not support deep ecology and its claim for biotic equality, presumably on grounds of lack of interest in the case of plants and non-living natural objects, one would nevertheless recognize an overriding human need for a healthy and high quality natural environment. An effective ethics of the environment, which I prefer to call a secular view of the environment, must be neutral between and equidistant from absolute adherence to either views of anthropocentricism and bio-centricism. Openness to explain environmental matters with the help of the one or the other or of both as the facts and situations demand is the key to this 'secular' environmental ethics. The basic intuition of bio-centric equality is valid and preferable in principle, but like all genuine ethical principles, it is also *defeasible* and overridable under demanding situations. In point of fact, in the process of living, species use each other for food and shelter. "Mutual predation is a biological fact of life", say Sessions and Devall, "and many of the world's religions have struggled with the spiritual implications of this"[57]. Some religious texts even try to offer some sort of a spiritual justification for it, e.g. the *Srimad-Bhagavata*[58] pleading that a creature used for food by another attains *moksa: 'jiva māriṇa jiva khāi, sé jiva vaikunthé basai'* and also the well known scriptural pronouncement that *jiva jivasya jivanam* (one creature is another's life in the sense that one lives on the other). This may sound like undue adherence to anthropo-centrism, but the other plea, for vegetarianism, fares no better either, in as much as it amounts to depriving the plant kingdom of any right to existence. Speciesism would only be replaced by sentienceism and biotic equality would be nowhere in sight. A workable version and the practical implication of this principle, therefore, is that we should live with minimum impact on other species and on our environment in general. Depending on the demands of the situation, motorcar racing may be as undesirable as deer hunting, but if the situations so demand, hunting for food may be morally justified and hunting for sport and enjoyment of the palate cannot be. Actions that cause moderate harm (harm that cannot be avoided altogether or harm that is caused in a greater interest) to the environment may be ethically dubious but not plainly wrong, though actions that are unnecessarily harmful would be plainly wrong from the moral point of view. The secular ethical view of the environment, which avoids fixed pictures of the environment and closed patterns of explaining it, makes room for necessary harms as distinct from avoidable ones thereto. We may recall the 'dirty hand' theory alluded to in the previous chapter: If it is not possible to avoid dirtying one's hands (as in business, for example) altogether, one must keep the dirt in one's hand as thin as possible. This does not, however, glorify the dirty hand theory nor does it denigrate the principle of biotic equality. This only pleads for facing the facts in keeping with the spirit of the principles concerned,—which

57. "Deep Ecology", *ibid*, p. 122.
58. Oriya, by Jagannath Das, 11th *Skandha*.

we have been pleading for as the key to applied ethics. A virtue defeated under a demanding situation is never turned into a vice, nor is a vice invoked in a similar manner turned into a virtue. Virtues and vices do have their categorial status. But one must never lose sight of the fact that absolute value is an abstraction, and a universalisable but defeasible moral principle is representative of the spirit of ethics.

Bibliography

Aristotle, *Nicomachian Ethics,* trans. by W D. Ross (Oxford, 1935).

Attfield, R., "The Good of Trees" in Willott, E. and Schimdtz, D. (ed.) *Environmental Ethics* (Oxford, 2002).

Aurovindo, *Essays on the Gita* (Aurovindo Ashram, Pondicherry, 1914).

Baier, K., *The Moral Point of View* (Cornell University Press, Ithaca, New York, 1958).

Baier, K., *The Rational and the Moral Order* (Open Court, Chicago and Illinois).

Baruah, B.H., "Person and Value: Sketch for a Theory of Moral Personhood" in Mohanty, S.K. (ed.) *Persons, Mind and Value* (Decent Books, New Delhi in association with DSA in Philosophy, Utkal University, Bhubaneswar, 2000).

Benthm, J., *Introduction to the Principles of Morals and Legislation,* ed. W. Harrison (Oxford University Press, 1948).

Benthm, J., *Theory of Legislation,* trans. by C.M. Atkinson (Oxford University Press, 1914).

Blackburn, S., "Errors and the Phenomenology of Value" in Honderich, T. (ed.) *Morality and Objectivity: A Tribute to J.L. Mackie* (Routledge and Kegan Paul, London, 1985).

Blanchard, K. and Peale, N.V., *The Power of Ethical Management* (Fawcett Crest, New York, 1988).

Bowie, N., *Business Ethics: A Kantian Perspective* (Blackwell, Oxford, 1999).

Bowie, N., "A Kantian Approach to Business Ethics" in Frederich, R. (ed.) *A Companion to Business Ethics* (Blackwell, U.K., 1999 and 2000).

Bradley, F.H., *Appearance and Reality* (Oxford University Press, 1963, first published in 1895).

Brandt, R.B., *Ethical Theory* (Prentice Hall, Englewood Cliffs, New Jersey, 1959).

Brandt, R.B., *Fact, Value and Morality* (Cambridge University Press, 1996).

Brandt, R.B., (ed.) *Social Justice* (Prentice Hall, Englewood Cliffs, N.J., 1962).

Brandt, R.B., *Morality, Utilitarianism and Rights* (Cambridge University Press, 1992).

Brink, D., *Moral Realism and the Foundations of Ethics* (Cambridge University Press, New York, 1989).

Bulchholz, R.A., *Fundamental Concepts and Problems in Business Ethics* (Prentice Hall, Englewood Cliffs, N.J., 1989).

Carroll, A.B., "Ethics in Management" in Frederich, R. (ed.) *A Companion to Business Ethics* (Blackwell, U.K., 1999 and 2000).

Clark, S., *The Moral Status of Animals* (Oxford, The Clarendon Press, 1977).

Dancy, J., *Moral Reasons* (Blackwell, Oxford, U.K. and Cambridge, USA, 1993).

Dworkin, R. *Taking Rights Seriously* (Harvard University Press, 1977).

Fagothey, A., *Right and Reason* (C.V. Mosby Co., St. Luis, USA, 1972).

Feinberg, J. (ed.) *Reason and Responsibility* (Dichenson Publishing Co. Inc., Belmont, California, 1965).

Feinberg, J., "The Rights of Animals and Unborn Generations" in Blackstone, W. (ed.) *Philosophy and Environmental Crisis* (University of Georgia Press, Athens, 1974).

Feinberg, J. "Rights of Animals" in Willott and Schimdtz (ed.) *Environmental Ethics* (Oxford, 2002).

Flew, A.G.N., *A Rational Animal* (Oxford, The Clarendon Press, 1978).

Frankena, W., "Ethics and the Environment" in Godpaster, K.E. and Sayre, K.M. (ed.) *Ethics and the Problem of 21st Century* (University of Notre Dame Press, 1979).

Frankfurt, H., "Identification and Wholeheartedness" in Shoeman, F. (ed.) *Responsibility, Character and the Emotions* (Cambridge University Press, 1987).

Friedman, M., *Capitalism and Freedom* (University of Chicago Press, 1962).

Gewirth, A., *Reason and Morality* (University of Chicago Press, 1996).

Griffin, J., *Value Judgement* (Oxford, The Clarendon Press, 1996).

Hare, R.M., *Essays on the Moral Concepts* (Macmillan, New York, 1972).

Hare, R.M., *Moral Thinking* (Oxford, The Clarendon Press, 1981).

Hare, R.M., "Ontology in Ethics" in Honderich (ed.) *Morality and Objectivity: A Tribute to J.L. Mackie* (Routledge and Kegan Paul, London, 1985).

Hart, H.L.A., *The Concept of Law* (Oxford, The Clarendon Press, 1961).

Hinman L., *Ethics: A Pluralistic Approach to Morality* (Fortworth, Harcourt Press, 1977).

Hiriyanna, M., *Indian Conceptions of Values* (Kavyalaya Publications, Mysore, 1957).

Honderich, T., (ed.) *Morality and Objectivity: A Tribute to J.L. Mackie* (Routledge and Kegan Paul, London, 1985).

Hook, S., (ed.) *Law and Philosophy* (New York University Press, 1964).

Hume, D., *A Treatise of Human Nature,* ed. P. Niddich (Oxford University Press, 1978).

Hume, D., *Enquiry Concerning the Principles of Morals,* ed. P. Niddich (Oxford University Press, 1975).

Hurley, S.L., "Objectivity and Disagreement" in Honderich (ed.) *Morality and Objectivity.*

Johnston, H., *Business Ethics* (Pitman Publishing Corporation, New York, 1956).

Kant, I., *Foundations of the Metaphysics of Morals* (1785), trans., by L. Beck (Macmillan, New York, 1990).

Korsgaard, C., *Creating the Kingdom of Ends* (Cambridge University Press, N.Y., 1996).

Lamont, W.D., *Principles of Moral Judgements* (Oxford, The Clarendon Press, 1946).

Leopld, A., "Land Ethics" in his *A Sand Country Almanac* (Oxford University Press, 1981).

Locke, J., *Essay on Human Understanding,* ed. A.S. Pringle-Pattison (Oxford, 1924).

Locke, J., *Two Treatises of Government* (Cambridge University Press, 1960; first published in 1689 by Leslett Peter).

Mackie, J.L., *Ethics: Inventing Right and Wrong* (Penguin Books, London, 1977).

Manheim, Karl., *Ideology and Utopia* (Routledge and Kegan Paul, London).

McCloskey, H.J., "Rights" in *Philosophical Quarterly,* Vol. 15 (1965).

McDowell, J., "Non-Cognitivism and Rule Following" in Holtzman and Leich (ed.) *Wittgenstein: To Follow A Rule* (RKP, London, 1981).

McDowell, J., "Values and Secondary Qualities" in Honderich (ed.) *Morality and Objectivity* (RKP, London, 1985).

McIntyre, A., *After Virtue* (Duckworth, London, 1981).

McKenzie, J., *Hindu Ethics* (Oxford University Press, London, 1922).

Merrill, H., *Responsibilities of Business Leadership* (Cambridge, Mass: Harvard University Press, 1948).

Mill, J.S., *Utilitarianism* (Library of Liberal Arts, New York, 1957).

Mill, J.S., *On Liberty* (Longman, London, 1859, Bert and Leby, 1999).

Mohanty, S.K. (ed.), *Persons, Mind and Value* (Decent Books, New Delhi in association with the DSA in Philosophy, Utkal University, Bhubaneswar, 2000).

Mohapatra, P.K., *Personal Identity* (First published by Santosh Publications, Cuttack, 1983; second edition by Decent Books, New Delhi, 2000).

Mohapatra, P.K., *Concepts and Problems* (Santosh Publications, Cuttack, 1999).

Mohapatra, P.K., (ed.) *Social Justice* (D.K. Printworld, New Delhi, 1999).

Moore, G.E., "A Defense of Commonsense" in Muirhead, J.H. (ed.) *Contemporary British Philosophy* (George Allen and Unwin, USA, 1925).

Nagel, T., *Possibility of Altruism* (Oxford, 1970).

Nagel, T., *The View From Nowhere* (Oxford University Press, 1986).

Nerlich, G.C., *Values and Speculations on the Ethical Life of Persons* (Oxford, The Clarendon Press, 1989).

Nozick, R., *State, Anarchy and Utopia* (Basic Books Inc., New York, 1974).

Plato, *The Republic.*

Plato, *Georgias.*

Plato, Laws.

Popper, K.R. *The Open Society and its Enemies* (Routledge and Kegan Paul, London, 1946).

Prasad, R., *Varnadharma, Niskama Karma and Practical Morality* (D.K. Printworld, New Delhi in association with the DSA in Philosophy, Utkal University, 1999).

Prasad, R., *Karma, Causation and Retributive Morality* (ICPR, New Delhi, 1989).

Prasad, R., "Social Justice, Retribution and Revenge" in Mohapatra, P.K. (ed.) *Social Justice* (D.K. Printworld, New Delhi—DSA in Philosophy, Utkal University).

Rawls, J., *A Theory of Justice* (Cambridge, Mass: The Balkan Press of Harward University, 1971).

Regan, T., *The Case for Animal Rights* (University of California Press, Berkeley, 1983).

Rolston III, H., "Values in and Duties to the Natural World" in Willott and Schimdtz (ed.) *Environmental Ethics* (Oxford, 2002).

Samkara, *Vedanta Sutra.*

Samkara, *Geeta Bhasyam.*

Sagoff, M., "Animal Liberation and Environmental Ethics: Bad Marriage and Quick Divorce" in Willott and Schmidtz (ed.) *Environmental Ethics* (Oxford, 2002).

Scanlon, T.M., *Morality by Agreement* (Oxford, 1987).

Sidgwick, H., *Methods of Ethics* (Macmillan, London, 1874, 1907 and 1962).

Simpson, E., "Between Internalism and Externalism in Ethics" in *Philosophical Quarterly,* Vol. 49, No. 195.

Singer, P., *Practical Ethics,* (Cambridge University Press, 1993).

Singer, P., "All Animals Are Equal" in Willott and Schmidtz (ed.) *Environmental Ethics* (Oxford, 2002).

Singer, P., "Not for Humans Only: The Place of Non-humans in Environment" in Godpaster and Sayre (ed.) *Ethics and the Problems of Twenty First Century.*

Singer, P., (ed.) *Ethics,* Oxford University Press, N.Y. 1994.

Singer, M.G., *Generalization in Ethics* (Alfred A. Knop, New York, 1961).

Snoeynbos, M. and Humber, J., "Utilitarianism and Business Ethics" in Frederich, R.E. (ed.) *A Companion to Business Ethics* (Blackwell, London, 1999).

St. John-Stevas, N., *Law and Morals* (Hawthorn Books Inc., New York, 1964).

Sternberg, E., *Just Business* (Warner Books, U.K., 1994).

Strawson, P.F., *Individuals: An Essay in Descriptive Metaphysics* (Methuen, London, 1962).

Taylor, P.W., *Respect for Nature* (Princeton University Press, New Jersey, 1986).

Taylor, P.W., "The Ethics of Rights for Nature" in his *Environmental Ethics,* Vol. 3.

Vlastos, G., "Justice and Equality" in Brandt, R.B. (ed.) *Social Justice* (Prentice Hall, New Jersey, 1962).

Watson, G., *Free Will* (Oxford University Press, 1982).

Willott, E. and Schimdtz, D., (ed.) *Environmental Ethics* (Oxford, 2002).

Wisdom, J., *Philosophy and Psychoanalysis* (Basil Blackwell, London, 1953).

Index